Delinquent Fantasies

PATRICIA MORGAN

Delinquent Fantasies

Temple Smith · London

First published in Great Britain 1978
by Maurice Temple Smith Ltd
37 Great Russell Street, London WC1

© Patricia Morgan 1978
ISBN 0 8511 7116 8

Photoset in Baskerville by
D.P. Media Ltd., Hitchin, Herts.
Printed in Great Britain by
Billing & Sons Ltd
Guildford, London & Worcester

Contents

Wherefore I deny not that men (even nature compelling) *desire* to come together. But civil societies are not mere meetings, but bonds, to the making whereof faith and compacts are necessary; the virtue whereof to children and fools, and the profit whereof to those who have not yet tasted the miseries which accompany its defects, is altogether unknown; whence it happens that those, because they know not what society is, cannot enter it; these, because ignorant of the benefits it brings, care not for it. Manifest therefore it is, that all men, because they are born in infancy, are born unapt for society . . . wherefore man is made fit for society not by nature but by education.

Thomas Hobbes *De Cive*

Part One

All Things New

1 New Barbarism

A railway guard is killed by a paving stone thrown by children, and a driver by an insulator flung down by boys: 'Vandals hid life-belt, so man drowned' (*Evening Standard* 22 April 1971); 'Church vandals leave £1m trail of havoc' (*Evening News* 4 July 1975); a factory goes up in smoke and the pets in a Children's Zoo are pulled apart. Rubbing someone out is as trivial and as random as flicking a dog-end on the pavement: 'Busker George, a single man with no known family, died on Tuesday—two days after he was struck in the face by part of a builder's breeze block thrown by youths when they were turned off a bus in Regent Street for causing a disturbance' (*Evening Standard* 28 October 1976). There are not many gangster power struggles here: no heroics, few million-dollar bank raids or ingenious English murders. There is an absence of value, not a distortion. When life becomes not just a cheap or exchangeable commodity, but worthless, and plunder is seemingly neither for consumption, wealth nor power, it is as petty as it is fearful, as oppressive as it is mundane. The violence, the destruction, and the youth of its perpetrators combine to produce a barbarity without splendour or honour; something tatty, haphazard and sordid, as trivial as baby talk in a world where we are increasingly sport for wanton little boys.

Many losses can be distinguished in the criminal and delinquent onslaught on public life. It involves, first and foremost, a dramatic reduction in freedom. So many other rights cannot be exercised unless life and limb and, at the very least, an elementary forbearance, are guaranteed. Freedom lies in not having to calculate the risk to oneself on every journey outdoors: negotiating streets that have become a gauntlet of possible challenges, threats and sudden attacks; making intricate and urgent manoeuvres to avoid other human beings—particularly those who happen to be under twenty, stationary and/or in groups. Need-less to say, the restrictions on freedom increase with one's vulnerability, and those who already have least of the former—women and the old—find it further squeezed. Those who still live in areas where the threat and possibility of viol-ence have not so intruded into everyday social interaction, are not only spared the extra watchfulness, planning and immobil-ity it demands, but the misanthropy as much as the fear and misery it engenders.

For violence and delinquency stifle altruism as they kill freedom. Calls for assistance are too convenient a trap. Don't open the door; don't try to help the person who appears to be in trouble; don't give directions, the time, change—certainly not in some areas. More and more the environment becomes a harsh place where others are out to hurt, where the young particularly are out to hurt. Far from adults voicing and demonstrating care and consideration towards, and pleasure in the young, they now increasingly maintain that they positively hate children and young people and go out of their way to avoid them.

Delinquency, needless to say, involves a wicked waste of resources in a world which is so often short of the barest essentials. The cost of crime was estimated by insurance com-panies, security experts, Government Departments and others as around £2,000m in 1975 but this does not include vandalism, nor does it include the losses due to the disruption of production and employment by arson and other destructive acts. The cost of vandalism runs to tens of millions, and we only know the tip of an iceberg, since most is not reported. Break it down into more manageable, smaller sums and think what they might buy. Kent council reported losses due to vandalism *in one month* in 1975 as £198,000—what might Age Concern, Oxfam, even a sanctuary for aged donkeys do with £198,000? Two boys in a very well set up family in the neighbourhood I left, have destroyed enough in their short lives to keep an Indian village going reasonably well throughout several reincarnations. Edu-cation authorities experience six times the vandalism of ten years ago and the bill for arson is now around the £6m level. How much can be bought, or built, how many employed for twenty-five million pounds—the annual cost now of the destruction in schools?

Delinquency brings a dramatic deterioration in the quality of life. Its routes are marked by the smashed phone boxes, broken trees, wrecked vending machines, disembowelled lamp-posts and burnt-out buildings. It affects the famous beauty spots, the ornamental gardens, the bus-shelters in the desirable residential area, as it does the new housing development:

> Vandalism is downgrading the quality of life of thousands of council tenants. People who rent from the council homes they could be proud to invite their family and friends to visit, now hustle them with furtive shame past wrecked glass, demolished brickwork, damaged doors and the general air of shabbiness that they bring with them. (Spokesman for Islington council *Evening Standard* 5 October 1976)

Public squares, public gardens, public communications, public playgrounds, public lavatories are 'done' and 'done' again until they are no more. Public workers, from bus-conductors to publicans, are increasingly becoming targets for violence. (In London in 1974, 473 bus staff were attacked badly enough to require time off work for shock and injury: there were 5,000 less-serious assaults reported. London Transport's estimate for assaults on tube staff in the same year was 700.)

In some places delinquent destruction could now be said to be the main cause of urban decay. I myself saw a perfectly sound area being bust up by it. A better known example is Kirkby, a new town with no inherited racial or religious problems, no more than 20 years old. It has community centres, sporting and recreation facilities and good schools, but it is now a social disaster area:

> The whole atmosphere of the town centre and the four community centre shopping precincts is marred by the fact that most shops have either bricked their windows or covered them with permanent and unsightly metal grilles, despite which graffiti abound.
>
> Insurance companies have in some cases refused to insure certain shops or have charged prohibitive premiums, thus driving shopkeepers out of town.
>
> About seven hundred dwellings, mainly flats in three-storey blocks of six, have been completely vandalised and it is estimated that it will cost more than £3.5m to renovate them. (*The Times* 3 December 1975)

Kirkby has many companions, though not always on so grand a scale. I visited an estate for young families in a rural setting in Kent—the personal and communal landscaped gardens, playgrounds and tennis courts, houses with shining, well-equipped kitchens, and the rest of modern comfort and convenience—all could have come straight out of an advertisement for exclusive suburban properties. *Could*—for the whole place was beginning to resemble the scenes of churned earth and blackened tree-stumps in First World War paintings: one was reminded particularly of Nash's *We are Building a New World*.

'There won't be anything left around here soon' is the ironic comment of a passer-by on another act of vandalism. Nothing is immune: the first week that a new high-speed train came into operation, it was seriously damaged by a heavy object dangled from a bridge by children. It was carrying 300 passengers and the driver very narrowly escaped death. Arson has been responsible for roughly a million pounds' worth of damage to five historic warehouses in London's dockland, which were to be renovated as part of a development scheme. During the summer drought of 1976, fire services claimed that the overwhelming majority of the fires which destroyed large areas of commercial and recreational woodlands, and the habitats of our rarer animal and bird species, were deliberately started by children.

If the cities are to be saved as centres of a civilised urban life, and not plunged into gutted and fearful wastelands, as in some American urban centres, delinquency will have to be tackled as a problem with high priority—perhaps as *the* urban problem. City life cannot exist without security in its open spaces, some unarmed trust and reciprocity. In Britain, as on the American pattern, there is a mass exodus of skilled workers and middle-class groups from the metropolis and other inner cities revealed by studies like that of the GLC. These areas are left with heavily welfare-dependent populations: the old, the sick, the handicapped, the uneducated, the dull, the retarded and the unskilled. This represents a loss of power, voice, social skills, support and informal help and funding. What is not realised here—or is unmentionable—is that although the movement from the cities has many other long-term causes, delinquency has now ceased to be merely a symptom of urban breakdown in *this* country (if it ever was) and has become a major contributor to it. It accelerates the same vicious social circle which one can see in some schools, where those teachers who can no longer stand it leave, thus further weakening resistance to the problem by the loss of consistency, experience and familiarity. A survey for Thames Television published in May 1977 found three-quarters of inner city dwellers wanting to move to the suburbs or further. Nearly half of those questioned felt it no longer safe to go out alone at night in central London, with the figure rising to sixty-five per cent for the over 55s. Some of the other reasons quoted, for example, squalid, dirty and deteriorating surroundings, could also be related to the rise in vandalism and the decline of civic values, or even simple politeness.

For it is not merely the discrete acts of violence and vandalism which so prompt the urge to escape. It is the spread of what could be called a delinquent syndrome, a conglomeration of behaviour, speech, appearance and attitudes, a frightening ugliness and hostility which pervades human interaction, a flaunting of contempt for other human beings, a delight in crudity, cruelty and violence, a desire to challenge and humiliate and never, but never, to please; where the individual gets his way and wouldn't think or bother to get it with anything but aggression. And, whether justified or not, any threat that this syndrome will spread into adjacent areas as yet relatively untouched, accelerates the stampede to an illusory safety. Illusory, because the problems are nationwide and essentially classwide. Areas of low delinquency today have a habit of becoming swallowed by high delinquency ones tomorrow, and no one escapes the cost. Very many 'desirable' middle-class areas, perhaps less violent, now display an accumulating squalor in their public places, a legacy of numerous acts of petty vandalism, pilfering and filthy habits.

People's desire for 'community' is a cant phrase. But if it means something, as James Q. Wilson mentions, it certainly does not mean just an emotional need to belong, a situation depending solely on *personal* relationships in which conformity and structure have no place. The word became too coloured by hippie commune propaganda and practice.

Community to most citizens is a rational self-interested desire for safety and orderly conduct in one's immediate public environment, an emphasis on formality, and predictability. One might add that norms and values are required *to be seen* to be in operation to be affirmed, and it is in their continual public reassertion and affirmation that belief in them is located. Human weakness may lead them to be betrayed behind people's backs, but you do not laugh in their face for all to see. Thus, the supposedly contradictory approach to law-abiding behaviour which has often been remarked upon (where, for example, surreptitious stealing from work 'does not count') in fact involves little contradiction in practice. Where the motto is 'what the eye does not see . . .' values are not frequently outraged, threatened or overturned; and the fact that the transgression is minor and concealed, is an inadvertent acknowledgement of these values. The odd can of paint that vanishes does not demonstrate the impotence of principle nor shatter the comfort and trust of community; it 'does not notice' as does, for example, the open looting of property, the swaggering challenge and assault. My friend's aunt who obtained most of her shrubs as discreet cuttings from the local park is not necessarily a hypocrite when she professes dismay and anger at the children who have pulled all the roses out of the beds.

If, to many people, times were getting better and people getting better as this century progressed, the days of improvement would seem now to have been brief. The ugliness and brutality of the past are back, but in a new form. It is as if effort has been overturned and achievement demolished, as so many older people watch with sadness and anxiety the dissolution of much that they worked for in far harder times.

Predictability: the fear engendered by much delinquency of the street-attack variety, is partly that people feel themselves to be at the mercy of capricious forces, which so frequently strike without much rhyme or reason, and which follow no discernible pattern of intensity. It is different from a wave of instrumental crime. That is intelligible, it is *understandable*, even if illegitimate. There they might have some clear idea of the ends sought and the 'economic cost' to which the criminal is prepared to go to attain them. However, killings have occurred for a few coppers, as hastily thrown away; assaults for a few empty beer-bottles—and for nothing. A passer-by might be sworn at, or he might be killed—it is all one. Increasingly, it fails to reassure people to tell them to 'get it into perspective'; to remind them that murder or assault can come as much from an intimate friend as from a stranger. If I have a violent husband I

know what I am going home to, and I know what I can expect;
and if I don't have a violent husband, then that is partly
because I have chosen not to have one. But I do *not* know what
to expect, and I have no choice over, what an anonymous
person may do to me on the street. I do not even have the
privilege of the knowledge that the footpad breaks an arm for a
shilling and a head for a pound. Is it robbery when the only
criterion is vulnerability, and there is really nothing to steal?
On what calculation was a 79-year-old, half-blind man killed
and robbed of about twenty pence? Or when bus-conductor
Ronald Jones died over a twopenny fare for a dog that must
have cost pounds a week to feed? You may be abused for your
class, your sex, your colour: that, in a way, you understand. But
to be abused because you are someone who happens to be there,
where even being your attacker's identical twin would not save
you? An environment may be full of risks, but it can at least be
navigated if they are known and calculable. Human beings seek
to organise and understand their social environment via some
meaning, and modern delinquency cuts it clean away; for
without meaning there is chaos and the unpredictability which
undermines the social world.

The population's experience of lawlessness all around
them tends to create an almost bizarre situation where people
not merely acquiesce, but themselves begin to participate in
acts they would initially, and still may, disagree with. They
choose to act in ways they cannot morally defend and wish were
different because they feel that their environment gives them no
choice. Everybody does it, and worse, there is disadvantage if
you don't. The rise in general lawlessness makes the initiation
of any solutions increasingly difficult for those who most desire
them. People connive more and more at the destruction of their
own environment and their own safety, while calling for acknowledgement and protection in their plight. Frightened for
themselves, some are also frightened of being left out of the
sharing of the spoils. One's own children might as well be
delinquent if everyone else's are. Honesty and consideration
are viewed with incredulity, and the ways of thieving, receiving
and deceiving gain open acknowledgement as the way of
modern life. In this way too community is undermined, and
fragmentation sown where there ought to be combination;
where it is too easy to take advantage of the vital short-run in a

situation where distrust has sometimes gone too far.

Without the possibility of a reasonably secure public life and the fabric and facilities for this, civilisation in all its aspects fares badly. The right not to be arbitrarily coerced is probably the most basic right and protection of the old and weak an elementary expression of care, concern and solidarity in human society. It is understandable—if perhaps over-dramatic—that many people in all walks of life have voiced anxiety, not only for the survival of city life and the preservation of some kind of public environment to use and enjoy, but for the associated civic and democratic values, when confronted with the prospect of a future so poorly equipped with the customs and norms essential for this. Even if we are simply less and less protected, ourselves and our property at greater and greater risk, and our resources providing more and more offerings to the children's potlatch, isn't the rapid growth of anti-social behaviour coming to the forefront as an issue of national importance?

Certainly, if asked, people will say so. A survey by the Liberal Party of the main problems facing Londoners, as defined by Londoners themselves, found, in May 1975, that violence and vandalism followed hard on the heels of inflation. The same result was obtained by the more professional and large-scale (international) Gallup Poll investigation, published in 1976, of attitudes to personal and social life. Disquiet at the fall in standards of public conduct also followed close on anxiety over the state of the economy. A very significant study carried out in 1974 by the Social Science Research Council and published in 1977 (*Encounter*, February 1977), attempted to relate voters' values and priorities to their self-designation as either 'left' or 'right' wing. Shown a list of eight 'aims and objectives which people say that our country as a whole should concentrate upon', and asked to indicate which they thought most important, a majority on both left and right chose, first, the maintenance of a stable economy. Then again, the fight against crime figured very high on the lists of both.

Yet further evidence that the fight against crime ranks high in lists of priorities by the people of this country was provided by the *New Society* 1977 national survey into British attitudes to money and work. Asked about the aims and objectives they thought the country should concentrate upon, the desire for a stable economy was followed by economic growth and the fight against crime coming in almost neck and neck to make up the top three priorities.

Yet, it is as if the powers that be have long ago turned their faces to the wall. Whatever the public may think, it is certainly not fashionable to be concerned with rising crime, delinquency and violence—street crime, the greatest fear, being the greatest taboo of all. It is a sign of the bigot, the reactionary, the law-and-order fascist and the vulgar in public bars who rant on about wogs. Ignore them, they will get fed up and go away. Indeed, the National Front marches against mugging—what more do you want?

Names do hurt, and some are effective enough to make cowards of many of us. According to the manner in which I have spoken, and the implicit stand I shall be thought to have made, I shall be called hysterical, repressive, punitive, emotional, even sick. But look at so much of the editorial material and so many of the contributions in highly regarded and widely read sociological and quasi-sociological publications, and it is clear that for *anybody* to be concerned with violence, delinquency and crime as a problem *in itself*, is *ipso facto* hysterical, emotional, punitive etc. Even the term 'moral' has become one of fashionable abuse. Are you shocked when people get robbed, bashed up, set alight? Do you find it worrying when the old are knocked to the ground for a laugh and a quid? Don't you like being pushed, beaten and abused? Are you terrified by being baited by a group of youths the whole length of a train journey?—because if you are, darling, then you are guilty of 'moral panic'. The sophisticated, the educated, the nice people of our age, know better; they are above all this and even if they notice, they affect not to.

To make their plight known, those exposed to the brunt of the anti-social tide, such as publicans, transport and hospital staff, have to resort to measures from strikes to buying space in national newspapers. There can hardly be a major city which has not been busless or trainless due to a protest against violence at one time or another.

One may assume that a public so concerned about the problem of crime and violence would be well disposed towards a vigorous attack on the problem. Thus, official shyness is not to be explained by fear of the public's resistance. Indeed, the public seem particularly well disposed towards the law, and agencies of social control. The survey by the Social Science Research Council mentioned earlier also asked respondents about their sympathies for various groups. The police came out top of the list for both those claiming to be 'left' and 'right' in their politics. The figures were respectively 84 and 88 median score on a 0-100 sympathy scale. Furthermore, the overwhelming majority of the population appear to believe strongly that this society deserves repair and support, rather than demolition. Using the same 0-100 sympathy scale, revolutionary groups scored lowest of any group in this study, both for those respondents characterising themselves as 'left' or 'right' wing. The median scores were 10 and 3 respectively.

A conclusion that one cannot avoid is that there exists a vast and widening gulf between the views of the public on antisocial behaviour, and the views of the intellectuals and professionals, not to say the politicians, who now shape our present policies and provide the influential voices on society and its problems. This is, emphatically, not just the natural and expected lag between advanced and lay opinion, but a very different kind of polarisation. Despite the belief that our age is supposed to exhibit more democracy, more mass communication and greater fluidity of class barriers than ever before, the distance between rulers and ruled on the issue of crime and delinquency is probably wider than at any time in recent history. And it soon becomes apparent that the differences are not just in emphasis or method, or sophistication versus naïvety, or scientific versus unscientific explanation, but often in fundamental goals and principles.

We have, in fact, reached a point where things have assumed bizarre proportions. While the public claims greater familiarity with violence from their own experiences, when railmen refuse to man stations, and busmen to drive certain routes, it is commonplace, for example, on Open University programmes for suave academics to deny in effect that street thuggery is real, remarkable or wrong. Given enormous time and a most deferential reverence which is denied to their opponents, these well-placed mentors insist that what *is* most reprehensible and significant is the very fact that people are making something of these events. It is not the crime that is wrong, or a problem, but the public's attitude to it.

This currently very prestigious view, that crime—particularly street crime—is simply an unwarranted dramatisation of events which are in themselves neither physically nor morally remarkable, has its roots in the fashionable muddle of 'deviance theory', with its appeal to minority groups. However, it is a recent development in a long tradition which denies the fact of rising violence and lawlessness and which has characterised much official and influential opinion. If the powers that be do not seem to be doing much about evil, then they have—by the same token—also been or disinclined to see it.

2 See No Evil

In the ten years 1960-70 the rate of indictable crime per 100,000 population almost doubled, and in 1975 stood at four times the rate of 1951. The number of indictable offences for 1975 had risen 7 per cent on the 1974 total, which itself was up by 18 per cent on the year before. Robbery rose by 31 per cent in 1975, and violence against the person by 11 per cent. The figures for 1976 again show a slowing *of the rate of increase* in indictable crime over the previous year which does not appear to have been held in 1977 (if the figures for the first quarter are anything to go by). However, violence against the person and vandalism continue their steep rise throughout the fluctuations in the general rise in offences, being respectively 10 per cent and 18 per cent up in 1976 over the previous year, and 14 per cent and 29 per cent up in 1977 (first quarter) over 1976. Since 1951 the most significant aspect of criminal statistics has perhaps been the *ten-fold* increase in those found guilty of violence against the person.

Violence, destruction, and youth, are the three distinctive features of rising crime. More than half the arrests for indictable crime are of young people under the age of twenty-one, a third between ten and sixteen. About a thousand children under ten fell into police hands in London in 1974. Overall, in fact, a fourteen-year old-boy is ten times more likely to be dealt with for an indictable offence than a thirty-year-old man, with two out of every three known burglars and three out of every five robbers being under twenty-one.

However, rising offence rates have been ascribed to faulty senses, short memory, and misinterpretation of the statistics, which primarily record police activity and are themselves part of that activity. As far as the police are concerned, they might be more energetic than in the past; P.C. Plodd may be more eager for promotion; all, or most, policemen may be suspected of misanthropy (which possibly led them to the job in the first place); or—more darkly—the police may be operating a vendetta against certain sections of the population such as blacks and working-class youth. As far as the latter is concerned, community and race-relations bodies sail as near as possible to outright accusation that the police invent both their figures and their evidence. The grand finale of this view involves the idea that the police are in some kind of massive conspiracy with other malevolent forces in society to increase the coercion and control of the population.

And the people? I was born and lived for thirty years in a very working-class neighbourhood. I know that now children smashing bottles against windows and stealing abusively from shops are quite commonplace, but that twenty to twenty-five years ago vandalism was virtually unknown and the theft of two shillings shook my school to its foundations. But, on the other hand, it can be claimed that we simply *notice* what is now more unusual or has become more immoral, or because the media tell us to. They sensationalise. And to some, they sensationalise for some of the reasons that the police fake.

There is of course an undeniable gap between crimes committed and those reported to the police. On the face of it, it would be theoretically possible to go on claiming that we have no *evidence* of a *real* rise in lawbreaking, if every alternate home were set on fire and every other citizen beaten senseless once a week. One study which should throw some light on these doubts is a project called the Sheffield Study on Urban Social Structure and Crime. It looked at how officially reported crime reached the attention of the Sheffield police. The project found that 'The results, interestingly, suggest that the official criminal statistics may be *not* just the product of greater or less police activity' (A.E. Bottoms and J. Baldwin). Indeed, the greater part of crime which reached the Sheffield police (80 per cent), was reported by the victim, or a civilian witness. Direct police observation accounted for only 5 per cent. There was no tendency for the proportion to be higher in the high offender-rate areas. As all reported offences are not necessarily cleared up—was there police bias at this stage? But tests revealed no tendency for the police to clear up more offences in the high-rate areas by calling on known offenders to question them.

Furthermore, a self-report study of juveniles on three council housing estates produced a rank-order of offender-rates in exactly the same sequence as the recorded official rates. So—in Sheffield anyway—as people are reporting more crime these days, it looks as if it is due to the surprising fact that crime is actually rising:

> . . . the recorded differences in offender-rates of our small area are real reflections of different levels of criminal action by the residents. The man in the street may not be wrong after all.

The man in the street can even be credited with 'an accurate perception of the reputation of estates' after the researchers had studied tenancy gaps in connection with crime and had employed their own observers. This study was to find that the complaint of residents on a highly delinquent council estate was that the police did not pay enough attention to it, rather than that they gave it a bad reputation.

Another investigation was undertaken in a medium-sized north of England city during 1972 (K. Bottomley and C. Coleman). Taking a random sample of one in two indictable crimes reported to, or by, the police, investigation was made of the nature of the police crime reports used as a basis for later Home Office statistics. Again, in contrast to the image of the police as crime-seekers, the survey showed that they were responsible for 'discovering' only 13 per cent of indictable offences, and a large proportion of these were revealed through routine checks or questioning in connection with other crime. Victims reported 57.1 per cent of personal injury crimes, 41.6 per cent of property loss, and 35.6 of property damage cases. Other members of the public, often employees or relatives, reported 21.4 per cent, 44.8 per cent, and 55.9 per cent respectively for the three types of offence. It was noted in this investigation that a large percentage of reported crimes *did not* lead to court convictions but were cleared up in indirect ways. Almost one-third of cases in the survey were cleared up either by being taken into consideration during the court hearing for another offence (20 per cent), or were thought not worth pursuing as the offender was already in custodial care for another offence (10 per cent).

The survey conducted throughout the USA by the National Opinion Research Centre of the University of Chicago found considerable under-reporting of crimes committed. For example, they gave a survey rate of 949.1 burglaries per 100,000 population in 1965, when the official rate was 299.6. Investigation suggests that the rate of crime experienced compared with crime reported is similar for this country.

A study of interpersonal offences by means of six-monthly random samples in 10,000 American households, revealed that victims' decisions to report offences were stable and related to a surprisingly 'economic' assessment of the offence, a rational calculation of harm which was stable not only over time, but over sex, race and socio-economic status (but not age—the young were frequent victims of violence and least likely to report it—see Wesley G. Skogan 1976). The effect of a prior relationship with the offender only decreased the tendency of the victim to report by 4 per cent (except in rape and theft with assault cases). Four characteristics of the crimes themselves were related to the decision to report—the value of the victim's loss, the success of an assault, whether or not weapons were used, and lastly, a more obscure variable—whether the offence was committed in what was roughly called the 'private-life sphere' of the victim, for example, theft and assault at home, rather than outside.

So overall, the evidence suggests that the layman's experience of the fluctuation in crime is related to rates of 'real' events rather than his increased or decreased sensitivity to them, but that he does not report very many offences he encounters. As crime rises, there is more reason to think that the percentage reported declines rather than rises. Evidence from America suggests that people in high crime areas are—from fear and resignation—less likely to report matters to the police. (See, for example, John Conklin, *The Impact of Crime*.) Is it necessarily in the interest of the police to swell statistics with offences they have little hope of clearing up, thereby demonstrating their own incompetence? The complaint that offences are ignored is aired less than the one that they are over-zealous. Yet some of those who report offences can be disillusioned when the police 'don't bother to write it down' or when they are told that they should 'put it down to experience'.

Although police harassment of blacks and sometimes working-class youth has now become part of liberal-left (and hence, sociological) coinage, it is still an open question whether there is any evidence for the accusation. Prejudice, and even bullying, is often confused with a systematic faking of evidence and statistics and the framing of individuals in certain groups. The two are not the same, and if the report of the Select Committee on Race Relations and Immigration (1977) admitted that some officers (like any other individuals) have sometimes been guilty of the former, it did not substantiate the latter. Wishful suspicion is no substitute for hard facts.

On other occasions the case seems to rest upon insinuations and tenuous extrapolations from data which only appear pertinent if police guilt is taken as axiomatic from the beginning. For example, police in the Metropolitan area have kept a log of offences which approximate to their definition of 'mugging' ('offences of robbery of personal property which follow a sudden attack in the open where there is no previous association between the victim and the assailant'). As with other offences, figures for individual divisions of the Metropolitan Police are not usually given; if they are (like those for assaults on the police as distinct from assaults on members of the public) it depends on the initiative of local commanders. In October 1976, figures were given to the public of the rates in some districts because the police claimed that they were unduly high, and rising, compared with other areas and with the previous year. That the figures referred to high immigrant areas brought criticism from the Community Relations Commission: the initiative of the commanders was taken as *prima facie* evidence of anti-black bias. It could also, of course, be taken as a *prima facie* case of concern at rising crime of a kind the public are very worried about, by a body whose responsibility it is to investigate and tackle it (see report in *The Times* 21 October 1976). In other cities with large immigrant communities, such as Liverpool and Manchester, police do not keep statistics of their own on 'muggings', or street robberies as opposed to other violent crime.

Even more devious is an argument from descriptive identities given of attackers and those arrested. In a Memorandum to the Select Committee on Race Relations and Immigration early in 1976, the Metropolitan Police included tables on offences of robbery and violent theft, which showed that, first: of 7,818 *descriptions* obtained from victims, a quarter were of whites, and 36 per cent of 'coloureds'. Secondly, of 2,294 arrests, 65 per cent were white and 31 per cent black. Not, so far, much evidence of bias. But the figures did not cover convictions, so the Community Relations Committee, seemingly convinced that things must be otherwise, have challenged the data (Report in *The Times* 28 October 1976).

In his self-report study of juvenile theft for the Home Office, William Belson found that black youths did not even report being picked up and questioned by the police any more than white ones. The data I have discussed, along with other available to date, suggest that the case remains open.

To turn to vandalism: Andy Sturman made a survey of all sources on malicious damage for one area in Manchester reputed to have a high rate of vandalism. He compared police records (including damage to property valued at under £20), records of local authority departments responsible for repairs, and figures for telephone-kiosk damage. He also asked residents in the area about their experience of damage to their property, and interviewed local shopkeepers and headmasters about damage to their shops and schools. Only *3 per cent* of all incidents in the Manchester area were found to be likely to find their way into the Criminal Statistics. This was not necessarily because most were of little value. There was a very low rate of reporting to the police from public bodies, and many—particularly schools—had a policy of not doing so. (This might be related to the ease of access to funds to pay for the damage.)

In another study in the same Home Office series on vandalism (summarised by Tony Marshall 1976), 600 Liverpool secondary-school children from all parts of the city were interviewed about their involvement in vandalism, as well as in other offences. It was found that 79 per cent of boys had smashed bottles in the street in the previous six months, and 48 per cent had broken a street lamp; 12 per cent had ripped train seats. With half the boys destroying a street lamp every six months or so, the cost to the local authority must be very high. Even what are usually thought to be 'low' delinquency, non-'problem' areas, for example, the borough of Hounslow, can have 4,000 out of 20,000 lighting units out of action every year due to vandalism. (Total cost to the borough – £100,000 per annum.)

The Fire Protection Association, largely financed by Lloyd's and other insurance companies, admitted in 1975 that the fire

situation in schools is now 'completely out of hand'. The public
has been aware for some time now of schools where the books go
up in smoke and the furniture out of the window; where robbery
is rife and gang conflict commonplace. Pupils tell of slashed
clothes and protection money. The stabbing that hits the head-
lines, produces in court the reaction of 'How did it get so bad
before anybody knew?' Busmen on many routes face four
o'clock with fear and trepidation, and can be forgiven for
drawing conclusions about speech and behaviour inside educational establishments from what they hear and see outside.

However, the classic reaction of head teachers, educational
authorities and the National Union of Teachers to information,
rumour or disquiet about rising violence and disruption in
schools, has been (a) that the problem is grossly exaggerated,
with the press sensationalising material which was none of their
business to begin with; or (b) that it has always been the same.

To combat accusations that both the public's and the
teachers' observations are purely anecdotal, the minority
teaching unions, like the National Association of Schoolmasters, have, in recent years, attempted to monitor disruption in
the classroom to 'prove' that standards of behaviour are actually deteriorating. Arguably, they are not employing the best
methods of information-gathering (in fact, they are most
inadequate) but they are trying.

Even should statistics be presented, of whatever worth, they
can still be met with the reaction that they reflect only the
observers' sensitivity and not the level of actual events. However, pressure from local levels has recently been making
inroads into the NUT's customary refusal to acknowledge a
real problem. In the light of a report of the Essex Teachers'
Association, where a working party of ten teachers found that
pilfering, truancy, obscene language, aggressive behaviour and
disobedience were on the increase in both primary and secondary schools, it could keep silent no longer, and the subject was
finally debated at the NUT's 1975 Annual Conference. (The
Essex report came after one from Croydon referring to monthly
increasing figures for physical attacks on teachers, serious acts
of disobedience, and teachers unable to cope with the strain
brought on by such events.) Many other reports and investiga-
tions all pointed the same way—that teachers were finding
violence a serious problem in the classroom, and that it was

increasing. For example, unhappy with the NAS survey of 1972, interviews were carried out by Leeds University, and questionnaires were constructed and applied to 250 educational workers, two-thirds professional teachers and one-third social workers. By two-to-one they found that violence was a major problem in schools (see Colin Pritchard and Richard Taylor's summary).

From more and more quarters, the fact of high and increasing levels of anti-social behaviour in schools has now been admitted. Clive Jones-Davies, assistant education officer in Cleveland and co-editor of *The Disruptive Pupil in the Secondary School,* claims that the evidence is so overwhelming that a significant deterioration in the behaviour of children in secondary schools is now beyond all doubt, and difficulties are reported by all involved with the schools down to infant level.

At Government level things have not quite got this far—not in public anyway. On Independent Television's *People and Politics* (15 November 1976), the Secretary of State for Education (Shirley Williams) still preferred to say that expectations of schools had risen, rather than that standards of what was euphemistically called 'preparation for life' had fallen. A short time afterwards, the Under-Secretary of State for Education and Science denied in the Commons (7 December 1976) that there was a national growth of vandalism, or even that there were any data widely available on the matter.

> It is my understanding that vandalism can arise in particular times and does tend to be a local phenomenon. There are not widely available national statistics. . . . It is not the case that there is any evidence to show there is a national wave of vandalism in schools or anywhere else.

Yet, behind the scenes, in June, the Secretary of State had already seen leaders of education and welfare organisations, when it was announced that a national inquiry was to be held into methods of reducing school disruption and truancy. At the same time a DES discussion document disclosed that more than half of the 104 local education authorities in England and Wales had, in fact, established 'behaviour units' in and outside of schools for children who 'can't cope' in the classroom (that is, the children teachers can't cope with).

But even if our information suggests that there really is more lawbreaking, violence, and vandalism, than previously, *why notice anything at all?* An argument frequently heard of late is that lawbreaking, and violence particularly, are in themselves essentially unimportant, and that it is rather those who worry about these things, or simply draw attention to them, whom we really need to watch. Two examples of this prolific genre which I shall discuss here are to be found respectively in the BBC Publication *The Lawbreakers,* 1974, (Paul Wiles: *Explaining violence and social work practice*) and in the Department of Health and Social Security Publication *Violence,* 1976 (Stuart Hall: *Violence and the Media*).

Violence, these authors maintain, is a matter of how we evaluate otherwise mundane, unremarkable events in the world. What matters is not that these events occur, but how we see them. We focus attention on one 'happening' rather than another and make it, and others like it, a subject of scandal, concern and prohibition. So, for people like Wiles and Hall, the problem is, why some events become so classified. To the obvious answer to why violence is seen as a social problem, Wiles' reply is to the effect that we have to die anyway, and we often get involved in accidents which injure us, so what's the difference between getting put down by an IRA bomb or a mugger's boot, rather than a virus or a loose stair rod? We don't label the latter violent and we don't get worked up over it in the same way as we might over the former.

> Why then is violent behaviour perceived as so socially prob-
> lematic? The answer may seem obvious: because it injures
> people. However upon closer examination such an answer
> turns out to be inadequate. Other forms of behaviour which
> are not legally or commonly defined as violence turn out to
> be much more injurious. In England and Wales you are
> more likely to die as a result of choking on your food than as a
> consequence of a criminal assault. Death and injury are far
> more likely to result from a whole host of other eventualities.

Where Wiles gets all these people who choke on their food is anyone's guess. But several things need to be said about this very silly, as well as perfectly callous argument.

If there is the assumption that we do not worry about—and hence take no precautions against—disease and accident, then this is palpably false.

A vast medical effort in money, manpower, facilities and research goes daily into the preservation of life of all ages and in the face of all manner of diseases, some of which affect only very small numbers of people. The child or baby suffering from some obscure complaint is a stock-in-trade of the popular press; and the merest suspicion that someone might be suffering from an infectious disease such as typhoid almost invariably makes the front page. Similarly, the law also enforces a host of safety regulations, including those intended to prevent the introduction of new dangers, such as the anti-rabies regulations. Even if the nature of a disease or accident is little understood and there is no real way to control it, this has never prevented people from dreading it and desperately trying to do something about it. If any disease had doubled its share of victims in the last ten years in the way violence against the person shown in the sum total of killings has done, we would be seriously concerned with measures to contain and reduce it.

(As Wiles does not give rates of choking on food, it is difficult to compare them with the claims made by the senior plastic surgeon for Manchester (*Guardian* interview 2 March 1976) who explained that the main cause of facial injuries in the North-West is now no longer motoring or other accidents, but street attacks, football violence and fights.)

Whatever he might wish, there might be circumstances where the individual may have to resign himself to a disease which is incurable or an accident which is unforeseen. But a reason why he might not so readily resign himself to becoming a victim of violence is that this involves deliberate acts which need not have been committed. Whether or not 'other forms of behaviour which are not legally or commonly defined as violence turn out to be much more injurious', these are non-intentional. Paul Wiles is part of the Faculty of Law of the University of Sheffield, and knows how central is the concept of intent to law in society. Other misfortunes may be partly avoidable if people avoid certain risks or take greater care—but an intentional act such as an act of violence is logically distinct from compulsion or accident: it *need not* have happened.

But if there is nothing special about violent events in themselves to make us notice them rather than other events in the world, why, according to these writers, do we in fact become concerned with them? Apparently 'to understand why we fear

certain behaviour of young people we must explain how that
behaviour becomes classified as violent behaviour.' It seems
that it becomes so classified by the media, which 'gives it a
certain meaning'. Some otherwise neutral events in the world
then frighten people, and moral condemnation ensues: there is
a 'moral panic'.

> . . . the role of the mass media in modern societies is to
> highlight and distort such behaviour with the effect of creat-
> ing a succession of moral panics. The rowdyism and van-
> dalism of youth is too everyday and commonplace to capture
> our attention (Paul Wiles).

Stuart Hall gives us a full description of how the media make
what should remain a morally insignificant, and naturally
unremarkable, phenomenon into a 'social issue' and a 'moral
panic':

> The media not only play a part in constructing violence into
> a social issue, they also have a role in the orchestration of the
> concern which they helped to create. For, without fail, sec-
> tions of the press and spokesmen on radio and television will
> use these causes for concern as a basis for stimulating the
> public into a moral panic, or for organising a public crusade
> and expressing public moral indignation.

And why?

> Thus, society's self-appointed moral guardians who desire
> greater social controls, more authority, discipline and
> restraint and who because of the progressive polarisation of
> society feel that things are slipping from bad to worse (i.e. up
> the threshold of violence), may have their worse fears daily
> and nightly confirmed by the relatively independent proces-
> ses of the media, who find it convenient to classify problem-
> atic or threatening events into and through these widening
> circles of disturbance. The effect of both working to reinforce
> each other is to promote a tightening circle of social control,
> a solidifying of the traditionalist world view, a moral back-
> lash and populist crusade – all in the form of an escalating
> moral panic about violence.

'. . . society's self-appointed moral guardians who desire control . . .' egged on by the media. Presumably those attacked and

robbed, and others who could be in just the same position, are either numerically insignificant or have no real objections to being attacked, until the media latches on to them. Or perhaps they mind a great deal, for Hall talks of a 'populist crusade'? Indeed, it is all very confusing. For on the one hand we have 'the progressive polarisation of society' and on the other, *everybody* seems to be in cahoots against violence by their 'moral panic'—authorities, the masses—the lot. (Except, that is, the violent themselves and sections of the intelligentsia.) The 'polarisation' discerned by Stuart Hall could be read as an unintended acknowledgement that nearly everybody, except its perpetrators, is fed up with violence. The 'moral scare' may, in fact, mean that a great many people *want* a social morality and a legal system which hold it wrong to take other people apart, and will exert sanctions against those who do so.

I would have thought that it was usual, unless one is a masochist, for all sentient creatures to avoid pain and injury and situations which inspire anxiety and fear. And, not only do things of flesh, blood and nerves desire not to be hurt, they also usually seek to stay alive. Even human beings who have never read a newspaper in their lives, who may not know the laws of the land they travel in, who have never watched television, who might be blind and deaf as well as illiterate, usually don't like being robbed, beaten up, maimed or killed, and they usually avoid circumstances where they might be. The accusation has now frequently been made that it is the use of the term 'mugging' by the press, which gives the offence its 'emotional' or frightening character. When Paul Storey brained a labourer with a brick and was ordered to be detained up to twenty years, liberal opinion blamed it on the 'alarmist' press coverage of 'muggings'. However, it is doubtful whether the use of any other term, whether robbery with violence, footpad crime and so forth would make the following events any more congenial, acceptable or less frightening:

> She was pushed and kicked and the youths tried to grab the rings from her fingers, which she folded under her arms in an effort to prevent the robbery.
> But they pulled at her clothing, ripped her skirt and poloneck jumper off. Constable Owen said they also tried to tear off her brassiere, knocked her to the ground, and continually kicked her.

There were cries of 'Let's burn her' as matches were struck
to help them see in the dark to snatch rings from her fingers
. . . (*The Times* 28 October 1976).

One youth described how a crowd of them punched and
kicked a couple under the West Way flyover in Portobello
Road, told police: 'They were crying for mercy'.

Husbands and boyfriends who tried to help wives and
girlfriends in danger of being robbed were beaten up and had
their wallets stolen.

A young mother with two small children was set upon and
£2, all the money she possessed, was taken.

Another youth told police: 'We really started doing the
muggings at the Carnival in Notting Hill and after that
everybody started going mad . . . there were a lot of us'. (*The
Daily Telegraph* 20 May 1977)

On the basis of the argument we have seen advanced here, why
should one regard the treatment of human beings anywhere, in
any way, as significant in the least—whether it be by Brazilian
or Persian or Chilean policemen, in South African or Russian
jails, by Palestinian guerrillas or Italian fascists, and so forth?
The victims, after all, will only be a small percentage of those
whose death and injury 'result from a whole host of other
eventualities'. Indeed, when Jews were beaten up on the streets
of pre-war Germany was the noticing, reporting, and the subsequent moral indignation abroad a 'moral panic' about street
violence?

The position on violence and the media is very different from
the one which we are accustomed to hear, and Hall, for example, is very concerned that we make that distinction. It is *not*
that the entertainment industry is arousing a taste for violence
or creating an insensitivity towards it, but the very opposite,
that it is creating a sensitivity and revulsion towards it which
are unwarranted. The example which is constantly brought up
is the massive press coverage of the seaside escapades of the
Mods and Rockers a number of years ago, compared with the
small amount of damage and delinquency which actually
occurred. (It was originally cited in the work of Stan Cohen.)
But, even in this case, the number of physical attacks was an
independent variable—the press was not inventing them. On
other more recent occasions, there have been, for example, riots

outside football grounds which have damaged and destroyed a great deal of property and injured people, which the press did not know about. The extent of the trouble only came to light after police investigation. In fact, residents near football grounds *themselves* urge the police to do something, and the newspapers to publicise their case.

That the press, in its coverage of incidents like those involving Mods and Rockers, might be helping to develop the behaviour in question in young people by providing such clear models to copy, I do not deny. News reporting has probably suggested everything from hijacking aircraft, to stoning buses, to people who would never themselves have thought of such things. And in the popular media the line between titillation and information is often hazy, particularly at holiday time. But, that the media themselves undoubtedly select according to their own current notions of what is a story, does not mean that these notions do not reflect some genuine popular attitudes. And that they can be irresponsible as well as frivolous in their pursuit of high circulations and audiences, does not in the least show that they are involved in any plot to strengthen repressive social controls. If authoritarianism means anything at all, the media would stand to suffer severely from such controls.

Stuart Hall betrays that paranoia, that obsession with a massive, hidden single-minded conspiracy of allied forces so common with extreme right-wing and religious sects, who see the real rulers of the world as International Jewry, Freemasonry, Popery or the Devil. But, unlike these, he is a learned man, a neo-Marxist, Director of the Centre for Cultural Studies at the University of Birmingham. And he gets his work into the publications of the Government manipulators and appears on those very media whose sinister machinations he is trying to expose.

In the denial or dismissal of rising delinquency, one moves quickly through a spectrum where arguments over the fact of whether or not it has *really* increased, by those who one presumes still deplore such activities, become a complete denial of its importance. Indeed, any importance that is retained is only to the delinquent himself. He is justified in behaving as he does, but the public is not justified in fearing him. The latter point I will take up in Chapter 10.

But if some authors now see nothing intrinsically wrong with

violent events, apart from the selective manner in which they
are represented, why should there have been an overall tendency to turn a deaf ear to the public, such a desire to keep them
in the dark and avoid the open discussion of the problem of
rising lawbreaking? Concealment and evasion have been with
us for years over trouble in schools, and statistical evidence for
rising crime has been constantly repudiated as inconclusive in
very many influential quarters. It is not simply that there has
been concern over the possibility of stoking anti-black prejudice; this is a red herring, for black street-crime has only
recently come to the fore in London. Ronald Jones was black,
and his death brought all London busmen and many tube-
workers out on a one-day strike against violence.

The explanation lies to a great extent in that fear expressed
by Stuart Hall of 'greater social control, more authority, discipline and restraint'. The public usually sees delinquency and
violence as a problem *per se,* and not a manifestation of something else. Their direct answer to it, almost unavoidably, is
socialisation and social controls. On the other hand, official,
professional and intellectually favoured approaches to the
increasing involvement of the young in delinquent and violent
activities have all implicitly or explicitly denied the need for
these controls. They are, in principle, unnecessary.

Varying explanations have been put forward which locate
the origin of anti-social behaviour in a range of emotional,
social and economic deprivations. There may be differences in
opinion about where the real defects in society lie, but all are
agreed that when they are genuinely and finally remedied,
there should be no need to uphold norms by sanctions and
law-enforcement. Favoured explanations all assume that anti-
social acts are a secondary symptom of other, quite distinct
problems. The psychological versions usually emphasise lack
of love, with subsidiary factors in the lack of 'outlets', or poor
provision for 'interests'. Economic and social versions sometimes blame low income, unemployment, the standard of housing (shared bathrooms, outside WCs, number of people per
room, etcetera), or larger and vaguer things, such as 'the
system'. (There are also biological versions of the kind which
blame such things as the concentration of atmospheric lead.)

The limits of the concession made to concepts of socialisation
and social control are that these measures form, at most, an

unpalatable stopgap, until we have THE ANSWER. Not only are they *not* part and parcel of THE ANSWER, but, like suppressing the body's manufacture of antibodies in the face of disease, they are even accused of exacerbating the problem, or complicating it, by preventing the expression of its symptoms. Delinquency and violence are not problems in themselves, but secondary manifestations of some unmet psychological, social or economic need.

Clearly, when you feel that the public are so ignorant about the true causes of anti-social conduct, you don't want them sabotaging the enlightened work being done on their behalf! Leaning heavily on the psychological concept of emotional deprivation, there has been a much-lauded change in the juvenile law with the passing of the 1969 Children and Young Persons Act. The move has been away from custody and deterrence, to treatment and rehabilitation, with children and youths in trouble being offered help rather than being faced with the force of law. But the results to date can only be embarrassing to the exponents of the New Socio-Psychological Expertise. The greater the groundswell of popular discontent, the more emphatically are deprivations of various kinds presented as the causes of the problem, and the more time has to be bought with denials of its severity.

Whether socialisation and social controls are simply believed to be unnecessary, or are disliked and repudiated for quasi-moral reasons, has been unclear ever since the beginning of the reign of the New Expertise. But, increasingly, the question has become more obviously one of principle. If certain ends can be secured only by what is felt to be impermissible repression, coercive authority, and so forth, then the ends themselves must be sacrificed. If it was unnecessary or counterproductive to impose and uphold norms, it now becomes something no one has a *right* to do. Better allow rising crime, delinquency and violence than capitulate to 'authoritarianism', is the implicit—if not explicit—assumption.

There is a more radical wing to this faction. For if delinquency and violence are problems only in the sense that they are made the occasion for political oppression and control, then the 'persecuted' delinquent, often with his deprivations still in tow, graduates from a passive creature to an active rebel against an 'unjust' system. He is now an avenger of our social

ills in consequence of the way in which he has been treated: it is
not that he has become 'sick' as a consequence – on the contrary, he is healthier than the rest of us! The final development
of this tradition where delinquent acts become political revolt,
is where the lawbreakers assume the mantle of revolutionaries
who will overturn the oppressive and rotten present, and usher
in the luminous, future Utopia.

Thus, attitudes towards delinquency and violence in influential circles have tended over the years to develop from factual
disbelief in the efficacy of certain means to deal with anti-social
conduct, to a repudiation of the ends; to a position where
delinquency and violence become the 'right' response.

Not, of course, that everybody has moved at once; and the
last thing that can be said about informed or educated attitudes
to delinquency and violence is that they are clear. At the same
time as the delinquent has become a revolutionary in many an
academic department, many of those who work the 1969 Act
and pronounce on childrearing still find him at a loss for love, in
the purest traditions of the Act's philosophy. The waxing and
waning of fashion in the social and psychological explanations
and panaceas which constitute the New Expertise, makes the
attitudes of the New Establishment, which carries them, a
rather jumbled assembly.

3 The New Establishment

In Britain, Government and public institutions seem to have been severely chastised by the experience of the Conservative 'fifties, when so many moves for reform were effectively blocked. The Establishment was unrepresentative and minority religious and traditional views were imposed on the majority. It didn't like birth control, divorce, abortion, unmarried mothers, or sex in the arts; it was none too keen on professional social welfare; it seemed to oppose all informal educational methods out of sheer obstinacy; the questioning of traditional norms was not respectable, and protest had an aura of almost treasonable shock. Indeed, the Establishment seemed none too keen on technology and science—especially social science. It was definitely, as so many said, Church, Crown and the Conservative Party.

But, by the mid-'sixties, anything new was suddenly to become, almost by very virtue of opposition or sheer modernity, scientific and progressive: objectively true and, by the same token—good. It was time we listened to the specialists and put our future on a firmer foundation. So, alongside the great promise of technology, the bringer of future prosperity, a tremendous faith was also invested in the emergent social sciences to settle our human problems smoothly and scientifically. The keys to the stewardship of human affairs were eagerly handed over: civil servants, MPs, Town Hall planners, educationalists, administrators of all kinds, fell over themselves to adopt the new experts' suggestions. Social science courses and Sociology departments blossomed. The Social Worker was the special practitioner of the New Establishment, and they were turned out in thousands to do its good works. Older trades and professions could no longer be trusted to deal with the public without the new knowledge (for years they might have been doing untold harm); and—fortunately—there was a widespread clamour for tokens of the new professional expertise by those ready and willing to receive it. Teachers, particularly, looked to professionalism to remedy their falling status and inadequate remuneration.

If science was the thing, those ambitious administrators and politicians who wished to be renowned for instituting its rule, assumed rather innocently that there already existed a body of accumulating experimental knowledge and expert opinion, as methodological and sound in the human sciences as in the physical. As there were chemists, physicists and engineers, so there were educationalists, child psychologists, sociologists and so forth—but how to recognise them? As the wish became the deed, courses were scratched up from a miscellany of notions about human beings and society, and the highways and byways were combed for the wise men who would lead us.

Fringe sciences, and marginal but recurrent strands in Western speculative thought, suddenly had the stage. For example, take the antecedents of the Plowden Report, the bible of the progressive upheaval in the schools. This was essentially a repetition of the largely ignored Hadow Report of 1931. That, in turn, belonged to a tradition which began in Froebel's Rousseauesque treatise of 1826, which spoke of man's social development as a pseudo-biological growth, thus the child should not be taught, but permitted spontaneously to produce of itself. A kindergarten movement on Froebel's principles flickered throughout the last century, and psychoanalysis added to it notions of the undesirability of 'repressing' instinctually programmed development. In the 1930s the pursuit of wholesome, natural man found sporadic expression in such things as the free school of A.S. Neill, or the aristocratic crankiness of the Russell clique, with its hiking, biking, nudity and pacifism. The pedigree of progressive education today is not essentially different from that of many of the pseudo-scientific cults and speculations of the last century or so—whether we think of Annie Besant and the Theosophy movement, Mary Baker Eddy and Christian Science, Phrenology, or indeed Freud and Psychoanalysis. The rapid dissemination of the latter as Psychology in the social science boom of the 'sixties, with its enormous influence on child-rearing, education and social work, was, in large part, due to the foothold it already possessed in the medical profession. Many doctors, as if looking for a justification for their quasi-priestly role, or for a source of knowledge about the human mind of which they were essentially as ignorant as any layman, had chanced upon, and with their status and title, legitimised the variants of psychoanalysis. And, as if the amateurs were making the professionals in their own image, the doctor-analyst was foremost in imparting his special knowledge of human development and mentality to the new generation of social workers and child-care experts who were to compete with and devalue him.

If scientific psychology was swallowed up, or swamped in its cradle, by the popular fancy for psychoanalysis, the questions which Sociology directed itself to, and the conclusions it reached, soon came to be decided by a vague Marxism. In turn, by the beginning of the 'seventies this had filtered down from academic departments to affect social work and education. Community work replaced Casework in the social services, and the emphasis on people's 'inner worlds' or personal relationships shifted to their handicaps and rights vis-à-vis 'the system'. The prescription changed from one of cultivating 'insight' into private dynamics, to advocacy and confrontation. 'Commitment' on the part of the professional became as important as 'Caring'.

We will make all things new. The social science expansion of the 'sixties, the vast increase in the numbers and tasks of the 'caring' professions, rode in on the back of a boom in the economy and in public spending. It rode, among other things, with the comprehensive demolition and redevelopment of whole city areas and town centres. It was a time when the very acknowledgement of limitations, or finite possibilities, was political death. Nobody dared suggest that perhaps *some* problems would always be with us, or that we might not be able to afford to solve every one of them. Nobody went to the people with the modest admission that they had renovated a thousand old houses: they had to pull them down and build ten thousand new ones. What was wanted was a fresh start, and for the first time in social history we could afford one. In education, that breakthrough in the understanding of the human mind—if properly financed—would bring us an effortless depth of learning, compared with the compartmentalised, dreary and often hard world of practice, exercise, repetition, instruction, 'talk

and chalk' that we seemed to have been caught in since the
ancient world. Again, old piecemeal and untidy methods of
social control were ripe for the great change to rehabilitation—a remaking of the offender: a radical change of heart and
mind that was here to stay—the final solution to the problem of
crime. Segregation and punishment, or custody and deterrence, were the crudest of stop-gaps, awaiting that ANSWER to
anti-social behaviour.

The appearance of the New Establishment is now broadly
associated with the Labour Party. However, very many of the
same ideas in education, penal policy and the social services
were in vogue abroad at the time, particularly in America. Any
government of a boom economy might have been tempted by
the dynamic image to cast itself as the backer of the scientific
future. It was only a sudden lack of funds which prevented
Heath's Conservative Government repeating the disastrous
American 'Head Start' programme with nursery education.
The official or 'consensus' psychology, with its figureheads of
John Bowlby and later Mia Kellmer Pringle, had as much
appeal for the Conservative Sir Keith Joseph as it has had for
The Observer and *The Guardian*. Its emphasis on 'the family', and
particularly, on full-time maternal care, has been acceptable as
an enlightened set of guidelines to all but the feminists.

However, reforming politicians, recently come to power, are
rather more inclined to opt for that Utopian sweep when the
resources are readily at hand. A two-way traffic has operated,
where long-standing ideals are held to have been vindicated in
fact, and what were believed to be scientific pointers forward
become, in turn, political dogma. Indeed, the vast public-
spending involved can be justified anyway as a redistribution of
wealth. And those that give feel righteously vindicated simply
by their good intentions; it is their critics who stand condemned
in asking for results. (Even in the teeth of the economy measures of the mid-'Seventies, Wandsworth council in London greatly
increased its social service personnel and expenditure. Part of
the money appeared to have been spent on full-page advertise-
ments in magazines consisting of pictures of quite ordinary
children and adolescents, accompanied by the vague but emotive claim that 'this' was the 'reason' they were not going to
comply with Government austerity.) Certainly Socialism, in all
its variations, has always cast itself as 'scientific' and 'inevita-

ble' as well as good and just. It seemed axiomatic that the way social science would 'prove' that society should be properly run, would be the Socialist way, whether it be Marxist or Welfare. The perfectibility of Man is central to Socialist assumptions, as is the idea that society is progressing or striving towards a culmination where this will be realised. History will be terminated as will politics, since there will no longer be any point in arguing about the rules, or conflicts to be resolved; no permanent necessity to manage, reconcile, restrain and sponsor permanently faulty men and institutions.

The 'sixties also saw the rapid rise of the 'sociological' pressure group, or the newly educated, statistic-wielding charity (Shelter, Child Poverty Action Group, National Council for Civil Liberties, etcetera) which, unlike older organisations, were felt to have an objective appraisal of the situation. Accordingly, their stance was that of impartial authorities in particular fields, rather than of fallible, partial and therefore biased interests, who simply pushed for what they thought was a proper deal for their own group. This quasi-scientific approach to what were generally acknowledged to be issues that could not *morally* be ignored, gave them considerable status and influence.

The changes which were to place the problem of delinquency largely in the hands of the New Establishment could be said to have had their beginnings in *Crime: a Challenge to us all,* a Labour Party research pamphlet, which was the report of a group of people headed by Lord Longford, published in 1964. In 1965, the Government was to follow this with its White Paper, *The Child, the Family and the Young Offender.* The aim was to abolish completely the whole legal apparatus of courts for the under-sixteens. In its place would be a local 'family council', a number of which would be appointed for each local authority area. The council would endeavour to reach agreement with the parents of the child on the treatment to be given, but, if there was disagreement, the issue would be referred to a court for determination. These special family courts would involve the magistrates in procedures to 'determine disputed issues of fact or decide treatment when agreement cannot be reached between the family council and the child's parents'. If the treatment required for a child under sixteen involved removal from home, then he would be placed in the care of the local authority.

Special provisions for delinquent children, such as Approved Schools, would cease to exist, since there would now be *no* distinction made between children who were 'delinquent' and children who suffered from other adverse circumstances: both were equally in need of help and care. The White Paper was an attempt, inherent in a 'disease' approach to anti-social behaviour, to spare the sick or deprived child involvement with the machinery and implications of the law.

But it was to anger the magistrates: and no wonder, for it bypassed them and what they felt to be their longstanding expertise; and it angered the lawyers. To many of them, the closed, secret nature of the proposed 'family' counselling, with no necessity to prove a case by standard rules of evidence, not only abandoned the idea of explicitly wrong acts, but demon-strated neither to the public nor to the young offender that justice was being done, or that it was at all relevant. It seemed a dubious precedent in a democratic, libertarian society, one of whose cornerstones is the rule of law. It was a way to kill with kindness, in that it appeared to strike at the basis of civil rights by taking away notions of responsibility. All young offenders would, in effect, be merged with those who were unfit to plead; their offences would be treated as a manifestation of depriva-tion which they could not help, and their legal rights conse-quently would be removed by paternalistic agencies operating behind locked doors and answerable to nobody.

In turn, society and its demands had apparently dropped out of the picture, on the assumption that the child's behaviour and treatment were something which concerned only the family, in conjunction with the social services. (But then, everywhere in the early 'sixties, the family—that 'greatest success story of the century'—was both the centre and the limit of human life and aspiration.)

It was conceded that, perhaps, too much weight had been given to the nuclear family to the total exclusion of society. But, apart from the lawyers' argument over the necessity to prove a case, all other objections were attributed to primitive, punitive bigotry. The belief of rehabilitationists in the Royal Road to Crime (whereby juvenile offenders almost invariably graduate into adult criminals) was long-standing, axiomatic and unquestioned. We must get at the root of the problem in the juvenile, if our adult prisons were to be emptied. Rehabilitation in the early stages was the only humane and effective way to nip anti-social conduct in the bud, and now, more than at any other time, we had the knowledge and skill to do this.

Proposals that would 'prevent the deprived and delinquent children of today from becoming the deprived, inadequate, unstable or criminal citizens of tomorrow' (James Callaghan, March 1969), were put forward again later, in a modified form, in a new White Paper *Children in Trouble*. This dropped the insistence on the controversial family councils, but kept most of the earlier features. The 1969 Act which followed abolished criminal prosecution for children under fourteen and made it tortuously difficult to institute for the under seventeens. (Only certain people would be able to lay a charge against a child; the police would have to consult the local authority first, whose social workers would investigate, etcetera.) The only way a young offender could be dealt with was by means of the care order, in the same way as any other child 'in need'; again, the distinction between deprived and delinquent was to be removed. Borstal was to be phased out for the under seventeens, and so were detention and attendance centres. Fines were to be abolished. There was to be a clean sweep of all punitive and deterrent measures.

Instead, offenders might be treated at home by social workers, or the social services might decide that a child committed to their care should go into one of the new Community Homes (ex-Approved schools), alongside other deprived and maladjusted children. There was much emphasis on treating children at home, and keeping them away from institutions as much as possible. The magistrate might advise about the type of care he thought the child needed when he committed him to the care of the local authority social services department, but he had no longer any power of decision. He could not, for example, decide that a child must go into a secure community home rather than a non-secure one. But he could still make a number of other orders, as he could for non-delinquents (for example, hospital care, a guardianship order, or an order for a parent to undertake proper care and control).

It might seem that the Act at least permitted the child, if he was an offender, to be put into care. Strictly speaking, this is not so. Although it contains an 'offence' condition for care proceedings, and although it insists on the offence being proved beyond reasonable doubt, the offender must *also* be shown to be in need of the care and control which he is unlikely to get from his parents. In one sense then, the Act does not deal directly with, and does not really recognise, *delinquents* at all. Delinquency alone is not *unambiguously* a ground for action to be taken. Should he break the law, a child from a comfortable home with supportive parents hardly fits into the vital second require-ment: that he would definitely not receive the necessary 'care' unless an order is made. Essentially, delinquency pure and simple is not the target of the Act, since the theory on which it is based sees delinquency only as a sympton of other difficulties.

Yet, even with the Act passed, many people still had qualms, and the return of a different government to power meant that it was not fully implemented. Being simply for the *status quo,* the Conservatives proposed nothing in its place. So an uneasy mixture of parts of the Act and pre-Act measures towards delinquency has remained to this day. It still remains possible to institute criminal proceedings against the under fourteens, and the obstacles to proceedings against the under seventeens were not enforced. Fining remains an option, as does Borstal for older offenders.

But the care order was central, and institutional treatment in the community homes has become increasingly therapeutic, even if it has usually been convenient in practice to separate delinquent from non-delinquent maladjusted children. The choice over what happens to a child in care, whether he should be sent home with or without social-worker supervision, or go into a secure or non-secure Community Home, still, of course, devolves entirely on the social services as intended. Power has not returned to the magistrates.

Yet in spite of not being fully implemented, the spirit of the Act has been complied with outside the care order and com-munity home system more than official changes would suggest. The trend since 1969 has been increasingly in the direction of more informal measures of dealing with offenders, often via police liaison schemes with social services departments, so that in many areas only a minority of offences are actually dealt with in the courts, and those are at the recommendation of the social services.

The deterrent measures which have survived from earlier legislation have, in fact, atrophied, if they have not been quite swept away. It is true that in 1975, for example, magistrates' courts fined 4,489 boys under fourteen for indictable offences (out of a total of 21,418 found guilty). They fined 1,298 boys out of a total of 2,694 found guilty of non-indictable offences. (Most of those found guilty would have received a conditional discharge, others would have received care orders and been handed over to the social services.) Of those 58,901 boys between fourteen and seventeen found guilty of indictable offences, 23,227 were fined; of those 30,739 found guilty on non-indictable offences, 22,867 were fined. However, the maximum fine to date (1977) that can be imposed on an offender between ten and fourteen is *ten pounds*. On an offender between the ages of fourteen and seventeen, the maximum fine is *fifty pounds*.

The coming of the 1969 Act cannot be divorced from the other changes wrought in the rearing and education of the young in home and school, in accordance with the new psycho-sociological knowledge. How much all this was represented as a tremendous liberation from the ignorance of the past can hardly be exaggerated, and what a marvellous future it was to have brought—a spontaneous feast, a blossoming of hitherto dormant talent, creativity, individuality and sociability, in which natural curiosity and gregariousness would equal learning, would equal happiness, would equal social responsibility.

It is not prejudice, but simply the truth, to say that the outlook which transformed so many things in the 'sixties, and whose aftermath we are experiencing and evaluating now, neither clarified its tenets theoretically, nor tested them empirically, before rushing them into operation. This being the case, whether the innovations would work might be said to have been largely a matter of chance. Extravagant promises were made, but half the time they appeared to be superfluous. For an arrogant certainty swept the new ideas into operation as if by divine command—one which had no truck with heretics. Axiomatically, these ideas were right: they must be implemented and those who quibbled would have to conform or go. 'Progressives only need apply.' It became almost indecent to ask if the new methods worked better to achieve specific goals, or even what the goals really were; everything from group therapy for delinquents to open-plan classrooms was introduced without its sponsors even contemplating testing it beforehand. Certainly prestigious terms like 'scientific' and 'experimental' were used, but only as a holy mantle to contrast these methods with the reactionary and traditional. In fact, they had nothing of the empirical spirit of scientific, controlled experiment. Such unreflective zealotry never paused to think that it might be mistaken; it simply demanded an allegiance every bit as rigid as that previously called for by that tradition it despised.

It had that double defence against criticism distinctive of ideology, forcing critics and doubters to fight on two fronts at once. 'Progressive' meant both factually true and ethically right, and calls for explanation, clarification or evidence could be rebuffed *both* as ignorant and as morally reprehensible, and opposition thus shamed into silence. Indeed, opposition could sometimes be psychologically labelled as 'authoritarianism', indicating not only error and repressiveness, but hinting at mental abnormality underlying it. This was particularly true in America, where the diagnosis of 'authoritarian' personalities was soon throwing its net not only over the outright fascist, corporate state supporter, militarist and racialist (as if such opinions, however nasty, were themselves symptoms of disease) but extended to anyone at odds with permissive, progressive policies on a whole range of social and political issues. Parental failure had warped the ordinary.process of development into optimistic, tolerant and permissive 'normal' people, and it was soon apparent that the amount of personal pathology in the general population was prodigious indeed. It is interesting that the sickness of 'authoritarianism' was supposed to show itself not only in morally repugnant and scientifically ill-informed opinions and solutions, but also to be distinguished generally by a faulty process of reasoning which saw profundity in empty clichés, tended to polarise views, categorise in black and white, was intolerant to dissonance, and very slow to self-examination! The progressives should perhaps have paused before casting this avalanche of stones.

In Britain, it is comparatively easy for Establishments to perpetuate themselves after they have made the breakthrough. This is done not only by self-selection, but by the accumulation of patronage that first brought them there. It has been alleged that a paradox of successive Labour Governments, as pointed out by Labour MP Maurice Edelman, has been that in order to carry through and implement progressive legislation, they have had to resort to methods of public appointments consistently resisted by radicals in the past, amounting to the creation of numerous offices at all levels under the personal control of Ministers and their subordinates. There is also the much-used jury idea of settling policy, the Royal Commission approach to distilling a consensus of acceptable 'expert' opinion among those who count. What are they now thinking? If the Morton Commission on divorce in 1955 was packed with churchmen, so today many similar 'independent' policy advice committees will be filled by the same socio-psychological voices which have already influenced Government and can be generally relied on to tell it what it broadly wants to hear. Being the Establishment means being able, without much justification, to rule certain attitudes or policies off the agenda. This is not necessarily sinister, but it is different from the way genuinely scientific opinion reaches a consensus. What perhaps causes some confusion nowadays, is that this Establishment was supposedly called into being because of some presumed expertise, unlike older ones which were known to be more clearly committed to principles, prejudices and interests.

Before the coming of the 'caring' professions and the new expertise, it is true that the medical profession had long been renowned for its tendency to dabble in an unholy mixture of morality and pseudo-science, and in doing so to peddle all manner of notions under the garb of 'science'. But again, the promise was that what the cohorts of the past had muddied would be clarified by the armies of enlightenment, not made into a morass. And when all is said and done, doctors do have a core of knowledge and expertise to fall back on, and if their moral prescriptions are unheeded and their fancies superseded, they still have something else to do. But the New Establishment laid claim to an expertise never tested before being put into operation, and the theoretical weaknesses, dubious origin and sheer confusion of so many of its ideas, make it by no means certain that they will repay the enthusiasm, trust and money invested. And if their remedies do not work, if the reforming tendencies are open to being undermined, what can it do? Mixing fact with value may be always illegitimate, but if you have some facts, they at least can be salvaged. If professions, accepted almost entirely on trust, cannot meet their promises, they can end with no task to fulfil and no position to defend but their own now entrenched interests.

So the questions surrounding the prevention and handling of delinquency in modern Britain go far wider than simply the 1969 Act; this Act has to be seen in the context of a whole new set of attitudes and practices surrounding the entire rearing of children, and all in turn are involved with the rise of a New Establishment with its own component professions. Indeed, one process in society which has marked the rise of the New Establishment is the trend towards the increasing professionalisation of more and more functions in human society which used to be undertaken in an unmystified manner by ordinary people. Few can be unaware of the writings of Ivan Illich, particularly on the medical profession. His claim that the medical profession is not only unnecessary but actually produces more pathology than it cures (with elaborate modern techniques) may be exaggerated. But none the less there is an increasing realisation that often functions have been taken away from ordinary people, or their representatives, and given into the hands of those who make a career of them but do them no better, and without proper accountability or any kind of control by the layman.

With delinquency, the procedures of social control and socialisation which have been utilised in human communities from time immemorial to teach and get compliance with norms and laws, have been largely taken away from lay experience and practice, and exchanged for a body of socio-psychological theory, whose special recipes only special practitioners are competent to apply. But the question has the gravest ramifications for delinquency, because here, in the takeover of the functions of socialisation and social control one enters deeply into the fields of law, civil rights, and social morality, to the very basis of order and values in society. If the New Establishment cannot deliver the goods, if its remedies to solve delinquency do not work, then unfortunately the problems do not stop there. Its ideological perspective can mean that the values which the remedies concealed assume a life entirely of their own. From their entrenched position they not only block other solutions as morally impermissible, but they come to redefine the very problem itself, and even become allies to the enemy they were first sent out to conquer.

Part Two

The Spirit of '69:
Psychology and Results

4 Rights and Wrongs: Disease and Disadvantage

The official shift from the older language of morality and legality to that of therapy and welfare, exemplified in the philosophy of the 1969 Act, has, as I have said, been presented as both a more humane and a more scientific outlook on juvenile delinquency when compared with traditional solutions.

The psychology which provided such strong justification for the stance of the 1969 Children and Young Persons Act, could be said to be *naturalist* in its orientations. Indeed, such a term does not apply simply to the 'deprivation of emotional needs' explanation of delinquency, but to very many, or all, explanations in terms of some kind of unmet 'need', whether psychological, economic or social.

In this psychology, concern has not been with how children come to understand and adjust to complex social requirements. It has rather been with what the innate 'needs' of the child are, which the adult world can provide for. The adult looks to the child and is guided by the child's behaviour, rather than acts as his initiator and instructor into the rule-governed tasks and arrangements of his culture. If the adult can provide for the child's needs, then development is assumed to proceed fairly spontaneously, resulting in a good, mentally healthy person who is favourably disposed towards his fellows and adequate in his dealings with them. With everything child-centred and child-motivated, not only is there no room for adult control, but the necessity for it would wither away. Here we short-circuit the cumbersome process of choosing, defending, transmitting and maintaining social rules. Only satisfy 'needs' properly and you can dispense with the imposition of norms and values, and the implicit element of coercion indispensable in securing obedience to them. We now deal in 'facts' about human development and have no further need for value judgements, and an externally imposed social morality.

In contrast, a conventional, socialisation view of the matter which is still broadly assumed by many of the lay public could be outlined as follows. A reasonably safe and congenial social existence is only possible if there are some broad, common rules of behaviour which people take seriously enough to demand from each other and, if necessary, enforce on unwilling members of their community. Society—any society—requires that children be compulsorily taught, at the very least, a code of conduct towards people and property. Without this, social cooperation, the learning of skills, the transmission of information, freedom from fear, and access to public facilities, are all imperilled, if not sometimes impossible. Before anything else can be decided about the way we want society, there must be a guarantee of elementary safety and predictability. Rights and entitlements—including the right to be different—can only be respected within this common code. To step seriously outside this code is to forfeit the right to tolerance. In the last analysis, a child must adhere to this code whether or not he understands the reasons behind it, simply for the sake of others. The code is, of course, broken by both adults and children, but corrections or sanctions of some kind are called for when it is.

Such a perspective can be characterised as crudely empiricist and voluntarist. It is not consciously based on any theory of developmental psychology, although it implicitly assumes the cultural nature of Man and the moral nature of society. It is compatible both with taking existing values for granted, and with the desire for alternatives. It assumes that human beings become what they are largely through social experience, and that the normal child, adequately taught, becomes responsible for his actions. And it assumes that people can learn consciously to adjust their actions in the light of surrounding circumstances and repercussions. It holds, moreover, that children have to be *explicitly taught* to take the feelings and rights of other people into account; the meanings and consequences of their actions must be pointed out to them. Their mere gregariousness does not suffice to make them considerate, any more than their natural curiosity means that they can arrive, self-directed, at the purpose of objects. Happy, gregarious children may merrily batter people with sticks and bricks, and if the toy guns fired real bullets, that might be jolly fun too. Right and wrong is no more spontaneously discovered than reading. It follows from this that children are hardly 'naturally good'; that they will not automatically become altruistic simply by being well treated and satisfied.

It would be wrong to see this view as one of original 'badness' or 'sin'. It is more correctly described as a belief in innocence; the child is, at first, just *unaware* of social rules, of the value of other people as things in themselves, and the value and significance of objects to them. He 'knows no better', and must be dispossessed of his innocence, rather than have some sort of primal evil stamped out. Society chooses to make some acts bad and forbidden, and many things which might seem stimulating or momentarily interesting to the child, are condemned by the norms of people around him. He is informed that he 'does not have to do it'. Adult control, and intervention in the child's learning and experience by the deliberate and open manipulation of social tokens such as encouragement, example, rewards and punishments, is the only reliable way to make sure social rules are learnt *and* obeyed.

A corollary to this view is that human nature is stable, and not capable of infinite improvement. It accepts that people can desire to exploit as well as to help, be aroused to cruelty as well as pity, can desire dominance as well as affection. Human vices will always be with us, and they must be tackled all the time and with each generation. Therefore, objectives are usually limited.

By contrast, in contemporary popular child psychology, if the child's needs are misunderstood, thwarted or unfulfilled, development will then be placed at risk and society will suffer as a consequence.

Those with a bad start are invariably spoken of as 'damaged'—like chipped china—implying some handicap or malformation of mentality, rather than inexperience or undesirable (but alterable) behaviour and attitudes. In the words of the Home Office Advisory Council on Child Care, 'Many of them [delinquents] have had severely damaging experiences . . . all of them have suffered some form of deprivation' (in *Care and Treatment in a Planned Environment*). The delinquent is thus more handicapped than irresponsible, more deprived than depraved; he is under the sway of compulsions or disabilities

beyond his control. According to *Children in Trouble,* delinquency is either a 'response to unsatisfactory family or social
circumstances, a result of boredom in and out of school'; or it is
'an indication of pre-existing maladjustment or immaturity, or
a symptom of a deviant, damaged or abnormal personality'.

On this view, the demand for adaptation by the young to
adult social standards, and the curbing of spontaneous
behaviour, is seen not merely as useless but dubious, and
sometimes downright dangerous. Thus, Mr Edward Short,
when Minister for Education, spoke for many then and since,
when he said that 'Sanctions and punishments in schools . . .
are the straight high road to maladjusted adult life.' For a long
while now it has been constantly insinuated, if not openly
stated, that to impose demands, to criticise, forbid, exhort,
condemn, set goals, point out failures; to threaten, reprimand,
or withdraw affection or approval, can all have grave and
possibly lasting psychological effects on the child.

Given this naturalistic orientation towards maturation, what
is seen as vital is not what is learnt, but what is felt or sensed.
Not common, shared content, but private, individual 'experience'. Human development is personal and emotional, rather
than social and cultural. So just what are those 'needs' which
were so constantly mentioned in the parliamentary debates on
the Children and Young Persons Act? There are discernible
demands for 'family life', for one relationship with a 'mother-
figure', for play, stimulation, exploration and, encompassing
all, the necessity for Love, as fixed and immutable as the
physical need for calories. 'The working party started from the
concept that the child normally develops a conscience, the
ability to care about other people and the maturity to find a
personally and socially acceptable way of life through warm
close relationships and a variety of experiences. These are first
with the mother . . .' and so forth (*Care and Treatment in a Planned
Environment*).

Very well, but what if he doesn't? The Government booklet
on Youth Treatment Centres (1971) sees, as do other
guidelines for dealing with emotionally damaged children, the
'damage' not as the delinquency itself, but as the underlying
condition of which the delinquency is merely a superficial
manifestation. And if the surface symptoms alone are dealt
with, and the deeper disturbance ignored, other symptoms may

appear in their place. As a child is stuck at the wrong phase of development, he will remain there unless he receives skilled therapy to 'heal the effects of past damage and to promote emotional and social growth'. The official view, well exemplified in *Care and Treatment in a Planned Environment,* regards the delinquency not only as the mere appearance of a deeper reality: it can even be tolerated and encouraged as part of the healing process:

> A therapeutic environment is one in which informal communication is encouraged, where there is understanding and tolerance of deviant behaviour, where the child has opportunity to express symptoms of his disturbance . . .

and

> . . . in our view immediate suppression of difficult behaviour, regardless of the circumstances in which it occurs, is unlikely to help children. A child may be better helped if such behaviour, which is often a symptom of underlying disturbance, is allowed to manifest itself. He may need to give overt expression to his feelings in difficult and hostile behaviour and also in verbal abuse.

The untutored, not conversant with the idea of residues of repressed and thwarted past needs, might of course take this 'acting out' simply as the sheer practice of delinquent behaviour under benevolent toleration, even approval, and feel that it could have the opposite effect to that presumably intended. But lay common sense, which rests on the obvious, is often quite unscientific. If it were allowed the deciding voice we should never, for instance, have had vaccination, which is so repugnant to common sense when it infects a person with the very disease it undertakes to prevent. So this in itself is no basis for criticising present therapy. (However, vaccination did deliver the goods and its practitioners were agreed from the start what these 'goods' were. It is these questions which are crucial to the 1969 answer to delinquency.)

If the damage to the child is emotional, then this is the aspect upon which healing must concentrate. In an institution for the damaged, staff must provide care and 'undemanding relation-

ships'. The techniques of individual therapy have been widely
used on a group basis, where boys explore their own and each
others' feelings, and their effects on each other. Rules are
conceded to be needed perhaps in the short-run, but are aux-
iliary and secondary to a process of developing satisfactory
personal relationships which will make the rules irrelevant
later:

> A very deprived and disturbed child is unlikely to benefit
> from help unless there are some underlying controls. How-
> ever, in our experience, in a residential establishment where
> the child's needs are properly understood and there is good
> communication between staff and child, relationships can
> develop between them which obviate the need for external
> controls. (*Care and Treatment in a Planned Environment*)

(As emphasis on the fact that social rules have been
broken—even unwittingly—is evidently avoided, would it be
possible for a child to be cured and not to know what of ? The
implication is 'Yes'. But if so, does he need, and how could he
possess, any conscious grasp of the right way to go about
things? Outside society, for which he is presumably being
prepared, *does have* 'external controls'.)

Naturalistic psychology appears to assume that law-abiding
behaviour and social morality somehow emerge spontaneously
from the satisfaction of 'emotional needs'. In turn, it is striking
how much it also assumes a lack of ability in people to adjust
their actions in the light of society's opinion and response. The
picture of Man which this and other 'needs' models portray is
of a creature of extraordinary rigidity. So unadaptable, so
unopportunist, he seems incapable of altering and adjusting his
behaviour to suit his contemporary surroundings. No concession is made to any sensitivity to perceived opportunities,
incentives and disincentives, and hardly much ability to copy
or emulate others. There seems to be the suggestion that the
satisfied, and therefore mentally healthy and wholesome person, will somehow feel and behave well, with his inner being
intact and sound, irrespective of the social influences around
him. (An argument invariably brought up to counter suggestions that people imitate violence from the media, is that 'they
would have done it anyway in a different guise'; suggesting that

the propensity for violence in a population was fixed at one time and is now unmanipulable.) *

It is because of this, that those solutions which on the surface seem to offer a recipe for perfect people are, in their repudiation of learning, in fact deeply pessimistic. The pervasive talk of emotional or other 'damage', with all its connotations of ruin and irreversibility, leads easily to a wringing-of-hands, a 'nothing can be done' attitude, because intervention was not early or thorough enough. The hopelessness is increased by the vagueness of the remedy which is often never of the 'right kind' and even, as we shall see with love, impermissible to describe or translate into practical policies. It comes total and spontaneous or not at all. This all contrasts oddly with the ostensibly harder, more 'cynical' traditional approach, which sees people (and children!), as altogether more resilient, capable of 'getting over it' and changing over time. Perhaps nothing better illustrates the gap between popular psychology (popular because of the way in which it has dominated education, social service and child-rearing policies and advice) and older views of human mentality, than a conversation between two mothers which was overheard at a bus-stop. One mentioned how, on a visit to her child's school, a particular seven-year-old appeared to be in the process of dismantling the classroom while the teacher stood passively by. 'Can't you stop him?' asked the mother. 'He comes from a broken home,' the teacher fatalistically replied. 'Well,' said the mother, 'he can bloody-well learn, can't he?'

What appears to be obscured in this assimilation of delinquency into deprivation, is the fact that it is *society*—not the deliquent—which insists on the 'cure', and is prepared, in some cases, to lock him up to give it to him! The smooth talk of healing somehow disguises the hint of coercion, and the impression is created that the interests of both the delinquent and society are the same. Sick and suffering people naturally want to get better, and so we provide the means to do just that. What is not faced is a conflict of interests. Society cannot tolerate

---

* For example, "On violence the evidence is inconclusive, indicating that violence on film might stimulate violent acts in those already predisposed to aggression, but confirming also that it is never a prime cause of violent or delinquent behaviour whose roots lie deep in family and emotional deprivation" (*The Future of Film Censorship for Adults*, 1974 Paper by Chairman, Film Viewing Board, GLC).

certain behaviour and thus something has to be done to stop it, because society's needs, and *not* the child's, demand it. The two *might* coincide, but there is no *a priori* reason why they should. Whatever the therapy may achieve for individuals—and that remains to be proved—the underlying philosophy guiding it will not acknowledge, even in theory, this basic difference between the treatment of deviants and the model of curative medicine. The slimiest sophistry is represented by the attempt in the booklet on Youth Treatment Centres (which have secure conditions) to justify close custody of young offenders as a denial of freedom which they themselves *really* want. It is '. . . a means of allowing an inner freedom . . . It offers the opportunity for the child to feel safe and to be safe while diagnosis, appraisal and treatment occur'. Glenthorne, a recently opened Youth Treatment Centre in the Midlands, is almost a nightmarish miracle of modern security. Most beautifully and comfortably furnished, with no suggestion of lock or bar, it is wired up with every trick of electronic surveillance.

In models which represent delinquency, or any other socially undesirable social behaviour, as a form of sickness or mental damage, is the 'client' or 'patient' still a citizen, once we deny our power to evaluate and judge? In the last analysis, without responsibility, can there be commensurate rights? In a community of reciprocal rights and obligations is it not intrinsic that people *do* judge each other; that they *do* ascribe intent to each other's moves—unless, of course, the other is mentally retarded or confused to a degree where he participates only marginally in the social process? If an incapacity for intent is to be extended to the lawbreaker, whether young or old, and it is held that he acts under some kind of compulsion, one might usefully ask just how humanity can be *fully* ascribed to him, except by courtesy. It is interesting that even some of the most notorious criminals have baulked at the notion of being considered irresponsible, or sick. The poisoner Graham Young emphasised that he wanted a prison, not a hospital, for he was bad, not mad. The notorious McVicar considered the possibility of a 'cure' for criminality, and even were it probable, rejected it on the grounds that when it took away responsibility and volition, it took away humanity.

Not, of course, that denying intent means treating the patient is treated cruelly or even unkindly—on the contrary—it would be no more justifiable than treating an animal or imbecile in this manner. It is frequently attractive to regard lawbreakers in this way, because it is nicer to pity than to judge, to provide comfort and solicitude rather than condemnation. (There is a whole publications industry in sociological weepies, tragic tales of individuals 'damaged' and inexorably destroyed by society's failures and mismanagement, to which the 'caring' are often addicted like some middle-aged women to romantic fiction.) And if the concept of responsibility has punitive connotations, with the public frequently berated for using the language of morality to child-batterers, juvenile delinquents and those it might consider lazy, selfish and downright wicked; so it also has inegalitarian connotations in the way in which it makes distinctions between people. No one should be out in the social cold. Volition can also imply that man must be accepted as being as much himself when he is nasty as when he is nice. The concept that the lawbreaker and the downright vicious are sick, conveniently hives off the offensive part of Man as if it were a cancer, or bacterial infection that is not part of his real nature. Such are some of the more immediate attractions of 'need deprivation' and particularly, sickness models of crime, delinquency and violence.

But however appealing such notions may be, it must not be forgotten that they also need to be backed by some substance in fact. There is no doubt, of course, that some offenders are sick, and some in enforced confinement are not offenders. Nor is there any doubt that what I have called the traditional, crudely voluntarist attitude was sometimes cruelly wrong in failing to recognise genuine cases of mental abnormality and lowered responsibility. At present these cases are explicitly recognised in the Mental Health Act, however much argument occurs over borderline instances. But no such clear status or general diagnosis is available for juvenile offenders.

Clearly, if a delinquent is sick, it is quite inappropriate for a court to deal with the situation, since courts presuppose volition and, in attributing responsibility and applying penalties, try and make sure that the future conduct of lawbreakers is in accordance with the rules. Enforcing conformity to rules by making their transgressors answerable before some tribunal of the people which has power to command and coerce on behalf of the group, has been part of many a society's everyday life.

Those representatives may be required to be legal professionals, or they may be trusted members of the community acting
on a lay basis. But sickness is a matter for specialists, and the
assumption of social control functions by social service professionals has been, initially, tightly bound up with, and to an
extent justified by, the denial of the 'normality' of the offender,
who now needs skilful diagnosis and correct therapeutic solutions. However, what weight can be given to the idea that the
delinquent is sick or damaged at all?

The view is always in danger of becoming a complete tautology. A person commits crimes because he is sick, and the proof
that he is sick is that he commits crimes. There is thus no
independent identification of 'sickness'. This can lead to the
entangled reasoning which seems to infect the 1969 Act,
whereby a child could not *really* commit a culpable criminal
offence (even though the rules of evidence are retained) since no
separate category of offences is acknowledged, other than as
aspects of deprivation.

Has it been established that all juvenile delinquents, or at
any rate a sizable proportion of them, are suffering from any of
the known psychoses? Not at all. Are they suffering from, or
prone to suffer from, the range of minor mental conditions that
afflict so many of us from time to time—anxieties, neurotic
habits, phobias, and so forth? Studies and observations seem in
agreement that, overall, such ailments actually affect delinquents *less* than others.

And psychopathy? This is itself only dubiously a 'mental
illness', and is usually accepted as the extremes of personality
traits found in varying strengths throughout the population. It
is associated with violent criminality. A significant number of
those diagnosed as psychopaths do seem to have a cortical
immaturity compared with controls, with an EEG pattern
similar to that of children, which leads them to seek strong
stimuli, and to be relatively unaffected by adverse consequences. (EEG abnormalities are found in approximately 50
per cent of psychopathic samples.) But there is a tendency for
many to 'grow out' of the condition at about the age of thirty
(for a full discussion see Robert D. Hare's *Psychopathy*). As
crime and violence have risen, so apparently have the numbers
diagnosed as psychopathic, and Broadmoor and other special
hospitals are as overcrowded as the rest of the prisons. But, as

in many of these psychopaths the neurological make-up does not differ from the rest of the population, that tautology rears its head again, as comment in the Butler report shows. Psychopathy has tended to become synonymous with the commission of violent crime, for the sign of a psychopath is that he commits rash and violent crime. For whatever reason there has been a rise in the number of violent criminals, whom some people have found convenient to call ill, or acutely disturbed, or mentally deranged.

Even given the known high genetic contribution to psychosis, it would be highly tendentious to argue that the rise in lawbreaking of all kinds could be due to the differential breeding rates of psychotics compared with normal people. The same might be said for psychopathy (where a pattern of inheritance of some behavioural dispositions is also suggested by research).

It may be argued that delinquents samples have shown differences in personality traits compared with non-delinquents: Eysenck and other researchers and observers have drawn attention to the apparent extroversion of delinquents. However, there is argument over the component indices of extroversion which are measured by the tests and the ways in which they relate to each other. When used on identical twins, for example, the test results do suggest a fairly large environmental contribution and, like other measured traits, inconsistencies are large in samples followed over long periods of time. But whether we adhere to a loose lay use of the term extroversion, or the definitions employed by psychologists and the criteria utilised in their tests, in no way is extroversion to be equated with mental illness or damage. The reported extroversion of delinquents may be reflected in, or have something to do with, their lower rates, compared with non-delinquents, for all kinds of neurotic ailments, such as phobias and obsessional disorders. (They have higher anxiety thresholds.) Speaking for the longitudinal Cambridge Study on Delinquent Development (where working-class youths have been studied for approximately fourteen years), D.P. Farrington and D.J. West (1977) ask that serious attention be given to their claims to have discovered a 'delinquency-prone personality type'. It found that eighteen- and nineteen-year-old delinquents were more likely to have been troublesome and aggressive from far earlier ages compared with non-delinquent boys. Yet, the (presumably innate) 'proneness' to troublesome behaviour of some individuals cannot explain the rise in delinquency in recent years, even if they will always be in the vanguard of rule-breaking of any dimensions.

However, if delinquents are not, in any conventional sense, mentally ill or abnormal, do they fulfil the criteria for a new category of quasi-illness—'emotional damage'?

Looking, for example, at the Government's *Care and Treatment in a Planned Environment,* we find the suggestion that those children who have been damaged emotionally may have been so because they came from 'circumstances which may include single-parent families brought about by illegitimacy or by death; separated or divorced parents; absent parents who may be in hospital, in prison or abroad; or "rejecting" parents, including adoptive or foster parents'. Or they may have come 'from homes in which there has been prolonged friction between parents or relatives; they may have had unaccepting step-parents, or they may have had unsatisfactory foster-home experience'. Or there may have been 'faulty upbringing by elderly parents, or serious ill-health, or severe mental handicap in the family'. Some children may not have had 'permanent relationships', or 'satisfactory identifications', and still others may have had parents who did not fulfil a 'significant role'. There are apparently even a 'number of children [who] have suffered from disturbed family relationships which were not outwardly apparent. Their parents may have appeared to function adequately, both as parents and partners', but—don't be deceived—there were 'disturbed relationships within the home', 'instability' or (intriguingly) 'other inadequacies'. The net cast by this emotional-damage syndrome is prodigiously wide. Who among us may not be emotionally damaged?

The upshot of all this is that, if *any* child turns out to be delinquent, some *ad hoc* reason can be cobbled up from his background to 'explain' his conduct, simply because it could be cobbled up from anybody's. These 'emotionally damaged' children show no common feature which distinguishes them from the undamaged—*except* their lawbreaking. Such catch-all 'explanations' are inherently unfalsifiable and hence scientifically vacuous. Since virtually anything is allowed to count as emotional damage, the theory must always be confirmed. In the same way one could 'explain' every case of influenza as being due to an immature streak in the personality—and never be proved wrong.

If delinquents are abnormal, then abnormalities in the population are very high. More than one in ten of all boys in England and Wales are now found guilty of indictable offences as juveniles. In a working-class area of London, the Cambridge study (D.J. West and D.P. Farrington 1973) found that nearly one-fifth of boys were found guilty of such offences. Similarly, William Belson's study of juvenile theft for the Home Office showed that nearly all London boys of all backgrounds and classes had stolen something at some time—haven't we all?

Many acts of lawbreaking could be classed as infractions or contraventions of regulations, and do not cross into morality, as clearly do offences against the person, and offences directly against property. The first continually vary; regulations may be imposed or enforced, or withdrawn and allowed to lapse over relatively short periods, as social needs for specific controls change. Obviously, the more persistent, the more wide-ranging and serious offences are thought to be on various criteria, the greater the chance a person has of finding himself in the statistics and becoming officially an offender. But overall, the idea that some sort of individual pathology constitutes delinquency or criminality is difficult to sustain in the face of the normality of lawbreakers and the social nature of moral and legal rules which are often so widely broken. As criminologist Austin T. Turk comments:

> Students of crime have been preoccupied with the search for an explanation of distinguishing characteristics of 'criminality', almost universally assuming that the implied task is to develop scientific explanations of the behaviour of persons who deviate from 'legal norms'. The quest has not been very successful . . . the cumulative impact of efforts . . . is to force serious consideration of the possibility that there may be *no* significant differences between the overwhelming majority of legally identified criminals and the *relevant* general population . . .

5 Those Vital Relationships

The vague concept of 'emotional damage' is cast so hopelessly wide as to be useless in identifying causes of delinquency. But, at least, doesn't it express, even if they are muddled, *some* valuable and sound hypotheses? Is it not true that insecurity in home background, disruption of relationships with parents, and lack of love in the early years, are known to have adverse effects in later life? Is there not a wealth of experimental evidence to support this?

There have been two main attempts to pinpoint the *crucial breaks* in personal relationships which predispose towards delinquency. The first is expressed in the now rather dated cliché 'Broken Homes'. The phrase is somewhat unfashionable because of its older censorious connotations towards divorce and illegitimacy; but the hypothesis of disrupted home background is still alive. Many delinquent samples show higher rates of broken homes compared with matched socio-economic controls, such as those of Hooke (1966), Carr Saunders (1942), Glueck and Glueck (1950), and Farrington and West (1973). Studies of corrective institutions also show a higher incidence of broken homes in the backgrounds of inmates, compared with the general population of corresponding age (Mannheim 1955, Little 1965). There are some suggestions that it is the more serious delinquent, or the more persistent offender, who comes from a broken home and that, in some instances, this is partly a product of the sentencing policy which selects those with inadequate homes. In the Home Office Liverpool sample on vandalism (Marshall 1976), the serious vandal represented 15 per cent of school pupils, and he was more likely than other vandals to commit offences of other sorts, to get caught more than once, and to come from a broken home. (On the other hand Belson's self-report study of boys' thieving gave little support to the broken-home hypothesis for this kind of offence.) Cowie, Cowie and Slater (1968) point out that particularly in the case of female delinquents, those with no adequate home, or none at all, are far more likely to end up in institutions than others (in their sample from the Magdalen Approved School only 20 per cent came from even superficially normal homes).

However, the cause of breakdown may be more important than breakdown *per se*. It is striking that there is very little connection between delinquency and the *death* of parents, but there is a strong correlation with divorce or separation. Douglas (1966), in the national large-scale developmental study, found that families broken by divorce produced 23 per cent delinquency rates compared with only 12 per cent in those families broken by death. If the Gluecks' (1950) figures in their very large sample are analysed, it can be seen that delinquency rises in proportion to less and less 'respectable' ways of breaking up the home. The shift in the delinquent direction is from separation by death, to divorce, to desertion, to both parents abandoning the children.

(However, throughout this discussion, we must keep in mind all those offenders who *do not* come from broken homes, as well as those broken homes which *do not* produce serious or persistent delinquents. A strong, but seldom-mentioned correlation found in delinquency studies, is the rise in offending with family size, for example, in Farrington and West (1975). Big families have been more acceptable than broken ones.)

The Gluecks (1950) noticed more hostility and interpersonal friction in the homes of delinquents compared with the controls. It worked all ways: parent-child, child-parent, and sib-sib. In Britain, Michael Rutter in his Isle of Wight study (1971) found an association between separation from both parents and anti-social conduct. However, this happened only when it occurred as a result of pronounced discord and disturbance, not because of illness, work or holidays. Children from disturbed homes were likely to be put in care or abandoned outright, and likely to have psychotic, hostile, violent and quarrelsome parents. The study for the Cambridge Institute of Criminology by Farrington and West (1973) also showed that the *conditions* of life surrounding family breaks were the really predictive factors. This, and the very low association of delinquency with the death of either parent suggest that if delinquency is higher in children from broken homes than in those from unbroken homes, the trouble lies more in the actual relationships themselves than in the mere fact that these are broken. This is supported by studies which suggest that delinquency is commoner in quarrelsome and neglectful, but intact homes, than in more harmonious, but broken homes (McCord and McCord 1959).

The second main attempt to identify the disruption in relationships which leads to delinquency has been the Maternal Deprivation Theory. The mother-child relationship has gradually superseded all others in the discussion of 'emotional needs'. Society and all its values, forms and institutions originate in the adoring pair at the crib. Maternal love is presented as an almost wondrous metamorphic force from which all things flow. It involves one unique relationship, yet the ability to relate later to a variety of people in all the complexities of human social relationships issues from it. It is of a quasi-natural, biological cast, yet it presumably must create the cultural state of man, involving intention and choice and a whole order of species existence which is basically artificial and constructed out of rules and symbols.

> Through this relationship—first with the mother, then the father and gradually through an ever-widening circle of other people, the child comes to a realisation of personal identity and worthwhileness. It forms the basis of all later relationships, not only with the family, but with friends, colleagues and eventually his own family. On it depend the healthy development of the personality, the ability to respond to affection and, in time, to become a loving, caring parent. (Mia Kellmer Pringle 1974)

Perhaps because of the biological connection of birth and lactation those who search for the child's pre-cultural, 'needs' which he brings to the human social world, are more likely to feel that there is this quasi-biological necessity for the mother figure as the child's first, somehow 'natural' relationship. Those relationships with other people, such as the father, are socially defined and more obviously employ modes of expression and expectation which are both learnt from and shared with other people. Therefore these do not constitute some sort of irreducible, instinctual requirement. In our tradition, the mother has been the parent who gives love. Thus a psychology which emphasises an *emotional* development of the human being as a substitute for initiation into the cultural process, makes the father superfluous, except in so far as he can become a second-class mother. And if a child-centred emphasis has found little or no room for the father's traditional role as the transmitter of more formal norms and skill; in so far as there might still be lingering connotations of authority and discipline, his function may even appear detrimental to the child.

John Bowlby originally launched the Affectionless Thief —the person who steals as an expression of his inability to make personal relationships, due to early separation from his mother; and he has haunted the treatment of delinquents ever since. To the best of my knowledge, the work of Bowlby and the studies of Rene Spitz and William Goldfarb are the *only* basis for the widespread conviction that maternal deprivation in early childhood can lead to delinquency. A detailed discussion of these studies can be found in my *Child Care: Sense and Fable*; I will simply mention a few points about the work of these three researchers.

The Affectionless Thief first puts in an appearance in Bowlby's *Forty-Four Juvenile Thieves*, partly published in 1944 and fully in 1946. Comparing forty-four thieves with the same number of controls, he claimed to have found that seventeen of the former compared with only two of the latter had suffered separation from their mothers for six months or more during the first five years of life. Furthermore, fourteen of the thieves had 'Affectionless' personalities. However, no standardised and publically utilisable criteria were used for selection or assessment at any stage of the study—on which Bowlby was the only worker engaged—which would enable another researcher to cover the same ground. In such circumstances the data can only be subjective. Beyond the claim that he matched his thieves with controls for age and sex, there is no mention of the number of possible controls they were selected from, or how otherwise they were selected, except that Bowlby treated them as patients at his clinic and knew their backgrounds. The thieves are described as persistent, and Bowlby spoke of 'permanent damage'; yet many were very young, four to seven years of age, and their crimes were sometimes trivial—stealing pennies from mother's bag, and in one case, stealing an ice-cream from a barrow. Not only were no standardised tests used for Affectionless personality, but it was accorded no stable definition, with Affectionless children at one point 'conspicuously solitary, undemonstrative and unresponsive' and at another 'energetic and active'. They had 'never since infancy shown normal affection to anyone' yet one child 'showed no affection for his mother, but much for his grandfather', and another was 'extremely fond of the baby and liked mothering him'. From these and other accounts, the term Affectionless-ness seems to be used, among other things, simply to indicate a lack of affection or trust of mother.

At the outset Bowlby admitted that the study was riddled with faults, and that his intention was not to test an hypothesis, but to frame one for future testing:

> This research was unplanned; it grew out of the practical problems confronting workers in a busy clinic and has all the defects inherent in such conditions. The number of cases is small, the constitution of the sample chancy, the recording of the data unsystematic, the amount of data on different cases uneven. Conclusions drawn in such circumstances are clearly liable to all sorts of errors.

But the conclusion was that '. . . *prolonged separation of a child from his mother (or mother-substitute) during the first five years of life stands foremost among the causes of delinquent character-development and persistent misbehaviour'*. And maternal deprivation was on its way, with Bowlby claiming that 'if you take a bunch of recidivists you would find at least 30 per cent, very likely 50 per cent, whose delinquent character has been caused that way, against 10 per cent to 15 per cent of the general population'. From his writings it is clear that he identifies Affectionlessness with Psychopathy. So the claim is that separation from mother makes a child a persistent thief and incapacitates his ability to relate to other people; he goes on to become an adult criminal, and what is more, is a psychopath.

However, not by the wildest stretch of a prison doctor's imagination could a third of either adult *or* juvenile recidivists be called psychopaths. Even allowing for the fuzzy and tautologous nature of the term (in that the condition is itself identified with a propensity for violent crime) the figure in the combined prison and special hospital population is probably under 10 per cent.

Has anyone else found Affectionless Thieves? Bowlby's *Child Care and the Growth of Love* (1965) suggests that legions have done. However, that volume provides little in the way of relevant and solid studies with which to grapple. Anecdote, hearsay, analogy, doctors' opinions, a host of *may's* and *might be's,* impressionistic observations, studies made without controls, and all manner of defects indiscriminately put down to maternal deprivation. This is never accorded a stable definition, but is used to connote any adverse rearing conditions. His maternal deprivation is all-pervasive because it is compatible with any outcome, and convertible into anything.

William Goldfarb (1943, 1944) in America compared children who had spent their early years in a bleak and impersonal institution with those who had been reared in foster homes. Doubts surround the selection of the groups, but the institutionalised children later showed lower IQs, and Goldfarb also claimed that the experience had damaged their personalities; they were said to have craved affection and attention and to have been inept at relating to others. However, one would think this not abnormal in children coming from an environment which neither provided them with much in the way of human company or teaching in social skills. They are equated by Bowlby with his Affectionless Thieves, although only one of William Goldfarb's institutionalised children stole.

The third study by Rene Spitz (1945, 1946 & 1949), which is invariably cited to back up the extreme claim that maternal deprivation can actually kill, was carried out in a foundling institution. Even the whereabouts of this place of appalling neglect, filth, disease and callousness has not been revealed to this day. If it existed then judging by the descriptive detail, the measles which was rife accounts for the high death rate, and the almost total lack of human contact and even sensory stimulation might go some way in accounting for the backwardness of the survivors, rather than absence of the physical presence of Mother, which we are told makes up for every other deprivation. Since the infants were too retarded, as well as too young, to be capable of stealing, nothing is indicated about delinquency. Thus in the three main studies proposing the general mat-

ernal deprivation thesis, only one of them, Bowlby's, found
'Affectionless Thieves'.

And that one even Bowlby couldn't repeat. For in 1956 he
hoped for a dramatic reaffirmation. Sixty children who had
entered a sanatorium for tuberculous patients before the age of
four (with separation experiences of between six and twenty-
four months) were compared with a sample of matched classmates selected by teachers. The age at follow-up ranged from
nearly seven to nearly fourteen years of age. The data for
comparison involved three items. There was an IQ test
administered by a psychologist, who also gave a report on the
child in the test situation; there were the teachers' answers on a
questionnaire covering the child's relationships, work and play
and designed to spot maladjustments; and there was a more
informal report asked of the teacher on the child's general
health, family and progress. The teachers did not know the
purpose of the research, even if they knew who had been in a
sanatorium. This was the only major study carried out by the
maternal deprivation advocates using something in the nature
of objective tests and independent, uncommitted testers.
Bowlby 'believed that the differences between the sanatorium
and control children might be sufficient to be clearly manifest
even with such a relatively crude instrument'. No significant
differences turned up. The results were so embarrassing that
they went unpublished. Instead, Bowlby and colleagues
decided that some of the teachers' reports might be 'unreliable',
despite earlier claims that this factor had been ruled out by the
research techniques, and the 'reliable' ones were sifted out. But
even then the resulting differences were very meagre and
related to daydreaming; reluctance to compete; having to be
told what to do; difficulties of concentration, and a tendency to
get a little rougher at playtime. These were automatically put
down simply to maternal separation, when the children had
been through the most harrowing times at home and in hospital
as a result of severe illness in themselves or families. And the
children were to find themselves described as stunted and
permanently affected people. Yet only one was ever reported to
have stolen, although Bowlby came to 'suspect' that more had.

If the hypothesis fails to stand up in the work of its main
partisan, how does it fare in later, more sophisticated research?

In 1959 Siri Naess in Norway selected delinquency cases

from the files of the Oslo Child Protection Council, an official body responsible for the treatment of all juvenile offenders in Norway. The boys were between ten and eighteen, and one criterion of selection was an explicit index based upon, as far as possible, Bowlby's notion of delinquent character development. The symptoms had to include stealing, and at least one police case referring to this or other offences. The other criterion for selection was that the boy had to have a non-delinquent brother. It was necessary to isolate the factor of maternal separation and this could be best done by ensuring that home conditions were as similar as possible. After checks were made for any delinquencies the brothers might have been engaged in, the mothers were twice independently interviewed about separations, and the records of children's homes and departments were searched for placement records. The result, on a sample of nearly the same size as Bowlby's original one in *Forty-four Juvenile Thieves*, revealed that the separation was significantly *higher* in the non-delinquent group, even for separation of six months or longer, whether before five years of age or ten. (The figures were: 10 per cent of delinquents separated for at least six months before age five compared with 20 per cent of brother controls, and for at least three months before five—15 per cent of delinquents compared with 27 per cent of brother controls.)

A second study on this hypothesis was conducted by Naess in 1962 to see what happens to the amount of maternal deprivation in the backgrounds of delinquents compared with non-delinquents, when other factors are allowed to vary, that is, when delinquents and controls are not brothers sharing the same parents and home. On a random selection method, another sample of delinquents was chosen from the files, and, as might have been expected, boys who did not have non-delinquent brothers (because, among other reasons, if they possessed brothers near in age they were likely to be delinquent also), were more delinquent than the group selected for the 1958 study, having more police referrals. The amount of maternal deprivation among these delinquents was higher than for the original delinquent sample of 1958, being slightly above that for the controls in 1958. This however was not statistically significant. It stood at 27 per cent for six months or more before age five, and 31 per cent for three months before five. Similar figures for maternal deprivation were also found in a group of children attending a clinic for psychiatric treatment, and a group under observation in a psychiatric hospital (cases were only included if they had stealing mentioned in their records). These lie between the figures for the control and the second delinquent group, being 24 and 26 per cent, and 25 and 30 per cent. So, maternal deprivation rises in delinquent samples *only* if other environmental factors are allowed to vary, such that it is an incidental function of these. From analysis of Norwegian delinquent samples the factor with which delinquency is more closely correlated is the broken home, and in turn, the home that has been broken through disturbance, such as violence, father's imprisonment or desertion.

Another very well conducted, large-scale study by Michael Rutter (1971), repeats the findings of Naess—lower rates of maternal deprivation for delinquents compared with controls when other factors are held constant. Rutter explores every avenue and pursues every angle to give the maternal deprivation theory every chance.

One of the groups of children he investigated was composed of nine- to twelve-year-olds in families from a community of small towns in the Isle of Wight; the other was a representative group of children from London families in which one or both of the parents had been under psychiatric care. (The first group had been selected originally for a large-scale investigation of the educational, physical and psychiatric handicaps of school-age children. The second group had initially been selected for an investigation of the difficulties experienced by families when one member becomes sick.) It was found that separation of the child from only one parent carried *no* increase in the rate of anti-social conduct. Fewer separated children were anti-social compared with non-separated. There was no difference between paternal and maternal separation. No difference was made by the age of the child at separation. There was an association between separation from both parents and anti-social conduct but this applied only to homes where the marital relationship was rated 'poor' rather than 'fair' or 'good'. In these cases separation from both parents was often surrounded by mental disorder or deviance in the parents, discord or abandonment. Where the child was separated from both parents because of holidays or physical illness, the rate of anti-social conduct was again low.

However, the issue has been reopened by Douglas's recent (1975) interpretation of data arising from the longitudinal study of children born in 1946. The findings appear to indicate an association between *prolonged* or *repeated* hospital admission in early childhood and an increased risk of disturbance or delinquency in adolescence, and Douglas has, accordingly, suggested a causal relationship. However, as Rutter points out (1975), among other things: data were missing on a very substantial proportion of the sample; even on the data given, the increase in troublesome behaviour associated with hospital admission contributed little to the total number of disturbed children in the sample; it seems that the association was still there when the child was admitted to hospital after the onset of delinquent activity; Douglas had no data on family discord or deviance, so that the findings could have been related instead to this factor.

None the less, Michael Rutter decided to follow it through on fresh data. This was provided by a sample of four hundred children taken from the two epidemiological studies of the general population of ten-year-old children living on the Isle of Wight and in an inner London borough, for which information was available on hospital admission and on a variety of detailed aspects of family functioning and social circumstances. The study confirmed that *repeated* hospital admissions were significantly associated with later disturbance, but then these children with many admissions were much more likely to come from homes where there were acute problems. The position on *prolonged* admissions was that children who had experienced them were also very likely to have experienced multiple admissions and to be likely to come from highly disadvantaged homes. When attention was focused on children who were troublesome, who had experienced a prolonged hospital admission and who did not come from homes where there were acute problems, *only three out of the initial sample of four hundred remained.* As Rutter comments, to see if these three children had directly sufferend from maternal separation because of prolonged hospitalisation would require an enormous sample for it to be investigated further: 'if there was a risk it must apply to a tiny proportion of children'. It could then be construed almost like an exceptionally rare allergy or deformity; it would then hardly be a response of *normal* children. So much for being 'foremost among the causes of delinquent character development and persistent misbehaviour'! (Bowlby 1946). If it accounts for the condition of three out of a sample of four hundred children (and in the circumstances, so could many other unexplored, surrounding factors), who are themselves a small sub-group of a far larger population, its role is so small as to be irrelevant to any discussion of anti-social behaviour and delinquency.

Other studies fail to show any connection between the type of crime committed, recidivism rates or the age at conviction, and maternal deprivation, whether before or after five (Little 1965, Field 1962).

The Nation's children are supposed to pay the price for women's freedom. Whether the speaker has heard of John Bowlby or not, a hoary old reason for delinquency is Mother Going Out to Work. Some of the most extreme renderings of the Maternal Deprivation Theory are to be found in relation to maternal employment. If the World Health Organisation Expert Committee (1951) regarded the use of day care as leading to 'permanent damage to the emotional health of a future generation', the well-known stand of Mia Kellmer Pringle of the National Children's Bureau does not seem to differ much from this. It is rather extraordinary that she should advocate, as the priority in the fight against juvenile delinquency, a massive allocation of public funds to mothers of young children to get them to remain at home for the first three years. Extraordinary, not only because the evidence of the effects of the employment of mothers during the child's infancy, on its adolescent conduct is sparse (see, for example, S. Yudkin and A. Holme), but because Kellmer Pringle herself acknowledges that only 4 per cent of mothers of pre-school age children work full-time and only 20 per cent work part-time. The level was lower for the mothers of our older children and adolescents during their infancies. Overall, one can conclude that if full-time mothers are being proposed as a solution to delinquency, then they have been well and truly tried and the result is the most delinquent generation this century. If they have not actually contributed to this state of affairs, the post-war homebound mothers of the Bowlby-boom have done nothing to counteract it.

The support still enjoyed by the Maternal Deprivation Theory is now largely the result of sheer self-reinforcement and repetition: 'I've said it three times, so it must be true'. Because it has been so influential, or because an uncomfortable number of reputations are affected, there must be something in it. The same could of course be said for the belief that masturbation is a cause of mental illness—a belief which lingered on for almost a century despite all evidence to the contrary. Even those researchers who know there is little or nothing in the theory, have come to invest it with such emotional share capital that many prefer to keep their knowledge fairly close to the family.

Bowlby, despite the negative results of his own research and that of others, has not altered his position, but has instead dogmatically stated (1954, 1956, 1969) that he will now assume the theory to be firmly established and proceeds from there to talk about the detailed mechanics of the trauma of separation which causes the unsubstantiated damage. The theoretical background of the Maternal Deprivation Theory is psychoanalytical; it was this which Bowlby claims led him and others to focus on the early mother-child relationship. Psychoanalytic hypotheses '. . . state in effect that the core of healthy adult personality is the ability to make continuous stable and cooperative relationships with other persons, especially love-objects, and that the satisfactory development of this ability in the adult is dependent on its healthy development . . . especially during the first five years of life. . . . These psychoanalytic hypotheses state further that the majority of personality disturbances, and neurotic and even psychotic symptoms, are the end result of dysfunctioning of the personality in the field of object [love] relationships' (Bowlby 1956).

Many of the adherents of Maternal Deprivation may be only vaguely aware of its origins in neo-Freudianism. It is often presented in a form which appears to be merely common sense, humane and empirical—a far cry from the wilder fancies of Sigmund Freud. None the less, not only the need for one mother-figure, but the whole idea of love as a kind of necessary psychological nutrient has come about from the latter rather than the former. The Freudians did not invent or discover love, nor did people need to be taught by them to value it. But what they did was to use a very particular concept of love—the Libido idea, the idea of a kind of ungeneralised, universal energy, capable of infinite transformations—in an attempt to explain the origins of human relationships, moral sense, mental disorders, and a good many other things.

Freud, as is well known, postulated that the infant comes into the world with a certain store of Libido: a raw, undifferentiated, instinctual energy, often identified as sexual. Early in baby-hood the infant derives his sexual pleasure by directing his Libido to his own body, and extraneous objects are ignored in favour of mouth and anus. When he directs it via an extraneous object he is said to make an 'object choice' and the outside world comes into existence as Libido is directed at it. The boy chooses his mother as object choice and—unconscious-ly—wishes to have intercourse with her, impregnate her, and kill his father. This is cut short by fear that he might be castrated. He gives up coveting his mother, and identifies with his father whom he introjects as his Super-ego, or 'conscience'. This primal adjustment of unconscious forces—and not any kind of social learning—is what establishes, among many other things, moral discrimination and law-abiding dispositions. All later difficulties are due to trouble at the Oedipal stage: trou-bles in the family circle before five that hamper the unfolding of the secret unconscious drama. Or, in the watered-down welfare and therapy version—to troubles in 'interpersonal relation-ships', especially in the early years. Somehow, if people are relating to each other emotionally adequately in the family circle—or indeed, simply co-exist—then social good spontane-ously comes out of it.

However, in Britain, Bowlby's 'special case' of psychoanaly-tic theory has been more influential. Melanie Klein's innova-tion at the Tavistock Clinic was to argue that the baby intro-jects the *mother* as its conscience, and at a far earlier age. To her, the baby's libidinal cravings are as much for love as sex, coming into the world as it does with 'an innate unconscious awareness' of mother's existence (1959, also 1936, 1932). He has an elaborate fantasy life centred on the behaviour and intentions of external reality—namely the mother. He feels persecuted, feeling 'unconsciously every discomfort as though it were inflicted on him by hostile forces'. He feels persecuted also because he has such violent emotions of his own towards his external love object, his mother. He wants to cannibalise her, destroy her. So when there is frustration of his needs, any absence of the satisfactions given by the mother on demand, this leads to the fear that he has lost not only his good object, but has been actually responsible for its destruction. The terror is made worse by the fact that quite early on in babyhood, the mother has ceased to be simply an external object, but has become introjected, in the way that the father was in the original Freudian story. He starts to feel guilty because he thinks that he has destroyed his 'objects'; the loss then becomes a punishment for the dreadful deed, as much as the boy's castration fantasy came from unconsciously wishing to kill the father in the original Freudian tale. Obviously, in such circumstances, nothing could be worse than actual separation; the baby is unable to correct the speculation that the ultimate disaster has happened:

> Phantasy, born of rage, thus distorts the picture of the real mother. A kindly mother who has put her child into hospital, a frustrating yet well-meaning mother, and a really unkind mother can, by this process, alike come to be regarded as malicious and hostile figures. ... The child becomes haunted by bad objects, with the familiar result that he comes to regard himself as a bad object. (John Bowlby 1946)

And the next stage cannot come about: the stage when the baby realises what his destructiveness might do to his love objects, and where he starts to make symbolic reparation to them. Then the 'capacity for love and devotion, first of all to the mother . . . develops into devotion to various causes that are felt to be good and valuable'—all are 'symbols of the good and protective mother' (Klein 1959). As in the Freudian model, super-ego covers all social capacities and accomplishments—and again all is achieved without social learning, without any explicit teaching, or any conscious thought. All you need is unbroken proximity between mother and child, and it all happens.

And it all assumes what it undertakes to explain. Klein's infants obviously come into the world with a fairly complete knowledge of it. Drawing heavily on Klein, a social case-worker explained to me how we got our sense of guilt from those fleeting moments when mother went missing and we felt responsible for her loss. She had not paused first to consider how a baby could ever feel guilty—as distinct from experiencing a sensory incongruity or deprivation—before he had learnt what it was to do wrong. Being able to use the concepts of guilt and responsibility presupposes at least some knowledge of rules which could be broken.

But, if the story is accepted, and if the libidinal strivings have nowhere to go during infancy, then clearly the individual must be unable to relate to anybody else later on; and, as obeying the law is part of the same business, he must turn out to be an Affectionless Thief. Theory tells you so: never mind what reality says. At the end of his 1956 sanatorium study, Bowlby classified his separated children's personalities on a psychoanalytic reading of their 'object relationships', particularly with their mother. Any category he assigned to them seemed to involve some deficiency in the child's ability to relate to her; either they needed affection, did not need affection, had tempers, were obstinate, needed reassurance, did not need reassurance, were dependent or independent, wanted approval or did not want approval, and so forth. The most deficient were those children in whom '. . . loving components in their relationships to their mothers are little if at all expressed, while hostile components or indifference are frequently prominent. Many are said to lack any feeling of attachment to their mothers and to get on well with strangers, known clinically [that is, psychoanalytically] as an ominous combination of features.' The suspicions aroused in *Forty-Four Juvenile Thieves* are confirmed. The meaning of Affectionlessness is simply lack of love, or suspected lack of love, for mother. Theory says that if you are separated from her then you cannot love your mother properly; and if you cannot love your mother properly, then you will not be able to make relationships or behave yourself. (Strangely enough, Bowlby finds it 'ominous' when children are seen to relate to others from mother—a queer state of affairs when the benefit of the maternal bond is supposed to be an ability to get on with others!)

It would seem that even if there is no mother to love, her absence—and hence the impossibility of the child having any relationship whatsoever with her—renders him *ipso facto* Affectionless—no matter what other relationships he has made. This being so, it is difficult to see how maternal deprivation can *cause* an Affectionless Thief, since they are one and the same thing.

Whether Klein's ideas are an improvement on Freud's is a matter of taste. One cannot say whether they are nearer the truth or not, because both are equally resistant to any clear testing. Nothing directly observable supports them unless we 'interpret' signs and events in terms of them. Nothing suggests that anyone unconversant with such theory would independently reach such conclusions by looking at child behaviour. 'First believe and then see' is the reaction one gets from Kleinian therapists and counsellors. 'When you put the children under analysis, you *know* it's right'. And accordingly, the children's play, prattle and squiggles confirm it, as the shape of sacrificial animals' livers used to confirm the predictions of ancient augurs. In psychoanalysis, anything in the world can, by sufficiently tortuous interpretation, be symbolic of anything else. Indeed, the more bizarre the explanation, the more impressive it seems, and all the more proven. As in so many pseudo-sciences, this unfalsifiability, this ability to reconcile itself with any possible result, is seen as a great strength of the theory, whereas it is the very opposite. Genuine science frames its hypotheses so that they *can* be falsified by test results.

Many in social work and education might be surprised and embarrassed if confronted directly with the wholly Kleinian basis of so much of what they have come to accept as psychology, such as the origin of conscience in the demonological fantasies of the infant. The reasons lie not necessarily in stupidity or credulity, but in the demand for instant expertise and instant theoretical foundations for the new social work establishment created so suddenly in the 'sixties.

Some of those who do know the full Kleinian tale are driven to defend it, not as literal truth, but as some kind of beautiful story, poetic symbolism or metaphor for what 'actually goes on' in the early formative relationships (much as Christians have tried to represent Genesis as a poetic description of geological ages). But if it is only metaphor, why is it appropriate? What do we know independently of the formative processes which make it an *apt* metaphor? Do we have other good reasons for thinking that specific early personal relationships or indeed the love that they are often equated with, are *all* that is necessary for social responsibility (among other things)? It is often at this point that it is hinted that one should not ask this question; it is not really seemly, or one only betrays one's own lack of 'feeling' by doing so. It is also suggested that one does not really need an explanation of the actual processes—somehow they are so close to us, such an immediate part of every mother's experience, that we all 'know' just what goes on.

In this way doubts are stilled and the mere fact that most mothers love their children is made to stand duty for a psychological explanation of personality disturbance and anti-social behaviour. But, is it so, is love enough? If we have enough love, will the misbehaviour take care of itself?

6 All You Need is Love?

Certainly the child care experts have been emphatic on the child's vital need for love. Maternal deprivation has often been synonymous with love deprivation as much as mother-child separation. As the king-pin of consensus psychology John Bowlby proclaimed 'Mother-love in infancy and childhood is as important for mental health as are vitamins and protein for physical health'. Now Mia Kellmer Pringle has the generous use of the Government's health and educational propaganda machine to beam out urgently and repeatedly the need for love. It is love that the mother must stay at home and provide in the child's first three years. After those vital years have gone it is very, very difficult to make good those deficiencies. And when the Minister of State for Health, Dr David Owen felt that in connection with our personal and social failures 'It is very worrying that mothering has gone wrong'. Pringle's claim is that the

> Prisons, mental hospitals, Borstals and schools for the maladjusted, contain a high proportion of individuals who in childhood were unloved and rejected. Their number is high too among the chronically unemployable and among able misfits. Anger, hate, lack of concern for others and an inability to make satisfactory relationships are common reactions to having been unloved and rejected. (1974)

So too are 'Vandalism, violence and delinquency . . . an outward expression of these feelings'. The child who puts bricks through windows and the bomber who blows up a crowded pub—both are sick for love. Such behaviour is a development of the way in which 'a young child who has been scolded or smacked, kicks his teddy-bear, or the table'.

Everybody believes in love. But few concepts have been more

exploited and abused. It is all things to all men, but to try and find out what it might mean for some and, moreover, how it might work, and towards what, is so frequently taken as a sacrilegious denial of what should be entirely self-evident. Yet, the very fact that we have so many problems with child-rearing and the behaviour of the young seems to suggest that there is either acute confusion over what is implied by the command to love, or that love is not doing some of its promised work.

Part of the way love is envisaged accounts for the very reason it is offensive, even perverse, to examine its role in child-rearing. It is an elemental, essential emotion owing nothing to social and cultural forms. The latter sully its purity, since however dimly the advocate may envisage it, what is social and cultural depends upon what is shared and learnt. And what is shared and learnt is, among human beings, endowed with meaning, which cannot help but be rule-bound and hence to that extent formal. So, it is felt, love is missed, destroyed even in the act of speaking of it. Something cold, mechanistic, denying human dignity and empathy, is put in its place, although the culturally derived understandings of human beings which give sense and shape to emotion are none of these things. And in reality very many parents who are informed from many sources that they must love their child, are putting into operation, or copying, social instructions or precepts: child-rearing advice could hardly have an effect in any other way.

Because of this, a distinction can be made between love as it is used in much of the child-rearing literature and a love which is more a social commitment to the long-term welfare of the child; an acceptance of responsibility for care and education. Being kind, patient, often when you may not feel like it: making the effort of imagination to perceive and predict the difficulties and requirements of another; looking after someone who is inexperienced, ignorant, vulnerable; speaking and acting for two. However, this draws upon the standards of a community, where there are social and moral demands that one behave in appropriate ways, even if it assigns responsibility for upbringing to particular people. Following this, it is difficult to separate as unique the feelings for children from all those that occur within groups of human beings sharing a certain complex of understandings; particularly where, whether in family, kin group, or productive unit, their fortunes, experiences, tasks and goals are tightly intertwined. People respond to the young because they respond to other human beings. What I have described is not at odds with temporary withdrawals of social pleasures and benefits as a check on an individual's behaviour or attitudes when these cross the boundary of acceptability, or undermine the group's other responsibilities towards itself or the wider society. Both this and the fact that kindness, perseverance, affection and support must often have to withstand the mood, the temper and frustration which threaten to disrupts them, means that human reason, for all that it is denigrated, enters along with socially acquired understandings and socially supported commitments to create and sustain emotional ties by tempering emotion itself. In this sense, love involves goodwill, even sometimes a rather disinterested concern, which might better be described in an old-fashioned way as charity or benevolence.

A contrast of our child-rearing attitudes with those of a radically different culture—that of present-day China—might illustrate a little about what we mean by love for children. In China (Kessen 1975), an extensive system of official and unofficial group-care and education means that no child is neglected or, indeed, unwanted, in a society whose future he is made to feel part of and contributes to. Upbringing is adult-centred, with the adult having specific expectations of the children which he assumes they will meet. Adults are perceived as totally supportive, consistent and reliable. Observers have found the children happy and affectionate, competent and low in maladjustment. In a system which is, in fact, very traditional, there is an absence of any mystique about the maternal tie vis-à-vis others, or the early years. Children are encouraged to relate to people and gain assistance and comfort through the development of social and verbal skills. Yet, by our criteria, Chinese children are not loved—or at least, not properly loved. We often feel that if the importance of the first few years is denied, this will result in a terrible neglect of children: that if attention is focused on practical programmes for social competence, it will further and cruelly deny the deprived children it is supposed to help, as will the children's involvement with people on any basis but the very personal, domestic one where love is the whole *raison d'être* of the relationship. But the paradox is that those cultures like the Soviet Union and China (for all their other faults), have been able to do far more for vast numbers of grossly deprived children in the aftermath of devastating war and economic backwardness, than we have been able to do in our affluence with a psychology so seemingly in tune with human sensitivities.

The way in which our consensus psychology has been apt to interpret love for children is in the most exclusive, possessive meaning of that word—as a particular commitment to one alone, with all the connotations it brings that this one being should be set apart and above all others, pleased and protected. On the analogy with the adult love affair, neither the tie itself, nor its commitments, are felt to rest properly or actually on social convention. Erotic overtones are, not surprisingly, very common. The psychoanalysis which consensus psychology has so heavily drawn upon finds Freud's infants seeking bodily gratifications which are all to be construed as sexual, and Melanie Klein's infants—in more romantic mood—crave the ideal, totally satisfying, partner.

Certainly the love that is conveyed by, or simply exists in, bodily contact, breast-feeding, fondling and so forth, is an old favourite in the child-rearing literature. If anything, claims for its efficacy as a solution to the problems of the modern world have increased of late, with a spate of books and articles offering a one-upmanship in child perfection, if you cuddle long enough or early enough (e.g. Liedloft, Leboyer). Leboyer blames war, violence and other human miseries on bright lights, cold gloves and instruments at childbirth; at being pushed and pulled out of the womb and slapped into life, and this is taken very seriously by eminent paediatricians and obstetricians, as well as Sunday journalists. The speakers at a DHSS conference on breast-feeding in 1975 spoke of its role in ' "bonding" the mental, physical and social health of the future generation'. Such an orientation, plus the necessity to cast the whole mother-child tie as something rooted in the dictates of Nature, and not the child-rearing patterns of a particular society at a particular historical period, has found the mechanistic 'imprinting' found in some bird species, and all manner of reflexes, useful in this context. It appears to be imagined that the satisfaction of a quasi-biological urge, whether to seek tactile stimulation, suck or cling, somehow transforms itself into later human social behaviour.

How can it do this? Are these urges, these needs, on the model of a hunger drive? If they are, then like those vaguer claims about love being nourishment, they seem to be suggesting a kind of stock-piling hypothesis where what a person imbibes at one stage he will give out later. Those who took in a lot will be generous, and those who were emotionally mal-nourished will, on the other hand, have little to give away. However, it is difficult to see how, if the need for Love operates like a hunger drive, it can possibly explain the effects of experience on behaviour over long time spans; only learning, whether in the behavioural or cognitive sense, can do that. 'Drive' theories are only of limited use in describing the effects on behaviour of conditions operating over short time spans. For after hunger or any other physiological need is satisfied, the behavioural index rapidly returns to normal: there are simply no residual effects that could accumulate over time. Nobody has yet managed to show that, all other things being equal, differences in child-rearing regimes related to feeding or con-tact patterns in early life are reflected in differences in the behaviour and personalities of adults (Orlansky 1949; Kagan and Klein 1973; Kagan 1976).

Harlow's monkeys have been bandied about *ad nauseam* as 'evidence' that the human child acquires everything from social morality to child-rearing skills from contact comfort. An osmo-tic education. Harlow's monkeys who had nothing cosy to cling to in early life later appeared to turn into violent 'delinquents', bashing other monkeys they came into contact with and mis-treating their offspring. However, it has largely escaped notice that the monkeys reared with nothing to cling to, or without a mother, were also reared in total isolation from their own species, and had had no opportunity whatsoever to learn from other monkeys who, of course, they had not even seen (Morgan 1974). Harlow himself came to abandon the idea that automa-tic instinctual mechanisms, such as clinging, had anything to do with monkey social behaviour. He correctly reasoned that if the monkey was instinctively compelled to cling, and if the consummation of the clinging mechanism was in doing just this, then clinging was the be-all and end-all of the business (and the same for any instinctual mechanism that you might imagine). Thus, the ways that monkeys interacted socially had to be dependent on something else which would endow them with a range of adaptable behaviours. In effect, monkeys had to learn, and experiments proved that they did just that; even those monkeys who had been reared in isolation became quite normal when they had the chance to learn from others (Harlow and Soumi 1971).

On top of this, human beings are not only non-instinctively programmed, but are cultural creatures. From the structure of norms and values which govern our conduct towards each other, to the absolute *basis* which makes it possible to understand each other, cooperate, or even know what we are fighting over, we are not dealing in re-directed love or any other emotions. And it is, in effect, grossly sentimental and erroneous ever to think that human social life could subsist on such a foundation. Human interaction is distinguished by being rule-bound, public (in the sense of conforming to intersubjective standards), and symbolic in that it employs systems of meanings, underlying all of which is the unique possession of language. Even emotions themselves have to be mediated and made intelligible by these processes.

If it is maintained that love does not necessarily exist in, but rather is conveyed by gratifications, then such a hypothesis is presupposing what it seeks to explain. It presupposes that the infant is equipped at birth with much innate social knowledge, so that he knows without more ado what things signify and how, in turn, to treat others from what is done for him. That he may come to do so as a child from the example and the explicit guidance of others is another matter, for here the child is learning patterns and principles of interpersonal conduct. (Certainly, it is common to hear the baby credited with a complex understanding at birth; the notions of people like Leboyer rest upon it. The infant has expectations; makes predictions and interpretations; has a very good memory, which presumes the existence of the most elaborate temporal, spatial and sequential concepts; he knows how to recognise rejection, good and bad, aggression and guilt, and so forth. Yet such things are the product of social experience, not prior knowledge.)

Certainly, it is easy to believe that like leads to like in a simple, one-to-one fashion. Good things must produce good ends, and bad means can only produce bad ends, hence the belief that it is self-evident that a loved child must become a cooperative, constructive, socially responsible, morally good adult. This often involves confusion between the moral conviction that good ends should not be bought at the price of bad means, and the factual belief that bad means must be counter-productive. Where it would be preferable, for example, to have a world without disincentives and the possibility of social rejection of the individual in some circumstances, it is easy to slide into the quite different, and perhaps false belief, that as a matter of psychological fact, these do not produce the desired result anyway. But nothing suggests that, for example, the countering of hurt with the granting of satisfaction, approval or tokens of love, will diminish the likelihood that the person will do this again—on the contrary, his success will probably increase the chance of repetition.

Should the child come to love others as he was loved, there remains the problem that conformity with the law and moral principles are very largely or wholly independent of whether one personally loves or even likes other people. Being considerate to those you love may be easy, but it is precisely because we do not and cannot love everybody (except perhaps within small groups with strong mutual interests), that morality and legal regulation become so critically necessary. As our child-rearing psychology has cast parent-child love in the form of the one exclusive bond, it is logically difficult to see how this is supposed to be applied to anything but another exclusive commitment to one—forsaking all others. Love of this nature has, if anything, been associated with an abandonment of obligation and responsibility; an obliviousness to social requirements, and the feelings of others. Applied to child-rearing, it can become 'my child, right or wrong'. I recall talking to a group of adolescent boys after watching a court case where a father broke down an old man's door and carved him up with a milk-bottle. The father's four-year-old child had reported to his parents that the old man had pushed him. There was no evidence for this, but much for the child and others ruining the old couple's garden and depriving them of any peace and quiet under the fierce protection of his parents; '. . . just do what you want and tell your dad if anything happens'. I found that the youths who had watched the case sided automatically with the father. If you loved your child, truth and falsehood applied no more than right and wrong—you *must* believe his word.

Again, it is true that sympathy, consideration, compassion and so forth, can be spoken of as 'moral feelings', but these denote also a capacity for moral imagination, an impersonal concern for others, a rational, socially cultivated and supported identification with those we may not even be remotely associated with, which must override our immediate reactions, moods and feelings, and to an extent counterbalance the claims of those we are more closely involved with.

There is a certain amount of evidence available on the complex question of how parental behaviour and the form of relationships in the home affect children, particularly in reference to their anti-social conduct.

First of all, there is the question of whether or not there is any 'carry over' of parental treatment of the child at one age into his behaviour at another, whatever the mechanism is which might be involved. This is very important, since, as we have seen, preventative policies aimed at delinquency and based on emotional deprivation hypotheses do emphasise early life. However, longitudinal studies of American children failed to provide support for the view that a mother's treatment of her child during the first three years of life is strongly predictive of adult behaviour. In one study by Jerome Kagan and H.A. Moss in 1962, ratings by direct observation of mothers and children at home, and of the children in the nursery school, were made during successive three- to four-year periods (at 0–3, 3–6, 6–10, 10–14 years of age). These ratings were compared with later ratings of adolescent and adult behaviour, and personality assessments based on extensive interviews. The results showed that there was, for example, no consistent relation between maternal hostility towards the child and variables involving anger arousal level or aggressive behaviour, as well as between other aspects of maternal treatment and later behaviour and personality.

Perhaps the first few years provide a foundation to be built upon: if you don't have this will things be far worse later than if you did? However, this idea is in direct conflict with some evidence that the effects of early life can be reversed by later experience if the child is placed in a different environment. (We do not yet know up to what age this can be achieved.) For example, Rutter studied sixty-five children separated from their parents because of family discord in early childhood and found that their later delinquency rates were half those of the children whose bad family circumstances had not changed, and were the same ratio as for those who had always lived in more harmonious homes.

The emphasis thus appears to need to shift to the influence of the home on the child in the here and now, rather than what it may or may not have been in the past. The Rutter study which covered the emotional climate of the home is widely held to vindicate the theory that it is the special intimacy or love unique to some mother-child or parent-child relationships which is the direct cause of non-delinquent, rather than delinquent, conduct. The findings deserve closer scrutiny and comparison with others. Quarrelling, discordant homes, homes with violent or insane parents were, as we saw in the consideration of separation, correlated with deviant behaviour. Another issue was the type of family disharmony. Discordant families were therefore divided into two types for research purposes: first, where there was 'tension', a persistent atmosphere of hostility and discomfort in the home; and second, where there was low tension, but a lack of positive expression, concern or involvement, where relationships were formally correct, but lacked any 'warmth' conveyed by words, voice or facial expression.

The second situation was infrequent, but was associated with lower anti-social disorder in the children, compared with the open hostility or high tension associated with significantly higher anti-social disorder. A combination of both further raised the level of anti-social conduct in the children. But it is not justifiable to assume that one factor alone (or perhaps several) is the only influence upon a certain outcome, or even a predominant influence, simply because others were not investigated—as they were not in Rutter's study. Concern for the children, friendly relationships, an absence of fighting and quarrelling, may be associated with other aspects of child-rearing which might be as, or more, important for a particular outcome. Rutter puts forward his version of the 'love alone' hypothesis to account for less anti-social conduct in low tension homes, but also asks:

Could it be that it is the child-rearing practices which are the main factor in the causation of delinquency and that the discord is important only in so far as it is associated with erratic and deviant methods of bringing up children? Secondly, experimental studies have shown how readily children imitate other people's behaviour, and how a model of aggressive or deviant behaviour may influence the child to behave similarly (Bandura 1969). Perhaps the family discord is important only because it provides the child with a model of aggression, inconsistency, hostility and anti-social behaviour which he copies (Rutter 1971).

In fact his work strongly suggested that adults affect children—at least partly—by acting as models. His research showed that hostility and discord in the home *between* parents had much the same effect in raising the levels of the children's anti-social conduct, as parental hostility towards the child. The child thus might imitate and 'learn' this way of behaving as normally as he might learn others. As well as providing a model at home, one must consider the model which parents might provide in their attitudes and behaviour to those outside the home.

In connection with his first point about 'erratic and deviant' methods of bringing up children, Rutter himself points to a number of studies which show that parents of delinquents tend to differ from other parents in their discipline and supervision of the children. As well as hostility in the home correlating more with a delinquent than a non-delinquent outcome, the Gluecks' (1950) large-scale study found that discipline was significantly more likely to be lax, indifferent, irrationally harsh and erratic, in delinquent-producing homes. Supervision, budgeting, housekeeping standards, planning—of anything—was poorer. In the Cambridge study delinquent boys were more likely to have received less supervision and more erratic discipline (West and Farrington 1973). Harriette Wilson found in 1962 that the factors related to delinquency in her problem-family study were the lack of supervision exercised by parents whose attempts at control were absent, lax or erratic. Difficulties of supervision also suggest themselves as partly, at least, the reason for the rise in children's delinquency with family size.

One might also consider the Robins (1960) study of the adult state of 524 people referred to the psychiatric clinic thirty years earlier—406 of them for anti-social behaviour. 22 per cent received an adult diagnosis for psychopathy (compared with 2 per cent in a normal control group of 100 subjects). Broken homes were, again, common in the backgrounds, and this again appeared to be strongly related to the fact that most also had fathers who were themselves psychopathic, violent or alcoholic. However, contrary to a love hypothesis, which has been so frequently advanced in the case of psychopathy, fathers who were strict supervisors and exercised consistent disciplinary functions, but were none the less cool and unaffectionate, still had fewer psychopathic children. How much this state of affairs can be compared with Rutter's 'low warmth' homes is not clear, because he denoted low warmth by lack of involvement and concern as well as lack of positive expression. One may not invariably accompany the other, and the Rutter study did not look at factors such as supervision and discipline in relation to the tension and warmth in the home. Although the outcome studied was broader than simply delinquent or anti-social conduct, research into intact families based on the National Child Development Study (see Lambert) suggested that the father's 'warmth' was insufficient in itself for a boy's social adjustment and educational progress; what was also important was involvement and the time the father spent with the child, time in which he might be expected to shape and control the development of skills, attitudes and behaviour.

A very recent Swedish study gives weight to the theory that it is a combination of the example set by parents, their involvement with the child, and the supervision they exercise which is crucial to whether or not children get into trouble with the police. Boys aged between eleven and fifteen caught for a first offence, *did not* tend to come from low-income, poorly educated, overcrowded or broken homes. But they *did* come from homes where parents frequently quarrelled and where consistent, interested supervision of the child was lacking (Olofsson).

It must always be kept in mind that although bad or broken homes could be presumed to affect males and females fairly equally, boys' rates of delinquency are far higher than girls'. However, boys are, on the whole, far less supervised. For a girls' level of supervision to fall to that traditionally thought normal for a boy might happen only in the most neglectful of homes. Certainly until very recently, delinquent girls could be assumed to come from broken homes in far worse conditions than those of delinquent boys, whose family circumstances were—on average—far closer to the norm. Contrast, for example, the appalling homes of many of the girls in the Magdalen study (Cowie, Cowie & Slater, 1968), with the many comfortable, well-off, intact homes of the boys in the Government's probationer study. In Black America, where there is little or no difference in the treatment of the sexes when it comes to supervision and discipline, the sex difference of high rates of broken homes for girls, and far lower rates for boys, vanishes (Daresman and Scarpatti 1975).

So the picture which emerges in no way suggests a simple association between the nature of the parent-child relationship, and the child's present conduct. The adult is as important as a model for the child in the way in which he behaves towards others, as he is in his behaviour towards the child. It is easy to envisage situations where the parent may behave badly towards other people, but behave well towards his child—will his influence be benign then? Or instead, will the presence of such a person serve to reinforce anti-social tendencies if, for example, the child is more pleased and favoured the more he emulates the parental example? Indeed, if we can get away from the concept of love as some kind of nourishment which automatically leads to good; something which doesn't enter the mundane process of learning as other influences do, then, its manifestations being desired, parental favours are potential reinforcers for all manner of attitudes and behaviours. A father of my acquaintance who dotes on his son, not only supports and cultivates his son's sadistic behaviour towards other children (from which they both derive great satisfaction), but instructs him in ways to lie and cheat his way through life. Other examples abound:

> . . . the husband made a favourite of the middle boy and when he had beaten her [the mother] he would take the boy out and buy him a present, so that by the time the boy was seven or eight his mother's beatings came to mean rewards and he would hang around and watch, laughing, to endear himself to his Dad . . . (Pizzey 1974).

If parents desire a very aggressive child, or a law-abiding, considerate child, then there is no reason why love cannot be used to produce the first as much as the second. What is central to the outcome is the behaviour and attitudes imparted: love is not *intrinsically* connected to any specific end.

It might be argued that on the basis of 'Do unto others as you have been done by', the child generalises in a simple way from the care and satisfactions given to him, to behave in a similar way to others. Rutter puts the case as follows:

> The third alternative is that the child learns social behaviour through having a warm, stable relationship with his parents, that this relationship provides a means of learning to get on with other people and that difficulties in interpersonal relationships constitute the basis of anti-social conduct (Rutter 1971).

However, it is an open question whether or not the child will learn in this way, simply by making deductions from the consideration and comfort given to him that, in turn, he must practise it on others, independent of specific instruction and support to do so.

Harriette Wilson's study of multi-problem families does not hold out much hope for this hypothesis. Among the boys in her sample, delinquency was eight times the national average for the 8–13-year-old group in the city, and, in the 14–17-year-old group, seven times; the girls' rate of delinquency was one-third that of the boys, compared with a national average of one-tenth. Even compared with control groups from two highly delinquent parts of the city, the research group came off worse. Probation reports spoke of children who were quite 'without shame or sense of responsibility'; whose creed was 'I see, I want, I take'. Their family ties were ironically exclusive, with the children possessing very little ability to make relationships, or even get themselves understood outside their homes, since their limited means of communication had grown up largely idiosyncratic to it. But siblings were observed to be very close and, despite appalling physical standards, many of the mothers were very affectionate to their children who, in turn, appeared at least to like them.

It is perhaps a strange world that has to be given quasi-medical reasons why it should love its children. It seems to want to believe that all manner of psychic ills will befall if it doesn't, as much as it hopes that love alone will take away the moral responsibility of prescribing and upholding norms.

What one simply cannot deny is that because social behaviour, by definition, concerns people's continuous interaction and identification with others, its rules, unlike those of arithmetic, cannot be divorced from the characteristics or behaviour of the teacher towards the taught. Those who are mistrusted, hated, capricious, unkind and negative, are hardly going to succeed in imparting much in the way of fairness, sympathy or benevolence. A positive, mutually satisfying relationship may be a very good tool to have when you want to develop the social responsibility of children, but it is not in itself an answer to delinquency, it is more in the nature of a blank cheque. And positive, mutually satisfying relationships are also credits in themselves, and not just means to other ends.

7 Cures?

So much for the psychology of personal relationships which exerted so great an influence on the 1969 Children and Young Persons Act.

What effect has the Act had generally on the rates of delinquency? And, more particularly, what effect has the change to the rehabilitative, therapeutic Community Home had on individual lawbreaking careers?

In answer to the first question, it is abundantly clear that the measures themselves have done absolutely nothing either to reverse or to hold the rise in delinquency, vandalism and violence.

In trying to make a sweep of punitive and custodial responses to delinquency, the supporters of the Act had wished to keep children and young people away from both the law and institutions, keeping them and treating them at home.

However, the trend in all forms of residential placement of juveniles has been sharply upwards. In 1966 the Approved School population reached a peak and then rapidly began to decline. This was before the Act and in a time of gradually rising crime. Norman Tutt, in a discussion paper *Care or Control,* claims that 'If the graph from 1966 was projected through to the 1970s one would have predicted a rapid demise of approved schools. However, the 1969 Act appears to have arrested or even reversed the process'.

Now, a somewhat greater proportion of available places in the former Approved Schools are occupied than before the Act came into force (87.2 per cent on 31 March 1974 as opposed to 83.5 per cent on 31 December 1970). Plans prepared by the regional planning committees in 1971–2 envisaged the development of 448 new homes by 1975 accommodating over 7,500 children. It must be remembered that the 1969 Act took the revolutionary step of removing the power of committal to these institutions away from the magistrates and gave it over entirely to the professional social workers who, it was assumed, would use it only in the most exceptional circumstances for a child placed in their care. But as Norman Tutt says, instead, the 1969 Act 'has precipitated an unprecedented demand from social service departments for increases in residential establishments. In the demand for increases in secure accommodation the voice of the social services is almost as loud as that of the magistrates.'

Indeed, the 1968 Home Office figure of 200 children needing special *secure* accommodation was sharply updated by Sir Keith Joseph's announcement in 1973 of the plan to bring this figure up to about 730 secure places by 1978. But this too is now dismissed as grossly inadequate. Marcel Berlins and Geoffrey Wansell, strong supporters of the Act, record their belief (in *Caught in the Act*), that there may be a need for as many as 2,500 more or less secure places in the Community Homes and Youth Treatment Centres.

There has also been a virtual doubling of the numbers of young persons being sentenced to detention centres and Borstals. In 1969 there were 828 sent to Borstal, in 1974 there were 1,645. In 1969 2,228 were sent to detention centres; in 1974 there were 4,451. It is still open to the magistrate to sentence older offenders to Borstal and detention rather than commit them to the care of the local authority. This punitive institutional option for the over fifteens but under seventeens remains from earlier legislation. If for their own reasons the social services are placing more children in their care away from home and in institutions, the reasons for the magistrates' increased use of detention and Borstal lie in their mistrust of these same social services. Uncertainties abound regarding the disposal of those put into council care, and the reasons for any particular decision. The magistrates might believe that a serious, calculating offender may be sent home or sent to an insecure community home whence he may abscond. The *Daily Express* (7 June 1974) printed a 'classic' report:

> JPs are being taunted on the streets by juvenile delinquents who have been let on the loose because approved schools [community homes] are full.

'We feel very frustrated', magistrate Mrs Grace Broadley told a court yesterday. 'We feel we have done the best for the children and sent them away from home.

'Then we see them walking along the road looking at the magistrates, shouting "Ha, ha, we've won, you have lost." '
Mrs Broadley is chairman of the juvenile bench at Accrington, Lancs, where five fifteen-year-old boys appeared yesterday after spending eleven days in the cells at top-security Risley remand centre.

Despite pleas from their parents, the boys were sent to Risley after social workers had failed to find any other place where they could be kept in care.

And yesterday, when the boys admitted stealing from houses in the summer holidays, Social Services official Alec Simpson said the county council still could not find anywhere for the boys to be kept. All five returned to their homes. (Reprinted with comments in *The Magistrate*, Vol. 30, No. 11. Nov. 1974.)

The Borstal or detention centre for the fifteen- to seventeen-year-olds alone remains related simply to offences and under the control of the court. It has the certainty that the delinquent will not be at liberty for a precise period defined by the court itself. Upholding a Borstal sentence on a fifteen-year-old, the Court of Appeal had this to say:

The court was concerned not only with the boy but with the public. It was not in the public interest that the boy should be roaming the streets just as he liked. He had to be given a course of training in secure conditions. It was most unfortunate that the only place available for him was a Borstal institution—unfortunate because he was so young. Very few boys aged fifteen were sent to Borstal in the course of a year.

. . . having regard to the way in which the Children and Young Persons Act 1969, had operated in practice, the limited resources which London apparently had for dealing with delinquent youngsters in its area forced their Lordships to confirm that the boy had to go to Borstal. (Regina v D (a boy), Court of Appeal, *The Times,* 21 October 1976)

(But the increased use of Borstal by magistrates for the over fifteens is also paralleled by its increased use by social workers themselves to deal with youngsters whom community homes cannot contain, or refuse to accept.)

This option is not open in the case of the under fifteens as the following illustrates:

> Mr Justice Kilner Brown complained at Liverpool Crown Court yesterday that he lacked the power to deal with a juvenile whose dangerous driving of a stolen car had caused the death of his friend. He said that was the second case in nine months in the court of a little boy who stole a car with others and killed someone.
>
> 'The public should know', he said, 'that judges have no power to do anything about it. Parliament, in its wisdom, has decided that in cases like this . . . the only thing a judge can do is to make what is called a care order'. (*The Times,* 7 October 1975)

The rise in the use of all forms of institutionalisation for delinquents by social workers and magistrates has perhaps been obscured by the concern about the increase in the numbers of juveniles being kept in adult prisons and remand centres (mainly remand centres): more than 2,000 under seventeens in 1972, and over 4,000 in 1974. These children and young people are there on certificates of 'unruliness', and are awaiting court appearances, disposal to other institutions, or supervision of some kind. Before the 1969 Act, they would have waited in remand homes or Approved Schools, rather than remand centres, where the atmosphere is close to that of an adult prison. Now the Remand Homes and Approved Schools have been transformed into Community Homes, *they do not have to take* children they feel that they cannot cope with or accommodate. Prior to 1969, these institutions *had* to take a child on the order of a magistrate. The question arises then, as to whether or not the juvenile delinquent is the sort of deprived child the sponsors of the Community Home in place of the Approved School thought that they would deal with, if they are turning so many away as unsuitable. The use of adult remand places may also reflect the refusal of social workers to use the alternative to custody, of supervision at home while awaiting disposal. In the case of the social worker not wishing to take a child or young person on remand, and after the refusal of the Community Homes to take him, the Chairman of the Court is often left with little alternative but to issue a certificate of unruliness. (It is curious that 40 per cent of the children and young persons on unruly certificates do not remain in custodial institutions after court appearance. So why was it thought so necessary to lock them up in the first place?)

Now, many who support the principles of the Act see unruly certificates as having another purpose. To them, they are an underhand way in which the police and the magistrates can administer to the alleged offender a short, sharp 'taste of prison', which they could not otherwise do under the present arrangements. This is claimed by the National Council for Civil Liberties and Russell Miller in a feature for the *Sunday Times,* 'Children Behind Bars' (9 May 1976). However, the police cannot issue an unruliness certificate. The only part that they may have in contributing to the remand of children to prison-type institutions, is in asking for time to prepare a case. Norman Tutt, well informed on a world shrouded in mystery, thinks that 'there is every reason to believe that it is the social service department which is requesting such a certificate in the majority of cases'.

But whether accommodation is wanted for children and young persons on remand so that they do not have to go into adult institutions, secure post-court treatment under care orders, or non-secure treatment, the situation overall is that more accommodation is being planned than at any time this century. Certainly, the writings of those favourable to the Act cannot fail to confirm that they have been in the forefront of the call for an enormous increase in residential accommodation. To Berlins and Wansell, it would kill two birds with one stone:

> It would render less virulent public appeals for lengthy periods of more traditional custodial treatment for children whose offences are particularly violent or anti-social. And it would also—and this is obviously the most important result—help the children. (*Caught in the Act*)

Indeed, these authors seem to regard the secure institutions, where children would remain 'for not less than eighteen months', as a golden opportunity to practise 'intensive treatment to suit their needs'.

There is perhaps at work here that tendency of professionals to increase their influence and numbers by the elaboration of

ill-defined tasks which are infinitely elastic and capable of
virtually any degree of expansion. Medicine is a good example.
To the founders of the Health Service, the demand for medical
services was finite, and might decline as the population grew
healthier under the impact of universal medication: instead, of
course, the opposite has occurred, and both the demand and
supply of medicine are apparently limitless. What about catering for deprived children's 'needs'?

> ... there is a natural tendency on the part of residential
> workers to prolong treatment indefinitely in the belief that
> another three months will do the trick ... the community
> home with education on the premises continually wishes to
> have a hostel on the site, in order that when a boy is ready for
> discharge from the community home he can be placed in the
> hostel in order to get the support and guidance necessary,
> since he is not quite ready for return to the community. This
> can be extended further. From the hostels one might wish to
> see the development of bed-sitters. All of these facilities,
> although apparently desirable, in fact have the effect of
> prolonging the institutional treatment ... (Norman Tutt,
> *Care or Control*).

This drift is extremely compelling because institutional treatment does not have clear goals, and cannot say when a boy is
'cured', or what would count as a cure. As Tutt says, a community home may aim at helping a boy reach maturity, but this
condition is so vague that it is always possible to argue that he is
not yet mature enough for discharge. 'Which of us is?'

This whole process is, of course, served rather than hindered
by the obvious difficulties of converting social sanctions and
controls into care and therapy. The social worker has to be-
friend the 'client' and 'help' him with his problems: authority,
coercion, rights and wrongs, should not enter into it. Can these
good intentions by-pass features present in all societies; or does
it simply mean that the social worker has bitten off more than
he can chew? Tutt sees trouble in this conflict of roles, engendered by the social worker taking over so many of the
judiciary's functions. For whereas magistrates in the formal
judicial setting look at the child's case dispassionately, make a
decision, and then hand the child over to the executive (in this
case the social services), the same clarity and detachment are

virtually impossible if the social workers themselves have to make similar decisions. The judiciary, whether its decision is good or bad, is not personally known to the child and his family and is not constantly involved with them. The social worker is. The clear division of traditional functions allows the judiciary, if necessary, to summon the police to deal with an offender and then forget all about him. But the social worker has the all-embracing role of deciding, carrying out, sanctioning and be-friending at the same time—all invested in one person directly acquainted with the offender. Even if he does summon police aid as a last resort, he still has to care for the offender afterwards. The near-impossible conflicts of this comprehensive task, Tutt thinks, are contributing to the desire for more residential places, as a means of getting the children off the hands of the area officers.

But all of this may be finally beside the point, if such therapeutic institutions really do work, as supporters Berlins and Wansell, along with so many others, axiomatically assume they must:

> Our society must reconcile itself to the idea that it is going to lock more children up in the future than in the recent past. We believe that this is the only possible way to help deal with the growing problem of juvenile crime and to help the juvenile criminals themselves. We do not come to this conclusion lightly, nor do we do so for the traditional reason of wishing to see the wrongdoer punished or deterred, but because we believe that residential institutions may offer these children, and therefore in the long run society as a whole, the best possible hope for their future.

Since the 1950s there has been a sharp decline in success rates of institutions dealing with delinquents. Official figures show that of boys released into after-care from the Approved Schools in 1954, 61 per cent had *not* been reconvicted within three years of release. For boys released in 1967 this figure had dropped to 34 per cent, and in the 1970s, to judge from recent studies, it has fallen to around 30 per cent. This has happened at a time of transition from regimes emphasising work-training and discipline, to therapeutic 'caring' communities, a change which promised to reverse the depressing trend to lower and lower rates of rehabilitation following release.

None the less, how do different regimes compare?

In a study published by the Home Office in 1975 and conducted by D.B. Cornish and R.V.G. Clarke, three house units at Kingswood Training School were chosen to take part. This school was the first Approved School to make a determined effort to employ therapeutic techniques, with group work, beginning in 1954. Once this was well established, a therapeutic community was set up in one of the houses. For the experiment the house with the most successful experience of group work—the 'E' House—was selected and compared with another group—the 'C' House. Indeed, so that the therapeutic approach could have every chance to prove itself, the selection of the boys to take part in the experiment was left to the staff of the therapeutic community. All this would make comparative lack of success or failure very difficult to explain or excuse on the grounds of lack of control over the variables:

> . . . research of the time suggested the existence of interactions between types of delinquents and types of programmes such that particular programmes might be most effective with certain types of boys. Bearing this in mind, it was thought that the most powerful and economic test of the effectiveness of the Kingswood therapeutic community would be a research design which, allowing the regime to select the boys with whom it preferred to deal, maximised its chances of success when compared with a more traditional type of programme admitting a similar group of boys. This form of design has certain implications for the interpretation of results. If, for example, the C House were shown to be less effective than the E House, the former could still object that this merely reflected its relative inability to deal with boys whom it would not ordinarily treat, and in this sense claim that its methods were not fully on trial. *If, on the other hand, the therapeutic community* [ie. the E House] *failed to produce better results than the C House, even using a favourable selection policy, it would be unlikely that the method could in any circumstances be more effective than the traditional programmes.* (D.B. Cornish and R.V.G. Clarke) [Italics mine].

The mean age of the 280 boys who took part in the research was 14.3 years; their mean IQ was 104.5; they averaged 3.1 previous court appearances. The 107 boys who were considered ineligible by the staff entered the school's Third House and did not take part in the experiment. The staff, after calls for clarification of their admission criteria, claimed that IQ below 90; mental illness; inability to form meaningful relationships, accompanied by an inability to learn from experience and to show concern and anxiety; and behaviour so excessive, aggressive or destructive as to endanger the stability of the House, all disqualified boys from the experiment. (Comparison by the researchers of the boys deemed ineligible and eligible by the staff, revealed that they differed little except in terms of intelligence, reading age and family size.) Eighty-six of the boys entered the therapeutic community which worked on principles of Democratisation (characterised by a flattening of the conventional staff hierarchy and the egalitarian participation by staff and boys in decision-making about all house matters); Communalism (where there is encouragement of an informal atmosphere); Permissiveness (characterised by the toleration of a wide range of deviant behaviour to allow 'acting out'); and Reality Confrontation (involving mutual interpretations of each other's behaviour). Eighty-seven other boys entered the Control Group, which offered a more traditional approach which 'may be characterised as benevolently paternalistic but cautiously liberal in its outlook'. Here the full-time staff took most of the decisions about house matters, boys' behaviour, and the rules and regulations, which were part of a structured environment in which habit-building and character-development were emphasised.

The results? No significant difference was found on a two-year follow-up between either the therapeutic group (reconviction rate 70 per cent) and the control group (reconviction rate 69 per cent); or—surprisingly—between these two and the Third House (reconviction rate 68 per cent), despite the fact that this took boys considered intellectually and emotionally unsuitable for the experiment (and that intelligence has traditionally been associated with better prognosis in previous studies). The therapeutic community had failed to produce better results even with a favourable selection policy, and it would therefore seem unlikely that these methods could be more effective than traditional ones.

But were the results an isolated fluke? Comparison with two nearby schools with similar therapeutic communities showed that these had almost identical reconviction rates (68.3 and 67.9 respectively).

It might be held that a 30 per cent success is better than nothing. So it is, but this assumes that without treatment *all* the boys would have returned to a life of crime. Is this a legitimate assumption? In the Home Office's previous *The Sentence of the Courts*, offenders under seventeen who received different kinds of disposal were followed up for a five-year period. First offenders sent to Approved Schools were consistently worse in terms of reconviction rates than those disposed of in other ways. These results could have been biased by institutionalised offenders coming from adverse environmental circumstances, which led both to the use of the method in the first place, and to their continued delinquency on return to it. But even with recidivists, other methods seemed to be as effective as committal to Approval School: fines, for example, seemed more effective.

A study in Inner London on reconviction rates of children committed into the care of the local authority in 1974, revealed that of 62 children sent home under the supervision of a social worker, because no place could be found for them in institutions, 46 (74 per cent) committed further offences in the twelve months after the order was made. But of the 102 offenders sent to an institution away from home:

> Of these, no less than 67 (66 per cent) committed further offences. (In four cases there was no information.) Almost as many in this group absconded as did not abscond—45 against 49. Secondly, virtually all those who absconded committed further offences—39 out of 45. Thirdly, of those in the group who committed further offences, two-thirds were absconders. Considering that those sent to institutions had less time at large to commit offences than did the others, their rate of offending after the care order was, in reality, even higher than that of offenders who were at home waiting for placement. (Michael Zander 1975)

Other research for the Home Office published in 1974 by Anne B. Dunlop suggests that the trend to the therapeutic, permissive regime may have accelerated the gross deterioration in institutional success seen in the 'sixties and 'seventies. In a study of nine Approved Schools with different regimes which began in 1962, after allowances were made for the differences in the intake which have been associated with differing success rates, it was found that the very traditional regime, which emphasised work-training and responsible social behaviour, had the highest success rates, with the lowest reconviction rates for the boys on release. Such schools were also characterised by low rates of absconding and self-reported misbehaviour. (It has also been suggested elsewhere by I.R.C. Sinclair and R.V.G. Clarke in 1963 that schools are more successful when opportunities for absconding, misbehaving and 'acting out' are limited.) The analysis of the nine schools was followed by these comments from Anne B. Dunlop:

> It has been surmised from the research results that at the time of this project there was a type of regime which was more successful in training the intermediate offenders which were sent to it to remain free from reconviction on release than were other regimes. Over the years this type of regime has lost favour and schools have come to place less emphasis on work and good behaviour and upon the part that instructors play in training. At the same time absconding rates have risen and success rates fallen. If, as the recent research suggests, there is a relation between the type of regime and behaviour of the boys within the schools and their success afterwards, the change which has taken place may be mistaken.

This study and their own research (looked at above), led the Kingswood researchers R.V.G. Clarke and D.B. Cornish to conclude that 'differences in success rates amongst schools are more readily explicable in terms of the omissions of the less successful programmes than the effectiveness of the more successful', so that 'those schools . . . which emphasise current control of delinquency by reducing opportunities for absconding may at least avoid providing boys with new delinquent learning experiences'. Thus, overall, we can say that 'it is more accurate to talk of the harmful effects of some programmes than to extol the virtues of others', that is, some schools perform a 'holding operation', while others actually increase the chances of recidivism. The permissive, therapeutic regime makes delinquents worse. All the changes over the last couple of decades, involving:

Developments in techniques of assessment and allocation to
different types of schools, the increased numbers of professional and trained staff, and the use of a more psychological
and humanitarian approach have not been successful in
raising the low success rates of schools.

The same conclusions are reached in a far wider-ranging and
intensive study for the New York State's Governor's Special
Committee on Criminal Offenders, by the criminologist Robert
Martinson. This exhaustive review and evaluation covered
modern rehabilitative techniques in use in the developed world
on lawbreakers of all ages. When the report was completed, the
Commission was so embarrassed by its findings that permission was refused for its publication. This was revealed only
when it was subpoenaed as evidence in court proceedings.

Martinson attempted to evaluate approximately a thousand
studies on the rehabilitation of offenders which have appeared
in the English language since 1945. After discarding those
which did not meet basic research methodology standards, 231
studies were left which dealt with virtually every form of liberal
rehabilitative treatment: educational programmes, individual
psychotherapy, counselling, group therapy, the creation of
humane and caring environments. None was found to be any
more effective than traditional penal methods. Even the highly
regarded work of Marguerite Warren in California, which
seemed to show that small case-loads and carefully selected
support with therapy for young offenders on probation made a
difference, was seen to depend for its reputation on inconsistencies in research procedures. The same behaviour in the experimental programmes, which in the control group was considered to indicate failure, was overlooked.

In the light of all of this, consider what Norman Tutt (following Sandford Fox in America) asks—what would be the effect of
a system, where, after a child was sent to an institution with the
express wishes of the court to 'cure' him of his deviant
behaviour, he could come back, legally represented . . . if his
treatment failed? Tutt concludes that 'Such an approach would
pose a tremendous threat to social workers and psychologists
and other "helping professions" in this country because, of
course, we have no evidence that *any* of our treatment . . . is at
all successful.'

A non-academic friend of mine believes, crudely, that the answer to delinquency is 'a kick up the bum'. Even at this level, can supporters of the therapeutic community honestly deny that, compared with their treatment, (a) this could be just as effective; (b) it would, at least, do less harm; (c) it is, unquestionably, thousands of pounds per case cheaper, and (d) it does not involve depriving anybody of their liberty for eighteen months or more?

Indeed, to take up point (c), can there now be any justification for the demands for massive expenditure on further institutions by the social services and other supporters of the principles reflected in the 1969 Act? These demands are, of course, the familiar answer to many a social problem: 'More of the same'; and the 'more' in question is, similarly, limitless. Berlins and Wansell, in their *Caught in the Act*, feel that even the decor left over from the repressive past conspires against healing:

> Resources are still desperately needed . . . for the building of all kinds of new institutions as well as new juvenile courts, some of which are still in extremely old premises, their gloomy atmosphere continuing to reflect the punitive approach to children in trouble. However sympathetic the magistrates, such surroundings are almost certain to be counter-productive . . . the effect of conditions like these on both children and staff is considerable and long lasting.

Renee Soskin, Chairman of the Camden Juvenile Court, outlines a truly mammoth claim for increases in expenditure and social services staff, necessary if the Act is to be 'given a chance':

> Had the government been able to service the 1969 Act as intended by its sponsors by providing a multitude of expert social workers, a wide range of short- and long-stay community homes, foster homes, a variety of intermediate treatments, enough secure accommodation, suitable educational opportunities for children of all abilities, small educational units where large ones are obviously unable to cope, there is a possibility that the Act might have worked. (Letter to *The Times* 10 December 1975)

And, equally, a possibility that it might not! Who is to say that laymen and others are necessarily prejudiced when they doubt that the ills associated with one dose of treatment will not be cured by a stronger dose? It is certainly difficult to see how it might raise the success rate of community homes. In some of these it is, in fact, difficult to see how more money could be spent. For example, a secure unit for 'very disturbed children'—St Charles Youth Treatment Centre, Brentwood—has a ratio of 40 'group workers' to only 38 'disturbed' children.

The question might be more fruitfully asked why there should even be the *present* level of expenditure on such projects in times of financial restraint. Yet the Government is still more inclined to heed demands for more money from those working with delinquents, than the pessimistic research findings on therapeutic regimes. The recent White Paper of 1975 on the Children and Young Persons Act urged the building of more local authority secure accommodation, and a DHSS Circular quickly followed urging councils to apply for grants for such building programmes. The cost per child, per year, in an ordinary (non-secure) community home is around £5,000 (the figure for 1976). In a secure community home—demands are primarily for this type of home—the cost can work out as an initial capital outlay of £20,000 per child, with an additional £10,000 a year thereafter. (This figure is based on the costs of Glenthorne, due to open in the Midlands in late 1977.) We know that some delinquents—arsonists, for example—can do thousands, even millions of pounds' worth of damage. But can we be sure that if they were completely on the loose, the majority of delinquents now taken by the secure units would consume £30,000 in a year? (Compared with the provisions now being made for delinquents, those for ordinary non-delinquent children in care seem pitiful. I have been quoted a figure for 1976 of £4 per year toy allowance per child in care in the Midlands and £1.90 to pay for their Christmas.)

Places at assessment centres cost between £6,000 and £8,000 per child, per year. These centres are supposed to diagnose the 'needs' of delinquents sent to them under care orders, and to dispose of them accordingly. But the needs are nebulous and the treatments don't work, so the whole exercise has the air of expensive futility. One would think that children might be better assessed at home or at school (in their 'natural habitat'), for delinquency-producing factors. The two pointers to recidivism have been found to be the age at the commencement of the delinquent career, and the number of previous convictions. To know either of these one does not necessarily even have to see the child in question.

And the same goes for those factors likely to predispose some children to more criminal convictions than others—large families, truancy, parental criminality, and low supervision (see the discussion paper on the subject by Penny Cooper). In 1974, D. Martin investigated absconders from community homes, for whom all manner of theories about emotional needs have been made to account. Originally he hoped to predict which children would abscond, and then provide them with a special type of therapy which their particular problems demanded. No variables of home background, psychiatric history, school history, work history, physical characteristics or personality (measured by objective tests), were able to distinguish the absconders from the others. However, some environmental factors distinguished the two groups—namely, the weather, the time of year, the circumstances of admission and the school regimes themselves.

As well as asking for more money as a solution to the failures of the Act, its supporters are also found claiming that many of the troubles and confusions could have been avoided or reduced and a real assault could have been made on the problem of delinquency 'had the Act been implemented as it was originally envisaged' (Berlins and Wansell). It is difficult to see how this would raise the success rate of the community home any more than would more money, since these are already more or less 'fully operational'. The pre-1969 powers of magistrates to impose fines have not been adjusted to take care of inflation, and the only effective action that remains within his power to take is to sentence the older juvenile to Borstal or Detention Centre.

How much the remains of pre-1969 penalty and magisterial rights handicap a proper attack on delinquency may be gauged from a comparison of the English mixture with the Scottish Kilbrandon system. This came into operation in 1971 as a result of the Social Work (Scotland) Act, and has similarities with the proposals made in England in 1965 in *The Child, the Family and the Young Offender*. Here, the Reporter (whose background might be social work or law), receives referrals from police, educational or other agencies, or private individuals. In about half the cases either no action is taken, or informal supervision by social workers of the child in question is arranged. In the other half the child is brought, with his parents, before a Hearing. This involves a lay panel, but a panel that cannot adjudicate on matters of innocence or guilt, since all attempts are made to avoid making distinctions between the child who has committed an offence and the child who is in need of care and protection. (There is the proviso that where there is dispute and denial the case can go to the Sheriff's Court.) The emphasis is on a decision that is in the best interests of the child. One child in two appearing before a panel is placed under the supervision of social workers, and one in nine goes into a list D school (the former 'approved schools' which now correspond to the Community Homes in England and Wales). The policy is similar to the 1969 Act as first conceived, in effectively abolishing *all* powers to bring criminal proceedings or otherwise take action on the basis of offence alone. It has been totally ineffective in doing anything about the rise in delinquency or recidivism in Scotland, although, here too, more children are sent to institutions than before the change.

Until far better results are shown than in the Scottish experience, it is asking a lot of the English and Welsh public to submit to the full extension of the 1969 Act, which would make care proceedings the only measure to be taken in the case of the under-fourteen-year-old delinquent, and make criminal proceedings very difficult with those in the age group containing some very dangerous members of our society—the fourteen- to seventeen-year-olds. Full implementation would, of course, further increase the autonomy, control and expansion of the professional social services.

Indeed, we appear to be well into a stage where the very need to produce results is seen as an irksome and irrelevant imposition on the real mission of the services in question, which becomes increasingly self-defined. This being so, an increase in their power and autonomy might be the worst step that could be taken to protect the public. The subtle change of ends becomes apparent when claims are made for therapy that it is meant to cure the deep-seated malfunctioning of the personality, and not the mere 'symptom' of delinquency. So it follows that when delinquent behaviour continues despite treatment it can be dismissed as merely superficial; perhaps, unfuelled by hidden conflicts, it will go away at some time or another. On the other hand, if alternative methods of dealing with delinquents appear more effective in reducing recidivism, or lead to a decline in offences, it can be maintained that this is not a 'real' cure, but could even be dangerous and counter-productive. 'Acting out' of the underlying disease has been repressed, and so it may now seek more devious, and perhaps nastier, outlets. Thus, as a test of methods of dealing with delinquency, such a viewpoint would see 'reconviction data as at best ambiguous, and at worst, misleading'. (R.V.G. Clarke and D.B. Cornish)

However, on such criteria it is clear that you cannot fail, even if you have a 100 per cent reconviction rate! It should be obvious to anyone that if a method is held to succeed *no matter what* the results, then it can never be genuinely proved either to succeed or to fail, since it is compatible with any outcome.

If there is supposed to be substitution of symptoms in those 'cured' of delinquency (as measured in reconviction data), the onus is on those making such claims to say what this looks like, and to see if it occurs more in non-recidivists (treated with therapeutic methods or not) compared with recidivists. Again, if psychic changes are occurring which herald the later disappearance of offending, it would be interesting to know what these might be and how we recognise them. Clarke and Cornish, who deal with this particular refutation of evidence in the course of their study, had found, as we have seen, that staff at Kingswood thought that they were selecting boys on the basis of a capacity for meaningful relationships, when they were, in fact, unknowingly selecting on intelligence. And indeed, boys who had been found guilty of offences during their stay, contrary to the 'expression of symptoms' argument, were significantly more likely to be reconvicted afterwards. Other investigators, like Sheldon and Eleanor Glueck, found that post-programme recidivism tends to be associated with continuing poor adjustment in other aspects of the person's life, since offending was in conflict with other avenues of social integration and success. (This refusal to recognise criteria for success and failure is now shared by all manifestations and offshoots of psychoanalytic therapy. Similarly, the failure to do anything about neurosis and psychosis—except perhaps make them worse—is 'explained' in terms of their incomplete application; the comparatively successful alternative methods are dismissed as treating only the 'symptoms'.)

The natural result of considering delinquency as merely one manifestation of emotional maldevelopment, and moreover, one which is equally compatible with the cure or continuation of the disorder, is to make delinquency itself irrelevant. If exploring personal relationships was originally supposed to have socially beneficial results by promoting emotional growth, then it is a small step from this to regarding just the emotional growth, the perfection of personal relationships—even the exploration of feeling—as the be-all and end-all of the therapy, (just as 'self-exploration' has been exchanged for promises of cure elsewhere in psychoanalytic therapies). The end of community home treatment thus becomes the cultivation of the personality of the inmates—all else is forgotten.

But do we agree to allocate such resources for children just to 'explore their emotions'; or indeed, send them away to community homes primarily to make them happy? To the argument that the community homes should not be judged by the criteria of reconviction and recidivism, Clark and Cornish have this to say:

> Firstly, it is because of their delinquent behaviour and not their attitudes that children come to the attention of the authorities and are committed to residential programmes. There may well be other unhappy, maladjusted and anti-authority children who are not delinquent and who, therefore, do not find their way into the schools. Those actually running the institutions are by no means the only, or even the most important, groups with an interest in deciding what the criteria for evaluating the effectiveness of such programmes should be. If it became known, not only that such institutions were relatively unsuccessful at reducing delinquency, *but that they did not see themselves even as primarily concerned with changing this behaviour*, it could be difficult to justify to the public the existence of the institutions, or the removal of the children from their homes. [Italics mine]

This view is shared, among others, by Logan, who maintains that outcome must be justified in terms of ordinary notions of success, which 'should refer to the correction or prevention of criminal behaviour, not to personal happiness, adjustment, mental health, or family relations'.

Yet the confusion of ends with means, and the increasing abandonment of the original ends runs throughout programmes set up to deal with delinquent or anti-social children far beyond the community homes system.

It is, for example, related by Christopher Sherratt (former Assistant Director, Stoke-on-Trent Social Services Department) that his county borough

> . . . had twenty-one play-leadership schemes. Objects were: (a) to provide a place of refuge and enjoyment, which can be expected to affect rates of vandalism and street accidents; (b) to care for children and assist in their development as part of the programme of family care; and (c) to introduce play leadership schemes as part of a wider community work process. . . . From the onset, the schemes have been *designed to enable children to develop at their own pace*. The city education department provided coaching schemes, that concentrated on developing abilities and skills, while the play leadership schemes concentrated on *enabling the children to be relaxed and natural*. We encouraged them to try a variety of activities, and to discover which they enjoyed, whether these were solitary or play with other children . . . [Italics mine].

It appears that the schools where the schemes were held got a bit of a bashing:

> Early on, there was considerable damage to the schools in which the schemes took place, of which much was the genuine responsibility of the schemes. In addition, our method of conducting the schemes has been a major source of disagreement with many people in educational circles in the city. Criticism was mainly centred on a lack of experienced staff, disrespect for and untidiness in school premises, and failure to keep the children under control.

But, far from recognising the incongruity between these results and the original anti-vandal aim of the provisions, anger is expressed at the teachers' audacity in criticising. 'It is disturbing that we as social workers should be accused, by people with considerable educational experience, of failing to keep control of children and of encouraging them to misbehave, and this emphasises the many barriers to understanding yet to be crossed between applied education and social work.' Did the scheme achieve anything else, apart from enabling the 'children to develop at their own pace', and encouraging them 'to be relaxed and natural'? Apparently, 'measurement of personal development is not likely to be possible', but notwithstanding, 'we believe firmly that this is the right approach, and that we are providing opportunities that many children would not otherwise have, following the child and discovery-centred methods.'

In similar vein, the units set up over the country in the last few years for violent school children who 'could not cope at school' have not taken long to reach the view that:

> Perhaps the centres cannot be judged by whether these teenagers make long-term improvements: totting up the successes and failures, those who have kept their jobs and those who revert to bad behaviour. (Joanna Mack, 1976, *Disruptive pupils*)

So what do these units do—except enable teachers to cope at school in more safety and peace? Why do they want 'panels of senior education officers, psychologists, education welfare officers, the heads of the schools concerned, plus an excellent staffing ratio'? Well, they need it all because the 'individualised attention given to each child is the key'. But what do they see it as the key to—particularly when the staff maintain that 'We've got to be careful not to impose our values on them . . .'? One wonders why they are there at all. Somebody has presumably decided that violence is unacceptable and thus somehow counter to *their* values, else why not save some money and close the place down? The staff appear to spend their time appealing to the children for guidance rather than giving it: 'The children, while doing other work, sometimes talk about their feelings and emotions, counselling each other. Their written work is open, revealing and frank, dealing with topics like the family, sex, emotions, and friends and enemies. In the afternoon, there are various group and individual activities – and again counselling and group therapy'. (Joanna Mack)

In Scotland the Kilbrandon Children's Panels, which have failed to do anything about the problem they were first set up to solve, are defended as having acquired a new purpose all their own by Professor F.M. Martin:

> Its underlying principle, the attempt to see the child as an individual person and not simply as an offender to whom
>
> certain procedures are automatically applied, has *intrinsic value* and a capacity to withstand erosion [Italics mine].

And, having lost all external reference, the worry becomes that

> . . . those serving on the children's hearings, particularly panel members, may lose morale and conviction in the face of repeated criticism, and come to feel that they are somehow failing the community by adhering to the Kilbrandon philosophy.

One can envisage very many other arrangements that see the child, or anybody else for that matter, as 'an individual person' and not as an offender, consumer or taxpayer, and so forth. But do they have to have an expensive apparatus to do so, and one, moreover, which is still presented to the public as having a responsibility for dealing with a problem which it has either failed to solve, or abandoned, and which might best be handed over to others?

Ironically, the only positive contribution made by the 1969 Act towards the protection of the public might be said to lie in its devious contribution to custody. Its supporters might wince at this and prefer 'treatment', but if we have to 'lock more children up in the future than in the recent past' to cure them, then, cynically, we know that institutionalisation is a good way of knowing exactly where they are, what they are doing, and that one is temporarily safe from them provided they do not escape. In the last analysis custody—whether comfortable or not—is a good means of self-defence. Cornish and Clarke, the researchers who compared the regimes at Kingwood, now look more and more like the demons in a progressive's nightmare. They say that since the rehabilitative functions of institutions appear to be non-existent, it is time we looked at their role (apart from straightforward care *qua* care), as agencies of social control:

> . . . any importance they [punishment and deterrence] may have is in no way diminished by evidence that residential

intervention programmes are of little rehabilitative value. To dismantle the apparatus of institutional intervention without adequate discussion and analysis of the role institutions of this kind may play in the process of social control, by reducing the likelihood that a non-offender will commit his first delinquent act, would be hazardous. The extent to which institutions can or do perform the functions of care, custody and deterrence satisfactorily (or indeed cost-effectively) should now be the subject of empirical investigation.

And in America, Martinson also asks for a fresh look at what he maintains are the two traditional functions of the penal system—to segregate and to deter—in the light of the seemingly worldwide failure of the medical or rehabilitative approach to lawbreaking.

8 Sordid Normality

Perhaps the therapeutic explosion of the 'sixties came too soon. It might profitably have waited for a more soundly based psychology to struggle out of its teething troubles, before buying a tempting package of pap which seemed to be saying nice things about care, love, Mum, and emotion. Alternatively, will institutional treatment fail, no matter what form it takes? Why, given the assumptions behind any rehabilitative programme, should it work anyway, whether run by therapists, scoutmasters, or guards from Devil's Island?

The assumption behind all programmes is that some fundamental change can be wrought in a human personality, on a par with an operation, or plastic surgery, by a spell under some kind of intensive regime away from everyday society whose impact on the individual is conceived as weak or neutral in comparison. Released once more into the world, 'fixed' or 'inoculated' as it were, the person functions henceforth in his changed state. Such notions have been with us since Christian reformers proposed solitary confinement and penitential regimes to develop a 'conscience' in criminals, to give them a chance of salvation, instead of deterring or punishing them with a fine or flogging. They obviously lend themselves easily to a medical or welfare model of unsatisfied needs which, when met, enable the person to 'grow' to his mature, socially responsible stature, as we perhaps see demonstrated in Lord Longford's role in the development of rehabilitative regimes for young offenders.

At first glance the failure of institutional regimes might seem to confirm the ultra-deterministic stance of so much consensus psychology about the irreversible, dramatic impact of the early years: 'we have not got the children early enough'; 'when they come to us they are already damaged', and so forth. The individual is 'fixed' irrevocably by a past environment, which the present is powerless to alter, try as it may.

Yet, there is evidence for the reversibility of excessive intellectual, educational, and social retardation in so many well-documented cases and studies going well into early adulthood. And this seems to belie the notion that the person cannot be changed in a relatively minor way, sufficiently to obey certain rules. Particularly relevant to the attempts at institutional change is the evidence from adoption studies, where children, often comparatively late in life, have entered into radically different environments.

One study by Alfred Kadushin (published in 1970), compared the outcome of adoption of older children from very adverse backgrounds to that of the more usual infant adoptions. His sample of forty-nine boys and forty-two girls were at a mean age of 7.2 years when placed for adoption, having experienced, on average, 2.3 prior changes of home since their removal from their original families as a result of court action to terminate parental rights because of neglect and/or abuse:

> The families from which they came were typically large, 52 per cent having five or more children. During their infancy they had lived in socially deprived circumstances, in substandard housing with families whose incomes were, most often, below poverty level. Natural parents had limited education. . . . The marital situation in the natural home was, in almost all instances, conflicted. In addition, the natural parents presented a picture of a personal pathology compounded of promiscuity, mental deficiency, alcoholism, imprisonment and psychosis.

Yet given this, neither the socio-economic background of the natural parents nor their pathologies were related to the outcome of adoption. Also, despite the fact that few adoptive parents initially want to take an older child, the level of success achieved was no different, in terms of statistical significance, from the level of success achieved with younger children.

Kadushin refers to other follow-up studies which add considerable weight to his own findings. For example, A. Roe and B. Burks studied thirty-six young adults who had been placed in foster care as children in the 1940s, because their parents were chronic alcoholics (and 81 per cent of the fathers and 44 per cent of the mothers mistreated them). They were compared with a sample from 'normal' homes which had been broken instead by illness or death (shown to have a low to nil association with anti-social or other adverse outcomes). No difference was revealed in life-styles or self-reported difficulties. It was found that 'most of these subjects have established reasonably satisfactory lives, including adequate personal and community relationships, and most of them are married', and were unlikely to differ from the unselected population if a sample were taken in comparison.

A study by E. Meier of sixty-one young adults who had grown up in foster-care, experiencing an average of 5.6 different living arrangements since removal from their own homes (usually on the basis of inadequate care), also showed that

> The vast majority of the subjects have found places for themselves in the community. They are indistinguishable from their neighbours as self-supporting individuals, living in attractive homes; taking care of their children adequately, sharing the activities of the neighbourhood and finding pleasure in their association with others.

Follow-ups of foreign children adopted in the United States after suffering gross deprivation in their own country, have revealed that both in the short run of six months and the long run of several years, the adjustment of these children is as good as or better than the native-born subjects living with their natural parents, whether adopted as infants or five-year-olds.

If people are capable of dramatic improvement in new environments, they seem equally capable of deterioration, although this is not so well documented. For example, Ann M. Clarke and A.D.B. Clarke draw attention to data from the British National Child Development Study, which showed that while children in upwardly mobile homes gained in reading and other intellectual attainments between the ages of seven and eleven, those whose families became downwardly mobile experienced losses. This seems to tie in with cross-cultural observations where individuals in very meagre cultural environments function at a correspondingly poor intellectual level, but when exposed to a more complex culture, their intelligence comes into the normal range (see discussion in the work of Wayne Dennis).

As the Clarkes say in their introduction to *Early Experience: Myth and Evidence*, the 'notion of continuity underpins all developmental theories. Each stage is held to depend upon, and be influenced by, the integrity of previous stages.' Yet 'longitudinal studies involving repeated measurements do not suggest the existence of *powerful* continuities'. So:

> It seems obvious that genetically programmed growth shows accelerating and decelerating phases, which are themselves responsible for changes in developmental phases. And in so far as learning (in its broadest sense) interacts powerfully with constitutional factors in development, it seems that part of its role is *unlearning* formerly appropriate responses which have become inappropriate. . . . Hence one would expect (and one finds) discontinuities in normal development even in a situation where there is some degree of long-term environmental constancy. Thus prediction of later from earlier characteristics is on the whole poor, not primarily because of imperfect measurement, but because it is confounded both by discontinuities as well as by individual continuities which show variability over time.

The idea of some kind of 'fixed stages' or stable continuity of individual development is seen to be more and more in need of drastic revision. The eminent American developmental psychologist Jerome Kagan now has strong doubts about his own earlier belief in a theory of this nature. He considers there is only modest empirical support for weak continuities in an individual's development, but that it tends to be rationalised by supposing that there is a firm 'underlying structure' to the personality behind the apparent changes. He is now sceptical of this supposition.

Across situations as well as over time, greater stability and endurance are perhaps accorded to personality than it warrants, because the environmental contingencies are taken for granted, rather than specified. People are seen in a constant set of environmental conditions, and predictions about how they might behave are made on the assumption of fixed personality, when in fact their behaviour and attitudes are as much a product of their present environment and cannot be widely extrapolated into changed circumstances.

The particularly bleak determinism of the 'cycle of deprivation' doctrine was investigated by Michael Rutter after it had already been made part of received wisdom by Kellmer Pringle and Sir Keith Joseph. Rutter found the hypothesis that disadvantage was transmitted through the generations wrong or not proven. With poverty, housing and parenting, no continuity was found through families. Where there were continuities in regard to intelligence, educational attainments, occupational status, crime and psychiatric disorder, the discontinuities were still more pronounced. Over half of all forms of disadvantage arise anew with each generation, even where there are regional continuities (which far outweigh family ones—particularly for poverty, parenting and housing); many people become disadvantaged without having been reared by disadvantaged parents. Continuities are even weaker over three generations than they are over two.

Overall, the picture emerges of human beings as very adaptable, and susceptible to their *present* environment. It is this which may account for the paradox in the failure of institutional attempts to 'change' the person, and the success of adoption, or other later experience, in reversing earlier disabilities. Man is *too changeable*, rather than too rigid. One might say that no matter what changes take place in the individual in the institutional environment, these changes will hardly carry over into his *post*-institutional environment, unless that too supports and sustains them. Human beings are capable of an enormous range of behaviour and attitudes; what they manifest depends to a large extent on their circumstances. Most people are volatile.

> The child could not make of himself what he was not. However, personality is multifaceted, and we are capable of a much greater repertoire of behaviour than we are usually called upon to manifest. The altered situation, requiring a 'change' in personality for the child, means an emphasis on the kinds of feelings and behaviour which helped him fit in to the adoptive home and a de-emphasis of those kinds of feeling and behaviour unacceptable in the present environment. (A. Kadushin 1970)

Early penal reformers who worked on the idea of personal transformation of the criminal, rather than simply deterrence, punishment or segregation, usually saw this in Christian terms, of saving the soul of the wrongdoer through self-examination, a change of heart and a commitment to live better henceforth. Ironically (when we consider the way that modern psychotherapeutic counterparts have resulted in more custody than ever before), the Quaker and other reformers' rehabilitative programmes often involved exceptionally long sentences of solitary confinement, and the most monotonous, continuous labour that the human mind could devise. (Considering the known mental effects of such sensory and social deprivation, a lashing, or a spell with the chain-gang might seem preferable and humane by comparison.) There is no evidence that the attempt to work on the depravity of the prisoner's soul, rather than working on his sick psyche, had any more impact on his post-institutional recidivism when he returned to his old haunts.

The modern psychotherapeutic version of rehabilitation bears a striking resemblance to those ideas of reform through salvation: not only in its emphasis on permanent change and autonomy henceforth, but also in the appeal to some purposive, controlling psychic agency. It is not the soul: instead, there is the pervasive psychoanalytic notion of an unconscious or at least of *something* behind the scenes which we have got to straighten out: a tangle of problems from the past, experiences whose disruptive effect prevents us from dealing properly with the present. Thus the necessity for 'insight', to try and interpret what is going on, to sort oneself out by introspection, instead of asking 'how shall I behave?' It is regarded as pointless trying to teach, to change behaviour or attitudes, or apply different environmental pressures to support alternatives, before the hidden source of trouble, the 'real' problem, is tackled.

Certainly, the memory of the past shapes the present, but only when it is applicable to our present condition: otherwise we have to adapt and cope anew. The supremacy of the past is often only an assertion of the presence of historical continuity. We are not so much products of environment as sustained by it, in that it has the power to suggest, reinforce and re-assert, but not to build in perpetuity. Yet, despite widespread beliefs in unconscious forces, there is a big conflict between how we, in fact, go about in the world, and many of our pictures of human motivation. As Kadushin puts it:

Social workers, together with mental hygienists, have tended to over-emphasise the importance, significance and power of the past. Although we say that the past is structured in the present and is *one* of the determinants of present behaviour, we tend to see the past as more powerful than the present and the most significant determinant of present behaviour. History, despite the historian's interest in the past, favours a situational psychology. Hitler transformed a nation in a decade so that there were few to support a democratic ethos; southerners who only yesterday swore not to ride in desegregated buses and eat in desegregated restaurants are doing that today.

Therefore:

We may need a reorientation in emphasis with a greater respect being accorded the present and the more recent, proximate experiences. The past does, of course, intrude to shape perception, and in the case of the psychotic and seriously neurotic it may even be decisive. But for those less ill ... the present is a countervailing force which exerts a constant pressure, demanding that we live in response to it.

The naive arrogance of people-changers protects itself in part by systematically ignoring the subject's own opinions of himself, to a point where he is virtually denied membership of the same rational community as his investigator. The comments of a Borstal boy, in a letter to his parents in the early days of therapeutic intervention, are illuminating. He was the material for an eager post-graduate's excursion into rehabilitation, and wrote: 'Dear Mum, hope you are well, hope Dad's well, hope the dog's well. I am alright. There is a bloke here now who keeps taking me into this room with a big chair. He sits me down and asks questions. He keeps asking me why I think I got here. *Well, if he don't know why I'm here, he must be daft.* Still, what I say is this, bugger them all, Mother Dear' (personal communication).

While adventurous and expensive programmes sought (and still seek) that momentous change in the delinquent's psyche which would send him forth transformed, vast numbers of lawbreakers appear to have been quietly rehabilitating themselves without benefit of, or even in spite of, treatment. In medical language, we have a widespread case of 'spontaneous remission'. In America, the Gluecks have long drawn attention to a phenomenon where, regardless of the age at which delinquency begins, delinquent careers run a fairly steady and predictable course. This led them to posit that juvenile delinquency is the result of short-term adverse educational and other environmental features, whereas persistence into adult criminality is more connected with long-term personal weaknesses with or without an interaction with the environment which might sustain it.

There certainly seems to be a decline in offending in the late teens and twenties. Contrary to general belief, the two groups of juvenile delinquents and adult criminals by no means consist of the same individuals over time. The Royal Road to Crime seems to hit a lot of complex intersections in early adulthood. The relationships between juvenile and adult crime are, in fact, very puzzling. Certainly adult crime has never been higher, and the prisons have never been so crowded, but how many of these criminals have entered the crime boom as adults, and how many have graduated as juveniles, remains something of a mystery. In several places there are indications that those children who get involved in lawbreaking at the earliest ages tend to be the most persistent delinquents, the ones whose delinquent career runs for the longest time: the later the start, the shorter the run (Glueck and Glueck 1940 and 1968, D. Farrington 1974). And so far as adults are concerned, the majority of 'first offenders' do not become 'second offenders' (N. Walker 1965; M. Davies 1974), whereas a much larger proportion of second offenders become third offenders. Of these *persistent* adult criminals evidence shows that a majority have no juvenile court records.

As we have seen, it is the person's sensitivity to the present, rather than rigid adherence to the past, irrespective of surroundings, which may be involved in the failure of institutional attempts to rehabilitate criminals and delinquents. The person will bring to his present environment possibilities from his past, which may or may not be relevant. If his new environment does not support the changes in behaviour and the attitudes he may have acquired in the institution, the likelihood is that these will not last. The conclusions of Cornish and Clarke on their findings from the comparative study of different Community Home regimes echo Kadushin and other researchers:

Past experience, rather than creating in the individual stable and consistent personality traits, equips him *with an ever-expanding set of potential behavioural responses*; but these behaviours, since they were originally elicited in particular situations, will only be repeated when the latter recur. Thus the persistence in the criminal behaviour of certain individuals, despite the treatment they are given and the measures taken against them, may largely be accounted for by the fact that there is little change in the environments which they normally inhabit.

The increase in recidivism rates of all institutions, from 39 per cent in 1954 to 70 per cent in the 1970s, with progressively more delinquents persisting in lawbreaking after their release, implies that young offenders are now taking far longer to withdraw from the offending scene as they get older. The reasons for this are probably the same reasons for the rise in lawbreaking overall among young people and children, and the corresponding rise in adult crime and adult recidivism following prison—that society is now generally more conducive to lawbreaking, or conversely that countervailing pressures against delinquency and crime are weaker now than at any time this century. As we have no real evidence that placing offenders in institutions even in the past worked significantly better than alternative non-institutional measures to reduce recidivism, it could be concluded that the social pressures which kept a child and young person from lawbreaking in the first place, which prevented adults committing crimes, and which worked for the 'spontaneous remission' of the delinquent behaviour of actual lawbreakers as they got older, have generally diminished over the years.

The lawbreaker's environment may change in that he enters circumstances which are incompatible with continuing to offend, or offending in certain ways. He may, for example, enter a job, get married, obtain an apprenticeship (in the past, he may have been called up for national service). All of these not only compete for time with delinquent activities, but may expect and discriminate more in favour of different actions and attitudes than the previous influences. He may lose entirely something which has become very important to him if he persists in lawbreaking. When comparative studies of delinquents and criminals have been undertaken with those of similar background who did not end up serious lawbreakers, it is commonplace to find the latter referring to, for example, relationships outside the family, job or army experience, as the factor which counteracted pro-delinquent conditions in their environment (W.E. Roper 1950, 1951). Again, there are the studies, like those of J. Campbell and I.A.C. Sinclair, which show that boys sent from institutions to lodgings, foster-parents, or to sea do better than those who return on release to their families and familiar surroundings. The anti-delinquent pressures of jobs, marriage, etcetera, are not inherent however. They obviously depend on how much an employer, a craft or union organisation, training schemes, or a wife, tolerate offences. One might say that if a boss is unconcerned about any conduct of his employees that is not directly related to job performance, if a union protects the security of lawbreakers, if it becomes acceptable—for whatever reason—rather than shameful, to have a husband in jail, then accordingly, less pressures work against, and more are compatible with, offending.

If some institutions perform a 'holding operation' in that they do not make the inmates less likely to persist in lawbreaking after they are released, then it may be because they are providing something which can be 'carried over' into post-institutional circumstances which conflict with, rather than support, continued offending. As we have seen, the old-fashioned work training institutional regime, now heavily out of favour, has been associated in studies with lower rates of recidivism than the modern, progressive 'therapeutic relationships' environment. The former may have provided a speedier introduction into employment, whereas the 'acting out' permitted by the latter simply provides more opportunities to add to one's repertoire of possible delinquent acts. It constitutes a rehearsal of lawbreaking, rather than a preparation for work. (Remember that Cornish and Clarke found that boys who had been found guilty of committing offences *during* their stay in a Community Home were significantly more likely to be reconvicted afterwards.) Nor is it at all clear how the stress on personal relationships is supposed to carry over positive tendencies into the world outside, since social relationships here may run on quite different lines from the 'exploration of feelings in group settings' of the therapeutic Community Home.

If marriage, like work, is traditionally associated with the 'spontaneous remission' of delinquency, it may be due to the factors I have mentioned above, which conspire to produce an atmosphere where the conduct demanded of a 'good husband and father' is not compatible with being in trouble with the law, rather than because (as psychoanalytical theory assumes), a better tone is achieved in intimate, personal satisfaction. Far from personal relationships being the basis on which social relationships develop, a socially understood code of behaviour in interpersonal situations is usually necessary *before* one can go on and develop more intricate and individualised patterns. It has long been the observation with behaviour therapy to treat anxious, failing neurotics, that instruction and practice of the 'right way to behave' in situations such as a restaurant, shop, approaching a stranger, complaining to an official, etcetera, also introduces far more confidence and success into personal relationships. Cornish and Clarke mention that one factor which may counteract delinquent recidivism is what they euphemistically term 'reality therapy', or practical help and informed guidance on how to deal with everyday problems, such as looking for a job, interacting with officials, planning and arranging various activities, applying for benefits, and attaining various ends legitimately. This can carry the delinquent into those areas of social relationships which are incompatible with offending, and also prevent conflict arising through ignorance. It has often been remarked how some delinquents possess no knowledge of the means to attain many ordinary, everyday goals, or make certain social impressions.

Again, it cannot be overemphasized that although some institutional regimes enable the delinquent to fit more smoothly into those social arrangements that counteract continued lawbreaking, no institution, no regime—however intense—*will do much to change the rates of recidivism if the outside society does not support its attempts, by pressures of various kinds on the individual to continue his constructive behaviour in normal life.* Take, for example, an institution run on learning-theory lines, where, in direct opposition to the 'acting-out' kind, non-delinquent conduct was reinforced, and alternatives to delinquent activities were cultivated. Even this would still make little or no difference to the success rates, if the later external environment continued to suggest and reinforce delinquency. As Clarke and

Cornish put it '. . . it is unfortunately the case that the more therapeutically useful the institutional environment is designed to be, the less it approximates to the real world outside, and the less likelihood, therefore, there is for behaviour to generalise'.

> . . . stress upon 'boy-changing', which has led them to try to treat the individual in isolation from his characteristic environment, has been to some extent misplaced. For while removal to an institution may protect a child temporarily from the environments which elicited and maintained his delinquent responses, attempting to change behaviour in one setting by working upon it in another does nothing—of itself—to alter the probability that delinquent behaviour-patterns will be resurrected when the offender has completed the institutional programme.

In other words, there is just no *key* that can be permanently turned in a person by a period in an institution. The most it can do is develop alternative behaviour and hope that it continues to be relevant, useful and *reinforced* by the outside world to which the delinquent returns. But once he does return it is that world, not the institution, that is the operative one.

It is therefore outside in the wider society that we are to seek the solution to delinquency—or rather—the perpetual management of human behaviour. If delinquent acts are always part of the possible repertoire of normal people, the problem is management and containment, more than 'rehabilitation'; creating a more vigilant atmosphere which is less tolerant of violence and delinquency than the present one. Almost unavoidable in all this are social control mechanisms involving first, the reduction of opportunities to commit offences, and secondly, the incentives and disincentives, rewards and punishments, which need to be present in the everyday environment.

The use of social controls to enforce compliance with the law is a matter of informal as well as formal techniques, particularly with children. The surrounding adults must feel able and willing to use them and, moreover, use them in the name of norms and values, which are also taught as they are upheld. This is a broader, more important sense of 'knowing how to behave', and goes beyond simply practical guidance on how to get along in society without clashes through misunderstanding.

Cornish and Clarke take a very atomistic approach both to delinquent acts and the control of them. Using car-stealing as an example, they speak of how the delinquent might first engage in it for a number of reasons, from being stranded late at night, or drunk, or encouraged by companions—or any combination of these and many others. Chance factors lead him to attempt something which is then completed successfully. The act becomes part of his repertoire, the experience of which he brings to new situations. Possessing this possibility does not automatically lead him to repeat the act, which will depend on being in a situation similar to the original one, expectations about the next outcome, and so forth. This is a specific act—car-stealing—which the person engages in, governed by specific factors—the setting, the repercussions, etcetera. It does not imply 'general' delinquency, although 'A particular individual may, of course, depending on the environment he inhabits, separately acquire a wide range of delinquent behaviours.' Much lawbreaking is undoubtedly discrete in the way Clarke and Cornish portray. Some people steal from supermarkets, others rape, others receive stolen goods, or dope racehorses—but are otherwise law-abiding. And, of course, many confine themselves to those offences which are often felt to be merely contraventions of regulations, rather than 'criminal' acts.

Such an atomistic approach seems unobjectionable as far as it goes, but there are large and very important areas it leaves out, mainly due to its distinctly Behaviouristic standpoint.

In a very complex, diverse mass society, the opportunities for lawbreaking are as numerous as the various social activities of people themselves. Rigorous supervision of individuals is impossible, and the certainty of applying punishment extremely difficult—that is if we consider only the overall operation of the law and administration in containing offences of the individual. If individuals carry around with them an expanding repertoire of delinquent or criminal possibilities; if they can only be stopped from applying these by restrictions on their opportunities and adverse repercussions, consisting in tight security precautions and the fear of punishment by courts, it is difficult to see why supermarkets are not permanently looted, or a single pane of glass remains intact. It would not be enough for the law to penalise specific behaviour, if the everyday attitudes of people in society approved of it or were quite indifferent to it. In general, major criminal laws—or more correctly, the principles underlying these laws—always require an informal, moral underpinning in the society for which they are enacted. The most serious crimes, such as murder, violence against the person, cruelty, theft, or destructive acts such as arson, do reflect violation of deeply held moral norms, which are expressed in informal techniques of social control: disapproval, ostracism, even spontaneous reprisals. Here, the community is not doing the job of the law, so much as crudely asserting the values which it expects the law to uphold on its behalf. Of course, some offences carry little or no social disapproval (such as tax avoidance, where the enforcing authorities have to operate elaborate surveillance systems—virtually to the point where the costs outweigh the gains), and much of the law is purely regulatory and has no moral connotation. But even underlying this is a broadly held rule that one should obey the law in general, provided there are no serious countervailing circumstances, and it is not unreasonable, unfair, and so forth.

One of the most important ways in which an individual might be said to be prevented from acquiring delinquent possibilities, denied the opportunity of using them, and punished when he does, is not through the law but through the limits of toleration of other people. The social pressures that can be exerted by one's immediate, everyday group are considerable—whether this is people at work, at school, in the same street or among one's circle of friends. For the most part, the likelihood of ostracism, rejection, contempt, or just disapproval by those one has to live with, is far more potent in initiating and/or preventing certain behaviour than the more remote possibility of punishment sometimes in the future by the anonymous power of the law. Of course, the norms imposed by some groups may not coincide with law-abiding behaviour, and many even demand lawbreaking. Also, an individual can be a member of several groups whose norms conflict. Thus the same youth may be rowdy and aggressive with his mates, but quiet at work with a different set of people.

Where all the important social groups the individual moves in uphold essentially the same set of norms, deviance is naturally rare, as shown in J.W. Eaton's study of traditional religious sects in North America.

It is, then, the approval or tolerance of the social groups with whom the individual must live from day to day, that is a major determinant in whether he behaves in a delinquent or criminal way. But it is important to stress—in contrast to the atomistic picture of actions suggested by Cornish and Clarke—that social approval or disapproval is not just contingent on rewards and punishments blindly following specific acts considered one by one. The individual is made to understand where he has gone wrong, to see his act as an act of a certain type, and to understand what is expected of him in future in different situations.

Underlying this is the fundamental point that human actions are not simply discrete physical events whose similarities are a given fact of the natural environment. Actions—as distinct from bodily movements or responses—involve intention and meaning, and these are defined by elementary *social* rules. These rules determine what counts as a relevantly similar situation, and what aspects of a piece of behaviour are allowed to generalise to future situations.

The socially naive have to be deliberately taught the actions appropriate to different social situations. If these actions cannot be recognised spontaneously, then they will not emerge simply as a result of positive and negative reinforcements unless their social meanings are pointed out. A child must be made to grasp, for example, that hitting someone, throwing something at them or shouting at them are all similar in being hostile, whereas accidentally knocking them down does not count. Thus, this teaching very quickly becomes instruction in broad, underlying principles and guidelines enabling the child to interpret the rules in new instances which cannot be laid down in advance. It involves increasingly intelligent guidance and uptake, and the acquisition by the child of broad attitudes or orientations (rather than a collection of independent bits of learning) which come to reflect a grasp of the relevant moral similarities which a community expects the young to acquire and manifest in their behaviour.

Earlier I argued against the idea that delinquency is generally due to strong and enduring personality traits, and emphasised instead a person's sensitivity to his *present* environment. If that fails to sustain and reinforce behaviour he has learnt, it will rapidly diminish. But I have also insisted on the importance of social and moral values, and on the face of it, this may seem contradictory. If you can change a person's values, do you not bring about a long-term change in his personality, disposition, way of life and image of himself and others?

But the weight of all the preceding remarks has been that an individual's values, and those of his surrounding group, are interdependent. There would be a contradiction only if one ignored the ever-present fact of the surrounding society in which the individual lives, and supposed that the *typical* way an individual's values change is in some kind of sudden, once-only personal conversion like Saul on the road to Damascus. This is the moral (or religious) version of the inoculation fallacy. Actually it is only where the continuous daily life of his society—or at least his immediate circle—reflects and supports the individual's values by and large, that they will continue to guide his actions. In fact, religious movements themselves have nearly always realised that 'conversion' is short-lived unless there is rigorous community support for the change. As Wesley so clearly saw, the person's new-found faith has to be sustained by a tightly organised group of believers if he is not to slip back again.

Returning to delinquency, it appears that learning constructive social behaviour and the maintenance of this behaviour are very much a continuous process, and not just a set of lessons with which the child or youth is programmed and then left to his own devices. If delinquency can only be prevented in the community, it must be part and parcel of that community that it transmits and upholds—by the same token—norms and values which are antithetical to violent, destructive and dishonest behaviour, and instead demand and promote more socially cooperative, responsible, law-abiding conduct. To do this, children and young people need to be involved with people who demonstrate desirable qualities and who are, furthermore, able and willing to cultivate and preserve them in others.

But, is this allowed?

Part Three
Salvation from Society

9 What Right Have We?

We have seen in Chapter 7 that the failure of 'progressive' measures to reduce delinquency has not weakened the attachment to them. Rather than abandon these means, the end itself is quietly being jettisoned and delinquency dropped from the agenda. The rejection of traditional approaches was not simply based on factual beliefs about psychology, but strongly mixed with certain values independent of fact, and these are being drawn in to bail out the failed remedies. The quasi-moral distaste for the imposition of norms and the use of any coercion, implicit from the beginning of the 1969 Act and the associated innovations in education and child-rearing, now moves into the open. At the same time as they denied the existence of any dichotomy between society's demands and the child's needs, the progressives were doubting the right of society to make demands at all. 'What right have we?' they asked. But in the face of the failure of their methods, there is not so much an abdication as a vigorous denial of anyone's right to interfere, and a determination to fight it. The public, having been sold policies, and having paid for all manner of facilities on the promise of high returns on their investment, are now faced with well-entrenched interests resisting the change to alternatives. If lower rates of delinquency can only be bought by what are believed or feared to be bad means, then they will not be bought at all.

In Chapter 7 we also noted the comments of Professor Martin on the Scottish Kilbrandon Children's Panels, that even if they did nothing to reduce delinquency, they still had an 'intrinsic value' and should be kept. They are defended, in fact, as an island of moral superiority in a sea of public reaction where '. . . the cultural pattern includes a number of markedly illiberal strands', and 'the moral climate is in some respects distinctly unfavourable to the development of non-punitive approaches to delinquency: this is apparent also in current controversies over permissive versus authoritarian styles of management in List D Schools' (Scottish community homes).

So we have guilt by association, and the existence of punishment in schools and even the unreformed Scottish divorce law are used to refute any criticism of the progressive Children's Panels! Both are seen as part of a general primitiveness that does not even deserve to be listened to or rationally argued with. The last thing that is appreciated is that public criticism and disquiet over 'progressive' or 'permissive' measures may have something to do with the fear, grief and uncertainty of human beings living in an environment which is daily becoming more dangerous and depleted; they may have cause to question the price they are being asked to pay for other people's sensibilities.

And the price of other people's scruples may be higher than it at first appears. 'We've got to be careful not to impose our values on them . . .' is something one hears everywhere in relation to the young. It implies logically that we have no right to teach that violence and cruelty are wrong, for this is 'our' value and is no more valid than its opposite. By the same token, we must no more discriminate against this behaviour than against any other. Could society exist at all on a basis where there must be *no* teaching of standards and *no* constraints of law and morality? If it is somehow a sin of arrogance to make a moral judgement or a moral choice about the behaviour of others, then who has been consulted about the view tacitly adopted in high places, that it is somewhat disagreeable for a rule-governed social order to continue at all? I also described in Chapter 7 a unit for disruptive pupils where the reporter claimed that the function of the unit for the children—besides being careful not to impose any values on them—was to allow them to explore their emotions. However, the reporter for *New Society*, Joanna Mack, was afterwards told by the co-director of the Leeds Young Persons' and Schools' Support Units, Melanie Guyler, that these very expensive provisions have as their additional function the more active one of actually *combating* any attempts of society to teach the children to behave differently, or even communicate to them its judgements about their behaviour.

> In our work we are fighting the labelling and the sacrificing
> of the individual to social systems.

and

> In our work, we attempt to live our belief that people have a
> right to be treated as individuals, who are meaningfully able
> to decide what is right for them. We believe that each person
> is the only person, who has the necessary qualifications to be
> the ultimate expert on himself. We attempt to cast aside our
> prejudices and preconceptions about what is 'best' for some-
> one else. . . .

Now there is a certain sense in saying that an individual is the
best person to know what is in his own best interests—that is,
what he *wants*. But his wanting it does not make it right. It is
pathetic nonsense and confusion to suppose blandly that 'the
individual can decide what is right for him'. If the individual
alone decides what is right, then anything that individual
chooses to do is beyond criticism or assessment—if he chooses
to help others or exploit them, in either case, it is simply 'right'
for *him*. He alone judges himself, and of course acquits himself.
Right is whatever he chooses to do, and whatever he chooses to
do, is right. This is to assimilate moral decisions to the model of
purely personal taste—an area where the notion of a 'right' or
'wrong' choice is meaningless.

The fatal confusion this illustrates is very prevalent, but
easily stated. It is true that the individual alone is responsible
for his actions: he alone acts, or refuses to act, and he alone is
answerable for his actions and may justify them according to
various reasons and values. But these values must be impersonal and external. A person who chooses to kill because of
intense authentic feeling that it is 'right' for him to do so at that
moment (like Sharon Tate's murderers), can never be acceptable in a moral community, even one which places high value on
individuals 'doing their own thing'. To be *responsible* for one's
actions means being required to justify them *according to common,
shared standards* independent of the actor. This is precisely what
distinguishes responsible choices from irresponsible personal
caprices.

Even more fundamentally, the notion that something can be
'right' *for me*, irrespective of whether it is right for others, is

simply absurd, for it abolishes the whole possibility of distinction between right or wrong, correct or incorrect, in anything at all. The very idea of doing wrong or getting something right, presupposes some rule or standard which is not arbitrary. Take that away, and the individual simply feels, acts, or believes just as he will—there can be no 'right' about it. If he alone is the judge of what counts, and nobody else is in a position to correct him, then there is no possibility of his ever being wrong—or right either. This may be called freedom, but it is a useless and empty freedom, like that of a man in a featureless desert who is 'free' to walk wherever he likes—a fact modern existentialists uncomfortably acknowledge.

The 'individual' is not to be set against the 'social system' as some pure metaphysical ego confronted with alien forces. This is a false and sterile opposition. In Western society the individual is indeed faced with wide choices, and can call upon different and often conflicting standards which suggest various ways of life. But there are none the less standards outside himself which he must share with others, and which demand elementary forms of social cooperation to enter into. Paradoxically, even the very cult of the 'individual'—autonomous, self-achieving, self-choosing, and the rest—is one which is defined, regulated and judged by very intricate social values which have evolved since the Reformation. In the broadest sense, it is modern Western culture which sets up, educates and equips self-sufficient 'individuals' and supplies them with their very concepts of total independence. It is our particular society which implants in us the conceit that we are free of it.

The continual castigation of 'labelling', never satisfactorily defined, has been made a catch-all to evade difficult but necessary questions of evaluation and assessment. If it is misunderstood or abused, the fault lies largely with those who have adopted and popularised it. Certainly, some people are hindered, discouraged or otherwise thwarted unnecessarily by crude and easy categorisation of themselves and their supposed abilities. But one can make sense of this only by assuming that this is because they are *wrongly*, unfairly, inappropriately so described—because it violates the true and fair assessment that should be made. What is hopelessly confused and self-defeating is the total rejection of *any* evaluation, the idea that 'society' violates the integrity of the individual self by applying descriptions and evaluations to it. People have worth ultimately only in the eyes of others (*some* others)—and this is only to say that human beings share common forms of social life, and do not consist of idiosyncratic private dreamers. One can reject one's 'labels',—that is, rebel against one's immediate group—but only with reference to some *other* social group, actual or potential, whose evaluations one will accept. It is logically absurd for someone to think they could consistently reject all values, for that would leave nothing in favour of which they are rejected. The only way in which moral principles can be genuinely rejected (a way which amounts to more than an infant in a tantrum shrieking 'No, No' at everyone and anything), is by appeal to some other, contrary moral principles. And where are these to come from, if they are not to be taught, supported, *imposed* and *shared*?

Of course, plenty of references are made to children's pre-existing 'values' which must not be impugned or infringed. But if this is to be taken seriously, if the child has any 'values' of his own, or even a few simple conventions, one must assume that they are acquired somehow from his environment and have continued with him because they have been supported, intentionally or not. If 'imposing' values means, not demanding blind and uncritical obedience, but simply teaching them, then it is very difficult to avoid imposition. Many modern educationalists are very eager that the child should 'question' or even 'reject' the values of his society before he has acquired any means by which to do this. (It is almost as if he must be denied an informed choice, since his educators are in terror that he might 'accept' instead.)

It should be clear that the attempt to 'save' the individual from social systems is essentially nihilistic. Those who attempt this are doubtless very well-meaning, caring and concerned, with their conception of the person as psychologically most fragile and morally quite inviolable. But it is a stand like that made by the Manichaeans, who called a halt to reproduction to spite sin—when it cuts off its own nose in advocacy of a sour Utopianism of social suicide for the sake of individual, therapeutic salvation.

The sincere but disastrous paralysis of the liberal conscience in asking 'What right have we . . . to judge, instruct, interfere?' has seemed so tolerant, humane and civilised—one might

almost say, morally *advanced*. Yet it is based, in part, on gravely
muddled ethical thinking—in particular, the failure to grasp
that there is *no* breaking out of the circle of moral obligations,
that refusal to choose is itself a moral choice.

Having recognised, correctly, that there are in society alternative and conflicting values, none of which wear any guaranteed mask of Rightness, there is a powerful temptation to feel
that relativism implies impotence, that all are equally 'valid',
and therefore one has no 'right' to assert one's own to the point
of action. ('These values may be all right for *us*—but perhaps
not for *them*?') At the back of this is the distasteful picture of the
insensitive missionary. It is as if, when the Divine Authority of
Judaeo-Christian moral law will no longer serve, there is no
kind of moral authority whatever, only opinion.

But the search for a cast-iron guarantee of our own rightness
is misconceived. What could possibly convince us that we had
found it? Certainly our values *may* be 'wrong', in the sense that
in various circumstances we would come to alter them. And
unlike the stereotyped missionary, we have to make patient
efforts to understand other codes of values, other moral view-
points. But if and when we do alter our values, then *those* will
become our values. In the meantime, what we have are the best
we know; and because moral values are about those ends which
are of greatest, most ultimate importance, they do apply, in
appropriate ways, to all human beings, including those whose
values are different. Tolerance of diversity happens to be one of
our values, but it is only one: some things, even practices deeply
embedded in other cultures (such as slavery or torture), we
may not in conscience wish to tolerate. The necessary fact that
we have to act with limited understanding, and from the particular position of our own cultural circle in our own lifetimes, is
no ground at all for not acting. Sins of omission are still sins;
and the injunction to proper humility in our moral attitudes
also extends to that brand of Pharisee who requires an impossible standard of certitude before he will act to prevent an obvious wrong.

The growing awareness that cultural learning is somehow
critically involved in human development, that it may not after
all be a matter of natural spontaneity given the right nurture,
has—paradoxically—resulted in increased squeamishness
about teaching. The tendency is, as it were, to wish to fix or

freeze the individual as he is first encountered, and render him immune and inviolate to any further acquisitions or adaptations. He is the savage brought home to exhibit at court, or the newly fledged moth pinned to the board. Culture, learning, are all right as long as they are in the nature of some kind of authentic folk impression that happened more or less accidentally. The individual may pick up something from his obscure past, even if it may amount to little more than a few grotesque habits, but no one else may commit the sin of being seen intentionally and consciously to impart anything he has not himself chosen (at least, no one outside his very intimate circle).

'Labelling' as a concept owes a lot to the increasing popularity of 'deviance theory' in social science and social service circles in the 'seventies, with the more explicit resistance to socialisation and social controls generally getting a substantial boost from this source.

Deviance theory prides itself on discovering—quite correctly—that laws are man-made and various, and that therefore, should you abolish the distinctions made by laws, you would thereby abolish offences and offenders. For an act to become deviant or criminal is not the result of any inherent properties it may have; it becomes so only through the existence of social rules. Depending on its rules, a society may make drinking, drug-taking, homosexuality, arm-breaking, or killing, deviant in some, or all, situations. But Nature, as distinct from social rules and artifice, is utterly neutral. The drawbacks of 'naturalistic' models of lawbreaking, particularly psychological ones, are therefore avoided. It is not that the mentally healthy person will naturally behave in a socially desirable way. Deviance theory has little place for notions that the criminal or deviant is sick. Deviants are the result of society's rules, the response to the breaking of those rules and the formal 'labelling' and 'processing' apparatus of police, courts, penal institutions and so forth.

All this is correct. But certain strange and vulgar conclusions are often drawn from deviance theory. First, it appears to be suggested that since it is society's 'labelling' which makes some acts criminal, the events have no real existence independent of that label: in effect that the experience of pain and injury are irrelevant to the sufferer once the descriptions of 'attacker' and 'victim' are withheld. And second, it is concluded that since laws and crimes are social creations they are therefore quite arbitrary, that there are no sufficient reasons for one set of laws rather than any other, or indeed for any set at all.

There are seldom victims in deviance theory, there are only 'audiences' to the 'labelling' of the rule-breaker. Accordingly, the deviance theorist Edwin Schur, for example, maintains that there is much the same amount of crime going on all of the time, with presumably the same number of houses stripped and faces slashed throughout eternity. When we notice, it is more or less arbitrary as far as the offender is concerned. The offender is quite unremarkable or indistinguishable psychologically, economically or socially from the non-offender. Those who become positively marked off as 'deviant' are thus really passive victims of a change of contingencies. The offender is simply Mr Anybody, who drifts into a position where the rules could make a distinction between him and others, and who is then 'processed'.

If all of this is so, if it is only because a society has laws that it has crime, and the only thing the laws achieve is the discomfort of the 'deviant', then it might seem the most blindingly obvious solution to the so-called problem of crime, to abolish it by abolishing the laws. Asking us to leave the kids alone whenever possible, this is essentially what Edwin Schur appears to be proposing in his *Radical non-Intervention: Re-thinking the Delin-quency Problem.*

The rather absurd position deviance theory ends up in, was put as follows by a critic:

> Rather, although those of this school come dangerously close to saying that the actual behaviour is unimportant, their contribution to the study of deviancy comes precisely in their conception of the impact of labelling on behaviour. One sometimes gets the impression from reading this literature that people go about minding their own business, and then—'wham'—bad society comes along and slaps them with a stigmatising label. Forced into the role of deviant, the individual has little choice but to be deviant. (R.L. Akers 1967)

The confusion which deviance theorists are apt to fall into between social conventions and the experiences covered by these conventions leads us to the suggestion that what the conventions do not cover is therefore not really felt, or even does not really happen. It is an obvious, convenient position for those like Stuart Hall whom we talked about in Chapter 2, who wants to represent public concern over street violence as the product of a concoction supplied by the media and the forces of social control. But abolish both the laws and the media defining violent crime, and will the pain of the blow or stab be diminished? Indeed, revolts have occurred among those who suffer injury, such as slaves, precisely because their society's existing set of 'labels' took no notice of their suffering and did not acknowledge its existence.

Or perhaps it all comes down to the argument that since crimes are social rather than natural facts, and since Nature makes no distinction how you go, and is unconcerned for what you suffer either way—why should human beings make rules which do?

Even if human beings are creatures who construct the means by which they live together, the 'artificiality' of the social order by no means implies that it can be dispensed with, or even that we can coherently envisage being without it. Popular conclusions drawn from deviance theory not only appear to be saying that there is no great necessity for, and even great harm in forbidding, condemning and penalising in the name of law and morality. They also intimate that there is really no need at all for shared standards of assessment in society; that to evaluate behaviour, to expect any conformity, is all 'labelling', all a distortion of individual life by oppressive forces. When there is talk of 'tolerating human diversity' a state of affairs seems to be envisaged where our actions would be not merely sometimes dangerous and fatal to one another, but generally unpredictable because unmediated by regular expectations. Human 'society' would begin to resemble a random collection of individuals whose lives and actions shared few meanings, each absorbed in his own idiosyncratic self, occasionally colliding.

It has certainly been widely canvassed—and by police chiefs—that many breaches of regulations (for example, some motoring and financial offences) which are now lumped together with crimes with distinct victims which also offend general morality, should be de-criminalised, and be left to civil action. In an increasingly secular society the law has already

withdrawn from many attempts to interfere in private life and
enforce specific personal choices in cases where no direct harm
is being done to another, for example, homosexuality, suicide,
abortion. Indeed, the proliferation of regulations, and thus the
possibilities for general law breaking, may be in danger of
trivialising all offences. We may become de-sensitised to lawbreaking generally if this includes a host of petty infringements
we are hardly going to avoid completely. Yet, when we come to
the 'de-criminalisation' gleaned from deviance theory, we find
Hall and Wiles berating us for making much of violence, and
Edwin Schur managing to avoid any reference to the problem
of crimes against the person and property—the offences which
the public are most concerned about.

   What has doubtless helped to form the conclusions drawn
from deviance theory, and has in turn been reinforced by them,
is the hyper-sensitivity of intellectuals and many 'informed'
and 'forward'-looking minds of the age, to society as a dreaded
bogey; it will gobble them up, or 'control' or 'condition'
them—and by the same token, all of us. In the writings of the
pioneers of progressive education, from A.S. Neill onwards,
society takes on the shape of a veritable monster, out to make
Man its Frankenstein. It is a cruel and capricious jailor,
lacerating the feelings and stifling authenticity, creativity—the
very 'self'. Laurie Taylor and Stan Cohen are preoccupied with
'escaping' from society to find the self—rather a forlorn task.
Their interest in delinquency and criminality is partly
because—to them—these represent break-out attempts. The
image of the authoritarian state: the idea that anything shared
is somehow degrading to the individuals concerned who aspire
to uniqueness; the psychological notion of environmental
determinism, where experiences leave permanent behaviour
patterns, and many more strands make up the dichotomy that
is posed between the individual and society.

   It is not just that social meanings and social rules simply give
us the framework from which to think and act, and that the
'self' is constructed from social concept, definition and judgement, but that very many people get enormous pleasure out of
what they learn from and share with others. The appeal of
rituals which owe nothing at all to 'personal' distinctiveness or
creativity, is a dramatic case in point. The participants do not
feel demeaned, humiliated or mentally tortured thereby. The

shame is that intellectuals who project their flight from society onto others can leave them, not uniquely flowering, but bitterly alone and impoverished.

In fact, to think that one can escape entirely the influence of the group, or keep others unsullied by it, is chasing moonbeams. It is trying to defeat the human condition, from which there is no way out. The question is not whether we should or should not be influenced by 'the group', but by *which* group, and *what* does it teach, sanction and uphold; what principles guide it and what room it has for participation in its choices. Is it better that the group should act within clearly delineated rules, or—like the children's peer group—only on the basis that might is right? The child has to learn, in time, that authority itself is in need of justification, and also the ways by which it is assessed and can be controlled, or made accountable. But this can only come from initial acceptance of *some* authority, and from those who will take some kind of lead to make sure he is informed and acts accordingly. Questioning, criticism, dissent and checking the power of those in authority are all skills that have to be taught, and from a basis of shared rules; yet the only thing which will lift the individual's oppression is condemned as a step in the authoritarian direction, with democratic authority held to be a contradiction in terms.

Revulsion at the particular element of *coercion* so frequently lies at the heart of the uneasiness about society's hold over the individual, particularly, of course, when it is a matter of formal or informal attempts to uphold law and normative standards. That deterrence relies purely and rationally upon the threat of adverse consequences from a greater power, makes it an option that is too reprehensible even to investigate. Coercion is what makes the whole area of policing and law-enforcement 'dirty', as when the social science lecturers at Kent University made it clear that the police were not welcome as students at their institution, and neither were law-enforcement studies fit to take their place as part of a degree course. The present low morale and dissatisfaction with their lot to be found in the British police force is partly the result of having to live under administrations and powerful influences which are uncomfortable about its existence at all. Often, in combination with psychological notions that it is mentally damaging, the concept of coercion extends itself to virtually all socially taught and reinforced behaviour: to standards of correctness, and judgements of right and wrong well outside the moral field. Since some pressure to conform is always implied, some token that one is failing, inadequate, out of step, employed throughout social life and learning processes, this is also 'coercion' in action.

The repudiation of coercion usually involves the central tenet that all kinds of force are morally equivalent. It rejects the idea of any special coercive rights of the police, the state, and the law; the policeman arresting a man for violence becomes by this very act just as guilty as he; a teacher who slaps or detains the pupil is no better than the boy who beats him up. The visible use of coercion by authority in society is felt to demonstrate a rottenness, an inherent viciousness, as if a society that had to fall back on such sordid means did not deserve to survive. 'Look,' it is proclaimed, 'the state is founded on force,' with all the outraged innocence of those who find that the vicar has been buggering the choirboys.

As violence, whether taught, imitated or discovered, is an effective way of getting what one wants and enforcing one's will, and as nothing suggests that some kind of switch can be pulled in nurture which will eliminate this propensity once and for good, it should be clear that eradication remains a pipe-dream. The only adult question is not whether violence should be totally permitted or abolished—because to do either requires power which can itself wield force—the question is, which rules govern the use of force—by whom, in what form, and for what ends? In modern societies the state has a monopoly of the means of coercion, and largely denies others the right of direct coercion. Indeed, the state came into existence to exercise violence—but to exercise it according to *some* norms. The disarming of the individual, with the state assuming power to coerce on his behalf in accordance with understood independent rules, has historically been felt to be the only guarantee of safety for citizens. This is to be contrasted with a precarious and unpredictable condition where the stronger coerced the weaker, and where self-defence was a matter not of right before the law, but purely of how many allies and weapons one could muster, and how well they could fight.

Protection was frequently bought only with self-enslavement. In the early feudal period, peasants suffered appallingly from the predations of plundering knights, who could help themselves to any amusement, sustenance and resources they liked in the absence of any overriding force to prevent them. The value of life would be virtually defined minute by minute and day by day, by the requirements or whim of the stronger. Long before modern notions of representative government, the 'King's Peace' was a desirable end *in itself* for almost all classes except the powerful nobility and warlords.

Politics has centred not on whether it is a good thing for the state to have this power of the sword, but rather how it uses it, what the rules are, who makes them, administers them and changes them, and to whom and how their actions shall be accountable. The crucial questions therefore revolve around *legitimacy*. But it is just this legitimacy or 'rationalisation' of violence, which some liberals seem to see as monstrous cynicism, and those who are its instruments (such as police and army), appear as disgusting as nightsoil workers in traditional China. This fact is felt to be a hypocritical affront to humanity whatever form this legitimacy takes—indeed, the more democratic the state, the more it is felt to be betraying these very values by relying on force at all—as if either they must be spontaneously upheld, or be wholly fraudulent. Such fastidiousness over these sordid facts of life resembles that of the ethereal aesthete over grossly physical matters, which are none the less facts of life. The move is from the one-ness of coercion to a position which finds the legitimate infinitely worse than the unlawful. Interference and control when wielded by the state are deliberate, whereas the individual's spontaneous action arises from the very core of his being, a pure thing free of contrivance (or it is in the nature of some kind of unavoidable accident). Hence the attraction of the deviance theory which finds the problem not in the offender's initial action, but society's reaction to it.

Hence, too, the marked lack of interest by respectable pressure groups in the coercion exercised by the criminal or delinquent on the citizen, despite assiduous interest in the individual's rights. The National Council for Civil Liberties defines these only one way. The fundamental civil liberties which they make their concern do *not* include freedom from arbitrary interference, attack, injury, abuse, invasion of privacy, and the destruction and removal of property, which so cripplingly restrict people in high delinquency areas. The interest is in, for example, ending completely the *loco parentis* tradition of teachers (which gives the right to punish and detain and so forth) and making changes which would make the police virtually impotent to apprehend lawbreakers. Only threats from government or officialdom are relevant to the preservation of liberty, not those from individuals. When there is such an exclusive concern with the individual's primary freedom of action, as if his acts had no repercussions for anyone else, it all makes 'civil' something of a misnomer: public life and mutual obligation to guarantee mutual rights have dropped completely away.

This concentration on the individual divorced from his impact on others gives us that blend of squeamishness and callousness which is such a hallmark of modern progressive opinion far outside the camp of specific deviance-theory disciples. Not only the public's 'reactionary' opinions, but their fears too are often held as tiresome obstacles to adventurous social experiments; they should be prepared for the risks of reform and freedom. 'The community has had to learn to live with its mad. Now it's a question of learning to live with its bad', said Jessica Blooman, Principal Probation Officer for Berkshire, to the *Guardian* in 1973. If this is to be construed that they will live with us *qua* bad, it could mean that attacks and robberies are some kind of little eccentricity which we could come not to mind.

This makes it a mistake to suppose that much liberal and progressive disquiet about coercion is because force might cause pain. The principle of the inherent wrongness of compulsion seems to be one of intrinsic evil and rests on no considerations of the consequences of coercion or non-coercion. Such a purist rejection is very similar to the Catholic Church's stand on birth control or abortion, or the strict Buddhist's on taking life. No matter what the consequences, whether the world perish from want, it is intrinsically evil to prevent a sperm from meeting an egg, or to kill germs. An act evil in itself cannot be made good by beneficial results.

So, far from the State's concern to see that its rules governing coercion are complied with thus demonstrating a desirable condition, it shows only the opposite. Where there is, for example, enquiry into police malpractice and findings of guilt—this is taken axiomatically to show just what bastards they are all along, not to show the wisdom of making force accountable. This puts the delinquent (or terrorist) in a privileged position indeed. Legitimate coercion will be regarded as no more, or even less worthy than his activities, while it is hamstrung by rules which do not curtail his. Moreover, it is then closely watched to see if it trips itself up in these selfsame rules, while no onus can fall on the offender since he has none to break. (Thus one finds the BBC justifying the need to give parity in broadcasting in a democracy both to the forces of law and to those which are now employing all manner of violent tactics to overthrow that democracy. But if it seemed to regard one force as no more legitimate than another, instances arise where the 'official' one cannot appear to answer the charges brought against it by terrorists because its rules forbid commenting while investigating!)

The failure to distinguish legitimate and illegitimate coercion occasionally takes the absolute about-turn that goes from nothing to all, like Ulrike Meinhof who moved from idealistic pacifism to unrestrained terrorism. If the policeman, the soldier, the state, can use it for particular purposes, why shouldn't anyone use the means of violence for his own purpose? And, making no distinction between who uses it for what, likewise no limits are placed on its scale. Thus the plushily brought-up adolescent, full of virtue, but virgin in the world of work and politics, may be a fitting recruit to terrorism after being raped by that horrendous discovery that the state is based on the monopoly of the means of violence:

> The major characteristic of terrorism is not its severity but its *indiscriminacy*. The conventions and the usages of war at least try and protect non-combatants, hostages, prisoners of war and neutrals. Military forces sometimes infringe these conventions, but there still remains the internationally accepted code as to how we ought to behave. Terrorism, by contrast, rejects all limits. Its distinguishing feature is that in pursuit of its political aims, it values neither mercy, nor compassion, nor conscience.

> Of course governments, too, may exercise terror, exercise it against their own subjects. Some do, and certainly any might. But when can we reasonably assert that a govern-

ment is using 'terror' against the population? Obviously, to
begin with, where it departs from the moral norms and
values implicit in its legal codes, to strike indiscriminate fear
into its citizens. Less obviously, but more damaging, where
it manipulates the system of the law, so that crimes and
offences are not clearly defined, judicial procedures are per-
verted, and the penalties are atrocious and arbitrary and out
of all proportion to the alleged offences; where in fact, the
government does anything it chooses to whomsoever it
chooses . . . (S.E. Finer *On Terrorism*)

Or, far more common, the progressive, the reformer, the
rebel intellectual is to be found satisfied or applauding on the
side-lines as society blunders into violence. Shocked at its
imperfections, its injustices, he feels that it deserves all it gets: it
deserves the lot, for it is ROTTEN.

10 Getting Their Own Back

Bad housing, poverty, unemployment, 'inner city stress'—the nineteen-seventies has seen 'social' replace 'emotional' deprivation, as the most reiterated cause of delinquency.

It is, of course, an old idea of reformers that crime is due to bad economic and social conditions, making it, as in the emotional deprivation story, only a temporary manifestation of abnormal environments which distort an inherent cooperativeness. It will go away with the conditions which produce it, when Man lives in the kind of society suited to his true nature and needs.

A complaint frequently heard about anxiety over rising crime rates, is that it is a smokescreen, distracting our attention from the 'real problems', the persisting injustices—thus assuming the implicit truth of a social-deprivation theory, with the delinquent as social scapegoat.

Speaking of the 1969 Act, *New Society* staff writer Paul Harrison said that '. . . in many ways all the concern with the 1969 Act has obscured the real problem. The rise in juvenile crime is not due to the act's inadequacies, but with . . . the pressures of poverty, and the inner city environment . . . the answer isn't providing more children's homes, or giving JPs back the power to send kids there. . . . It is nothing less than an all-out attack on urban poverty and deprivation.'

The eclipse of emotional by social deprivation, on the face of it, seems to spare the delinquent the stigma of personal pathology: society must be 'fixed', not him. However, the distinction is more apparent than real. For example, maternal deprivation was seen as a pathological condition of the *environment,* and the individual's reaction to it, in becoming delinquent, is as 'normal' according to this theory as when it is considered to be a reaction to unemployment. The impression that 'emotional-needs' models put the blame on the individual, not society, comes partly from the former's emphasis on the power of the past, which leaves the individual to be fixed, not the system which sustains his condition.

However, claims about social and economic need as a cause of delinquency and violence are usually even more confused than those about emotional deprivation. It is not made clear whether these needs are taken as naturally fixed, or socially given. Nor is it clear whether some kind of environmental determinism is being proposed, whereby the delinquent is somehow compelled, or driven to commit offences, as when a starving man steals food, or if he is as much in command of his actions as everyone else, but is simply *justified* in what he does. If the latter, then the question is an ethical, as well as an empirical one, for it is implied that we are in effect entitled to commit certain acts of violence, theft or destruction against others if we do not have certain things in life.

The notion of social and economic deprivation seems too tempting for many deviance theorists to miss. In an area where confusion and schism reign, a combination of deviance and social-deprivation theory is now highly popular at many academic levels. It allows the delinquent, or rather the commentator, to have his cake and eat it too. 'Classic' deviance theory is a little limited. If the delinquent is simply Mr Anybody, who justs gets labelled and processed, then particular delinquents, assumed to be selected almost at random, can hardly be credited with making a point about their social conditions. A step forward is to suggest that only people in certain groups are picked on. (To the co-director of the Leeds unit for disruptive pupils, Melanie Guyler, whom we met in the last chapter, the rules of society, whose labels she fights, are 'but designed to uphold the *status quo* of a society in which underprivileged individuals are used as pawns'. The children she is saving have already 'suffered the worst conditions of emotional, social and material deprivation'.) The next step is a curious hybrid, deviance-revolt theory, which maintains that the delinquent has a reason for acting as he does, whereas for the victim, or anybody else, to attach meaning and moral significance to it, is simply malevolent. It is all very strange. Surely when the delinquent attacks because he is making a protest or demonstration, he must intend people to take notice.

If they made nothing of it, how then would the delinquent publicise his case?

Paul Wiles explains how the social worker should concern himself with the meanings of the deviant, while ignoring those of the public: 'Behaviour which becomes designated as violent during the course of a moral panic may well lead to clients being referred to social workers accompanied by a magisterial statement which, as itself part of the moral panic, may imply a particular cause of the behaviour.' So, understanding 'the meaning of the deviance for the deviant' may pose problems for the social worker with such court directives; they may even 'themselves enter the world of the moral panic' [*sic*]. Wiles wonders 'how long it will be before we see British social workers putting forward clients' reasons on their behalf in court'.

If we are ever going to assess social deprivation theories as explanations for lawbreaking, we must make a distinction between the reasons of the lawbreaker's motivations and the rhetorical threats that political opportunists put in his mouth. It becomes increasingly common to find propagandists for various causes and reforms (often very good ones in themselves) using the lawlessness of others both as evidence for the truth and justice of their claims, and vicariously, as a lever to shift a slow or uninterested authority and squeeze the public purse. ('The government has received a "civil war" warning from an immigrant group. The Confederation of Indian Organisations says a war can be averted if the Government revolutionises its approach to poor, inner-city areas where a large part of the coloured community live'. *Evening Standard* 30 March 1977.) This use of other people's violence to push a cause often makes the claim that violence is due to social and economic deprivation so much of a tautology. The more violence and lawbreaking there is, the more it *proves* that the instigators must be suffering desperate circumstances, else why would they do it?

If the social and economic deprivation model is at all correct, one would expect to find some significant correlation between indices such as poverty, bad housing, unemployment, and the level of offences. Running through the argument is usually the thread that some sections of society are getting either absolutely or relatively worse off as the years go by, and becoming progressively trapped.

To maintain that offences are a simple reflection of poverty, one would have to maintain that social and economic conditions were something like sixteen times worse in 1970 than they were in 1900, for that is the rate of increase in indictable offences known to the police during those years (adjustment for differences in record keeping and population will not greatly alter the facts). The rate of increase also shows an accelerating trend: between 1900 and 1935 crimes known to the police trebled; however, between 1950 and 1968 the trebling was to occur in only eighteen years. This gives us a graph which shows only a minimal rise (with fluctuations) between 1900 and 1940; a more pronounced trend upwards until the early 1950s, when a decrease temporarily set in, before the curve turns sharply and rises steeply throughout the 'sixties and 'seventies. By rights, the decline in the 'fifties should have continued, or stabilised, and the graph shows a pattern for the 'sixties and 'seventies similar to that for the pre-war period. (This is because a rise in offences following wars is a common phenomenon; it is the sudden upsurge of offences in the 'sixties, when 'normalisation' was already under way, which needs explaining.) If the social and economic deprivation argument is to hold, one had even more reason to predict a sharp *decline* in crime and violence as our society gained in prosperity. However, the upsurge in offences coincided with the movement of Britain into a boom period and a mass consumer society, in which real incomes rose fast and consumer goods spread rapidly throughout the population. Also, poorer societies in the world today, whose inhabitants have the most meagre diet, shelter and rudimentary domestic provision, are not necessarily afflicted by the atrociously high levels of crime and violence which the deprivation hypothesis must suggest.

That living standards have been squeezed slightly in the mid-'seventies cannot be used as an explanation for a phenomenon which was well in evidence before this happened. On the face of it, there is not the slightest reason to believe that offences will fall if and when living standards rise again.

However, a sizable proportion of the population from which delinquents are drawn, are perhaps proportionately or absolutely worse off than they have ever been before. Paul Harrison, whom we have already referred to above, describes modern working-class existence as 'more like hell'. I assume that he must mean that the working-class exist in something like the conditions Engels described as conducive to crime over a hundred years ago:

> The manner in which the great multitude of the poor is treated by society today is revolting . . . they are relegated to districts which, by reason of the method of construction, are worse ventilated than any others; they are deprived of all means of cleanliness, of water itself, since pipes are laid only when paid for, and the rivers so polluted that they are useless for such purposes; they are obliged to throw all offal and garbage, all dirty water, often all disgusting drainage and excrement into the streets, being without any other means of disposing of them; they are thus compelled to infect the region of their own dwellings. . . . it is they in particular who are packed in the least space . . . they are penned in dozens into single rooms, so that the air which they breathe at night is enough in itself to stifle them. They are given damp dwellings, cellar dens that are not waterproof from below, or garrets that leak from above. Their houses are so built that clammy air cannot escape. They are supplied bad, tattered, or rotten clothing, adulterated and indigestible food.

In 1925 Cyril Burt was to claim that one in five delinquents (or 19 per cent in his sample) fell into 'very poor' groups, defined by possessing income insufficient to maintain basic physical health—a bare subsistence. However, it appeared that although delinquents came disproportionately from the poorest sections of the population: 'The biggest of my batch, 42 per cent, came from classes E and F—those designated by Booth as "comfortable" ' (meaning 'high-class labour, well-paid foremen and artisans' and lower middle-class shop-keepers, and so forth).

The 'rich' and the 'poor'—such terms, still very much in use, suggest a polarisation of life styles and an absolute criterion of poverty, which perhaps Burt was applying. You can just survive and keep going physically by rationing out each slice of bread and remaking clothes with remnants from the last. Such, indeed, were the conditions experienced by many a person still alive today. However, in the post-war world a tremendous social effort has gone into trying to see that such self-evident want—in diet, clothing, sanitation, warmth and furnishing—is as far as possible, eliminated. Since 1948 the agreed aim of British Governments has been that nobody should be allowed to fall below a certain minimum level, geared to the general level of either incomes or prices; and that all should benefit according to need from a range of freely available social provisions. The 'social wage' including supplementary benefit, educational, housing and health provisions was held to be equivalent to £1,000 a year in 1975 for every adult in the population. For over twenty years—from the early 'fifties to the late 'seventies—the social wage as a proportion of the consumption spent directly by people themselves not only kept pace with the rise to affluence, but rose from 33 per cent in 1955 to 59 per cent in the early 1970s. Over the last ten years we find the cost of education rising from £1,636 million to £5,388 million: health costs from £1,319 million to £4,094 million; social services costs rose from £109 million to £769 million, and social security benefits rose from £2,499 million to £7,165 million. The result of a virtual eradication of self-evident want (except for example in pockets of over-crowded and dilapidated housing), the total rise in standards of the population as a whole, and the diminution of differentials in income, has made the concept of 'poverty' in modern Britain very flexible and frequently conflated with remaining inequalities in income. When this concept is used to denote those who earn below two-thirds of the average wage, or those who fall within the bottom 20 per cent of wage earners, or those whose income from any source is less than supplementary benefit level plus 20 per cent, either way, when living standards rise, poverty becomes a matter of comparative participation. On such criteria, it is clear that in advanced industrial countries, no matter how high our average living standards may rise compared with those less fortunate who still have an enormous problem of basic want, in theory there will still be poverty.

There are some difficulties apparent in collecting information on poverty in a country where living standards are more homogeneous and the 'poor' themselves do not constitute an easily definable group of the population. Lucy Syson mentions in *Poverty Report 1976* that low income households are never identified in any consistent way with factors such as size, ages of children etcetera. Investigation is further confounded by the fact that the number of low-income households in any group which crops up in national surveys is very small, and makes cross-analysis very difficult.

Certainly, income levels do not correspond very well with social class categories. A survey for the Mirror Groups of the income and expenditure of 7,832 individuals (over fifteen), and 3,828 households in Britain, revealed that two-thirds of the top income earners were in social classes C1, C2 and D; conversely, a third of those in the second from lowest of the four income groups used were in social categories B or C1. The households which were conspicuously badly off as a group compared with the rest were those of pensioners, widows and casual workers. The majority of people on supplementary benefit are retired, as are the majority of those whose income falls within 20 per cent of this level. However, it has been suggested (by Fiegehen and Lansley in 1977) that official figures for household income underestimate the amount of money available to the poorest tenth. This is because households with low incomes are often smaller households than households with higher income. When, for example, you ignore the size of household, the poorest 10 per cent of the population have incomes of only 29 per cent of the median, but this rises to 45 per cent when allowance is made for the number of adults and children. Based on the quality and quantity of the fundamentals of life consumed by households, the Government Expenditure Survey identified those worst off as low wage earners, rather than pensioners and those on benefit. (Some of the lowest male wage earners are white collar workers.) In modern Britain the poor do not fit any stereotype of the manual, particularly unskilled, working class.

Housing is a key subject in any discussion of poverty and it would be quite wrong to ignore the fact that some groups live in housing that is still seriously unsatisfactory by present standards. However, one must also avoid equating these with the appalling rookeries of the past, or suggest that they are general or typical of the working class now. In this area, we have some information about the living conditions of both delinquents and the age group generally from which they are drawn. The Home Office study of *Probationers in their Social Environment* found that housing troubled fewer than 5 per cent of their sample of delinquent boys and their families. Most of the subjects came from homes where material conditions were generally high.

The report found that 84 per cent of the sample lived in a self-contained flat or house, and that more than half had their own bedrooms. The standard of furnishing and cleanliness was generally good, and only 5 per cent did not have television. Compared with other categories of offenders, juvenile delinquents seem comparatively advantaged. The Cambridge Study of Delinquent Development compared boys who had committed no offences since age seventeen with those who had admitted to, or been convicted of offences since then (Knight and West). The temporary delinquents were less likely to have come from socially badly-off families.

As for the total young population from which delinquents are drawn, the longitudinal study of child development, conducted for the National Children's Bureau, and following up all children born in a certain week in 1958, recently provided information on the living conditions of Britain's sixteen-year-olds (Ken Fogelman 1976). It found that 90 per cent lived in houses or bungalows and 9 per cent in flats (the remaining 1 per cent lived in rooms, caravans etcetera). In 50 per cent of the families accommodation was owner-occupied, and in another 41 per cent it was rented from the council. As far as amenities went, 92 per cent of the families from which the children were drawn had the sole use of a bathroom; 97 per cent had the sole use of a hot water supply, and 95 per cent had the use of at least one indoor lavatory. Over 80 per cent of the families had a refrigerator; nearly 50 per cent had central heating; 41 per cent had colour television, and 65 per cent had at least one car.

Moving now to the housing of the general population: 99 per cent of this lives in 'conventional dwellings', that is, not in shanty towns, squatter settlements, caravans or other makeshift or mobile accommodation. Homelessness affects 0.05 of the population and only 3 per cent of households have to share with another. (Ten years ago double this number had to share.) By 1973, the proportion of households without sole use of fixed baths was down to just over 6 per cent. It is difficult to convince oneself that this is Paul Harrison's 'more like hell'. The information that Britain has now more or less achieved its objective of one fit dwelling for every actual household may seem odd because our picture of housing conditions in this country is shaped by the very visible, loud propaganda of pressure groups on behalf of small minorities. Even here, residual housing problems may not always be solvable by non-coercive, democratic means. Some people, for example, don't want their homes improved, they want to spend money on something else.

Certainly organisations such as the pressure group Shelter have frequently urged that poor housing and the continued existence of pockets of overcrowding are themselves a *cause* of lawbreaking. The lack of an indoor lavatory is quoted so frequently that one almost comes to suspect that Shelter imagines some psychological compulsion to delinquency, activated by whether one passes through an internal or external door to urinate (or perhaps up against the wall?). However, the possession of indoor lavatories, like hot water supplies and separate rooms for children, has grown hand in hand with delinquency and violence. If the former used to be uncommon in the area in which I grew up, then so was lawbreaking. But Shelter is simply exploiting the emotive potential of any data that might serve as grist to its mill. A simple correlation between delinquency and children who come from ill-equipped or overcrowded homes shows, of course, no more causal connection than does a correlation between the lunar cycle and women's ovulation. Other factors simply have not been controlled for.

We know from Chapter 5 that large families are more likely to produce delinquent children, probably because supervision is poorer. (There has already been criticism (Tyrrell Burgess 1975) of extrapolations from the reading ability of children and its correlation with overcrowding to imply that bad housing is at the root of educational backwardness. The relationship vanished when family size was controlled. For large families in any social group have always been shown to do worse educationally compared with smaller ones.) We know also that quarrelsome and violent homes are more likely to produce delinquents; Shelter itself admits that the main cause of homelessness is now conflict with relatives and friends and the break-up of marriage. Thus self-selection may be occurring, whereby conflict-ridden families in their fragmentation have to settle for the worst accommodation. However, this point should not detain us too long, since the great *majority* of delinquents do not come from overcrowded homes, or homes lacking basic facilities, any more than the majority come from broken homes.

Other studies between housing and either offence rates or

offender residence *do* show a relationship, but it is emphatically
not of the 'poor housing produces crime' variety. The Sheffield
Study on Urban Social Structure and Crime found no association between the age and rent levels of estates, the economic
well-being of the tenants and the residence of delinquents when
other variables are controlled (Bottoms and Baldwin 1976;
A.E. Bottoms 1976). What did emerge was that the offender
rate varied according to different types of tenure, that is,
whether it was predominantly owner-occupied, privately
rented, council, or 'mixed', and it varied in a complex way. For
example, there was a contrast between council areas and rented
areas in the relationship between the social class of convicted
offenders and the social class level of the area. In council estates
the lower the social class of the area the higher the
conviction rate of working-class people. On the other hand, in
privately rented areas, the working-class conviction rate rose only
when there were fewer than about one-third of working-class
people in the locality. These and other relationships suggested
that the housing *market* was related to delinquent residence,
not the *nature* of the housing. It was very interesting to note
how estates tended to polarise as they aged into high and low
offender-rate areas, without other distinctions of social class or
quality of the housing within them being correlated with this. It
is suggested that once an estate or area acquires a reputation for
lawbreaking compared with others (which was found not to be
imaginary, but related to actual offence rates), then 'respectable' or 'responsible' tenants move, and those people indifferent
to the area's reputation stay, or don't mind moving there. It
would seem that individual preference, and bargaining power
or ability to manipulate the housing market, get one in and out
of certain areas. In turn, those who remain in these areas have
their own behaviour affected by them, and conform more to the
delinquent or non-delinquent pattern.

As well as these rather complex correlations between housing
and delinquency, studies show that council accommodation is
far more heavily vandalised than private (Tony Marshall
1976). This relationship is also found for facilities like 'phone
boxes, which are highly vandalised on all types of council
development compared with those in areas of private housing
(R.I. Mawby 1977). The 'poverty' of council tenants is, at least,
not suggested by what they spend on their housing. In 1976,

housing cost the council tenant 5 per cent of his income, compared with a 15 per cent average (after tax relief) for owner-
occupiers.

Thus the social behaviour of people is more vital than bricks
and mortar in making an area desirable or not to live in. As
offences go on rising, much more of our cities may become
undesirable places to live in. Both the initial movement out and
the subsequent greater deterioration of the physical environment are directly related to delinquency *per se*. Delinquency is
an independent cause of the vicious downward spiral which
occurs:

> 'This area has deteriorated fast. People get out if they can
> afford to but I was born here and it's a shame to keep
> uprooting . . . the estate is smashing really, only the kids are
> turning it into a slum with their vandalism and gambling
> and swearing.'
>
> Her friend a few doors down—the door had a splintered
> hole in it said: 'Tottenham has deteriorated by leaps and
> bounds. Let's face it, it's a slum now. Living on these estates
> is murder. No, it's not predominantly coloured kids; Greeks,
> Cypriots, Italians, the white kids are just as bad.'
>
> . . . another house in Tynemouth Road . . . had a *For Sale*
> notice outside. The woman there, an Irish Catholic, said:
> 'I've been here twelve years and I don't want any more of it.
>
> 'Everyone round here is living in terror. I don't go out in
> the road after dark. Two of my sons have been mugged. One
> was beaten up outside the hospital and the other was robbed
> of 25p. He came home covered in blood.
>
> 'But who's going to buy this house? Look at the place next
> door' ('Tensions in Tottenham', *Evening Standard*, 6 July
> 1976)

If the social and economic deprivation theory of the causes of
delinquency were true, how is it that when very many attempts
are made to give urban populations a more congenial environment, this is so often destroyed? It is like a man in a desert
throwing away a drink of water. Thamesmead, for example, has
everything for the community life and leisure of the inhabitants
(including boating lakes, plentiful play-facilities, as well as the
most modern of homes). None the less, the innards still hang

out of the lamp-posts and much the same can be seen in a multitude of other attempted solutions to 'urban deprivation':

The discovery of 'danger' ceilings on the Pepys Estate came about through vandalism.

At the same time there would have been no problems for tenants if the vandals had not gouged holes in the ceilings, releasing the dangerous asbestos dust.

Pepys Estate, opened in 1966 by Earl Mountbatten, was a show-place.

There is a youth club, football pitches, a paddling pool and swings. There is a hall for the Tenants' Association, parks, and organised coach trips and holidays for the children.

There is a purpose-built promenade on the river with a library and theatre. But for the past few years the cost of damage on the estate has run into hundreds every week.

It is a place now where a mother cannot leave her pram unattended without it being stolen; where it is not uncommon for rubbish to be thrown from the windows; where every light on the promenade is regularly broken; where parked cars are scratched and trees ripped up. (*Evening Standard* 20 April 1976)

In their booklet *No Place to Grow Up* Shelter show a picture of a group of thoroughly vandalised and consequently uninhabited flats. These are low-rise and recently built, of a design described as 'luxury' on the private market. Tripping over its own propaganda, Shelter's caption is that 'Slums breed crime', when it perhaps should have read that 'Crime creates slums'.

And down in the slums? Glasgow's post-war council housing schemes, quickly built to replace the nineteenth-century tenements, have a reputation for overcrowding and violence. Yet, as the schemes are being improved, violence and crime go on rising (G. Weightman).

Immediately following the last war, the inhabitants of countries such as Germany and Russia faced quite devastated cities. Here was social and economic deprivation *par excellence*; a life among the rubble. On the hypothesis, they should never have rebuilt; instead, their people, in appalling anguish at their conditions, should have sunk into savagery and endless marauding destruction. In our case, it is not that we have to build all that much. What we want is largely there, but we seem powerless to muster the non-material resources to prevent it being knocked down.

Is delinquency due to high unemployment? This has certainly risen in the 1970s as have offence rates. However, only a short memory could jump to the conclusion that the first must be the cause of the second, since in the 1960s offences were rising in a situation of labour shortage and virtual full employment. Hermann Mannheim (1940) traced the relationships between crime and unemployment in Britain over the best part of a century and found little discernible correlation. Between 1919 and 1920, for example, crime rose when unemployment was static, yet it failed to do so when unemployment jumped in the next year (except, that is, for begging offences). There was even a decline in violent property crimes. By eliminating distortions due to changes in recording procedures, and by breaking down offences into age groups, Mannheim showed a distinct difference in the patterns for different ages, which the overall figures had tended to conceal. For much of the first half of the century, there seemed to be a relation between crime and unemployment for those over twenty-one; but in the younger age groups delinquency appeared unrelated to national unemployment levels. And it was predominantly the young age groups which contributed to the total rise in crime. For adults, analysis of the prison receptions following the First World War showed that the introduction of a token unemployment benefit dampened these considerably. (The prisons were being used as shelter and a means of subsistence by the destitute.) Fifty years later, benefits for the unemployed have increased considerably in proportion to wage levels, and trade unions, worried about the levels of unemployment, have demanded—and largely got—good levels of benefit from the Government as the price of their economic cooperation. Although many commentators try hard to discover that things haven't changed much since the days of the Hunger Marches, because so many efforts have been made to cushion its effects, unemployment—however undesirable—cannot now be equated with the grinding helplessness of the pre-war Dole, not that is without a lot of new evidence from somewhere. The public have, in fact, shown minimal concern, with MPs claiming that—if their post-bags are anything to go by—it is a dead issue. Recently, the Child

Poverty Action Group forwarded to *The Times* details of cases of what it considered to be poor families living in a poverty specifically related to unemployment. A few extracts from the third and concluding review may be of interest:

> The state provides £60.65 a week in unemployment pay, sickness benefit and supplementary benefit, including nearly £5 for a special diet for Mrs Upshaw. They also have £7.50 a week family allowance.
>
> The rent for their four-bedroom council house is £7.10 a week. They spend about £8.50 on coal and electricity, allowing them to keep a good fire burning in the living room . . .
>
> Other regular outgoings are the television rental, telephone bill, and food for a small dog, three chickens and a cockerel.
>
> An overall impression . . . is that where unhappiness exists it lies in illness and worry about jobs and status rather than in financial straits. The children were happy, and that is a heartening finding, especially as their outlook would have been bleak indeed without the welfare state.
>
> . . . they are clearly not a representative sample. Real poverty does exist, such as among those without proper homes . . . among families who may never come to the attention of the voluntary welfare organisations [like CPAG] and among those who are too ashamed of their inability to cope to allow themselves to be interviewed by a newspaper. (*The Times* 24 December 1976)

If there is any relationship between unemployment and law-breaking in modern Britain, it must lie in factors other than the manifest misery that the former causes. Adult recidivists have poorer employment records than adult first offenders, but their income is no lower. The former may be as much a consequence as a cause of lawbreaking (N. Walker). The recent Home Office study of young probationers and their families which I have already mentioned found no connection between juvenile delinquency and the state of the labour market. Few of the boys in the study could trace their difficulties to unemployment in the area, and only in 7 per cent of cases was it considered a severe local difficulty at the time of the study. Of course, many delinquent children and adolescents are not in the labour market at all. But the lack of a statistical relationship between unemployment and juvenile delinquency at any particular point in time does not necessarily mean that the two are not linked, over the life cycle. It is not that the child's delinquencies are then a reaction to adverse conditions which he would not otherwise show; but that his entry into employment in late adolescence and young adult-hood often terminates his delinquent career. However, there is no guarantee that it must, as illustrated by many a report of the occupational status of older juveniles and young adults on violent robbery charges. Another suggestion is that the possibility of unemployment might drive the prospective school-leaver to actually improve his behaviour, since he is more dependent on references and qualifications to secure a job. This is of course assuming that he wants a job at all; crime may pay bigger dividends.

> He (Gary) has had jobs: office cleaner, fixing parts of tele-phones; and working as a carpenter . . . His highest pay of £50 a week, was as a carpenter. 'If I wanted to, I could make more money in an hour going out dipping, and put my feet up for the rest of the week'.
> He (Wilfred) reckoned to make about £200 a week. He thinks it's easy. 'I don't like this organised thing. Pickpocketing is nice because you can exist very easy on that.' (*'God lets me pick-pocket'* Gavin Weightman)

The unemployment argument often swings into one which says that it is the possibility of getting only certain kinds of jobs—the dull, routine, or unskilled—which drives the young to crime.

Only 7.3 per cent of the male working force can now be characterised as unskilled manual, and we know that juvenile delinquents have a far wider occupational distribution; both in family origins and their own destination. However, what is dull or routine is in part subjective, and hardly coincides with occupational and professional distinctions. A large number of humble middle-class occupations (working in a bank; an insurance office; for a local authority; etcetera) are hardly enthralling or even well paid. Being more highly placed as a professional frequently involves a great deal of work which is repetitive and tedious (consider the dentist or GP). Such occupations demand qualifications and training, and a lengthy postponement of more immediate satisfactions. Often boys seeking unskilled work will not face the demand on time and consumption required by training and study (David Downes 1966; Paul Willis 1976), and they are uncomprehending, even contemptuous of those who will (particularly now that differentials have narrowed). If the argument turns on frustrated expectations, then there must be even more frustration among those with qualifications; very many graduates and post-graduates now have to do work which uses only a small portion of their abilities and little of their education.

The complaint that dull and dead-end jobs produce delinquency tends to involve itself in a vicious circle, when it so often goes hand-in-hand with the assertion that the schools, too, are not 'interesting' enough. Yet in an attempt to entice the young to make use of them, children's attention has been permitted to dart after all manner of 'interests', and pursue the attractions of passing stimulation in the belief that this makes for 'relevance'. This sabotages any acquisition of qualifications or even the concentration necessary to complete a task. Add to this the desire not to interfere with the child's 'culture' by fitting him for work in the adult world, and one creates an impasse. (This will be discussed more fully in Chapter 13.)

Indeed, the argument over the connection between dull work and delinquency sometimes appears to be saying that *employment,* rather than unemployment, is the cause. Delinquency is a reaction against the 'slavery' of the factory system, or even the demands of the work ethic. (When some deviancy theory fans have enquired why certain behaviour is characterised as 'deviant' and criminalised, they have explained it in terms of the necessity for the work ethic to suppress the pursuit of satisfying and self-expressive fun.) Yet, again, in modern Britain the hours worked by all groups of employees have decreased as lawbreaking has risen. And it is never clear whether it is being proposed that technology, or simply systematic economic activity is detrimental to human welfare. It is very doubtful that without technology a population as numerous as ours could be kept in the style to which it has become accustomed; and it is quite certain that no human society could survive without routine work. There is so much idealisation of pre-industrial and primitive society, that exactly what it was like to plough a medieval strip, and just how impoverished were the living conditions that went with it are conveniently over-

looked. (To read Marcuse, for example, one might think that
before the capitalist work ethic, a typical peasant's day was
spent listening to the birds and rolling the wenches in the hay!)

It is no exaggeration that members of the public are deeply
puzzled when they hear that delinquents whom they see every
day—are socially and economically *deprived*. The puzzle might
be solved by the answer that, as with the expression 'emotionally deprived', 'socially' or 'economically deprived' is simply a
pseudonym for lawbreaker. There is a tendency, for example,
for *any* housing to be designated as depriving—whether the
tower block, the recent Parker Morris council flat, the pre-war
council house, the Victorian terrace house, new town or old—if
it is inhabited by juvenile delinquents.

And because deprivation itself seems to be defined in such an
abundant *ad hoc* way to suit the circumstances, it is difficult to
avoid the conclusion that what the social and economic argument is about so often is simply scarcity. Given that resources
are by their nature limited, and human wants infinitely extend-
able, deprivation is therefore the normal condition of all human
beings.

There is a certain unacknowledged logic in the madness of
those who appear to be proposing a sort of 'cargo cult' solution
to anti-social behaviour. (Inhabitants of certain Pacific Islands
who have seen the fruits of the white man's technology, but not
the machinery which produces it, believe that if they erect
something resembling his radio masts, good will come in abundance from the sky.) To take a typical instance:

> The main function of the police force is to look after property,
> not people. Its business is to combat that most elementary
> form of wealth redistribution—stealing.
>
> *In a socialist society want, the fundamental cause of crime, will
> disappear.*
>
> People would no longer have to struggle and sweat to get a
> house or to furnish it with decent equipment like studio
> couches, stereo systems and washing machines.
>
> They'd have these things as of right and in abundance. So
> there would be no need to steal.
>
> This would enable us to abolish the police force and to put
> the massive resources presently wasted on maintaining and
> equipping this organisation to some useful purpose.

... socialism would fairly swiftly result in a fairly significant reduction in the murder rate.

All the tensions associated with poverty would disappear.
There'd be no worrying about money, there would be more
human solidarity.

There'd be less overcrowding and therefore less conflict in
people's living units.

The result is obvious—unquestionably fewer murders,
suicides, and person-to-person violence. ('Do we need police?
A new series on the alternative to capitalism. *Socialist Worker*
28 February 1976)

A similar view that any scarcity is abnormal seems to be
implied in the opinion of the National Association of Probation
Officers that people are driven to smash up (in this case), what
they do not or cannot themselves possess:

The public park is vandalised by those without satisfactory private gardens; public telephones by those without a
personal telephone; public transport by those without private transport.

It is as though, in a society where the private acquisition of
goods is worshipped, those most acutely aware of their inability to attain those cherished ideals seek to vent their
anger on the public, common, shared substitutes. (George
Marshall, NAPO discussion paper Nov. 1976)

And, presumably, street lamps are vandalised by those without
electric light bulbs. Besides the fact that the ownership of cars
and 'phones has risen alongside delinquency, it is neither clear
why delinquents should destroy their chances of, at least, a
share in the things which they are held to need so desperately,
nor why commercial pressures, which affect us all, should make
them so disproportionately angry, or angry at all. Even without
modern consumerism it is diffcult to imagine a society beyond
the very small and very simple where people do not differ in
what they possess. To bring about an almost total equalisation
in very complex societies would itself demand social controls on
a massively pervasive and coercive scale, incessantly enforcing
a rigid conformity.

There is a marked lack, one might say an absence, of any
historical perspective here. There have been so many cases

where people have had access to all they desire, but it has not diminished their anti-social proclivities one whit. An interesting case is recorded for AD 1012, when Viking warriors, already loaded with furniture, money, clothing, and other valuables, took the Archbishop of Canterbury for ransom. Afterwards, helped along by the unlimited supplies of food and drink, they decided that they would hardly miss the extra cash, and preferred the amusement of pelting him to death with bones from the feast instead. If delinquency is at all related to the standard of living, why is it not as a potlatch, more than a hunger-cry? The reason it may not be so prevalent in poorer countries might be, partly at least, because they simply can't afford it!

In this context it might be necessary to say a few words about the hypothesis, touched on in a very confused way by that National Association of Probation Officers' discussion paper. This states that a mass consumer society, in promoting acquisitive attitudes, encourages crime by making people want what they would otherwise, and quite happily, have done without, and to want it enough to take it. Certainly the dramatic upturn in crime during the 'sixties coincided with an economic boom, and throughout the non-Communist world offences have had a habit of rising with the trend to prosperity. However, this might provide a superficial explanation for theft, but hardly for the most dramatic rises in violence and vandalism (the latter could indicate, to the contrary, that people have all they desire and goods are so easily obtainable or provided that they can be smashed up). Also, during the period of Victorian prosperity, when mass-produced goods became widely available for the first time, and large numbers of people with rapidly rising expectations were entering the social groups who could afford them—although not as fast as they might have liked—the street crime which had so characterised eighteenth-century cities was on its way out.

Those societies entering modern prosperity often also experience a sudden growth of communications. But, as well as a barrage of advertising for goods, the media have also promoted violence as entertainment. On top of violent entertainments one must also consider the plethora of newsreel which brings *any* war, *any* civil disorder, in any part of the globe, into the sitting-rooms of those not remotely concerned as combatants or contestants. Crime and violence rise after wars anyway, even in civilian populations who have experienced no social dislocation. It has been suggested by investigators Dane Archer and Rosemary Gartner (1977) that the reason lies in the lowering of inhibitions against violence, and the breaking-down of norms among the general population, due to the licence given to soldiers. This effect may be permanently created in societies not engaged in their own warfare, but suffering its after-effects through news reports and documentaries. This possibility deserves consideration, although nations in the Western orbit have also been affected by changes in child-rearing as they have entered Western-style prosperity. It must be remembered that some groups associated with commercial success and living in prosperous communities, Jews for instance, have low delinquency and violence rates.

What must also be considered is evidence which suggests that because the economy has entered a bad period in the last few years where growth in living standards has remained static, or has been reversed, people have lowered their expectations rather than felt more materially deprived. The *New Society* 1977 survey into British attitudes to money and work (reported by Tom Forester), found a quarter of the British population not feeling materially deprived at all, only a third slightly deprived, and the overall majority asking for little more in terms of material satisfaction. It revealed falling expectations, with people feeling that they were not going to get much richer in future and, what is more, not particularly wanting to.

If we want to know why delinquents act as they do, the horse's mouth may seem undeservedly far down the list of information sources. Where they have been asked, delinquents put the pursuit of fun high on their list in a substantial number of cases. Far from being miserable, they are enjoying themselves. Additional reasons for stealing and vandalism are, commonly, that it impresses and satisfies peers, or that the support of peers makes such activity perfectly permissible. Non-instrumental offences decline with age and an appreciation of penalties (as revealed, for example, by B.J. Knight and D.J. West, 1977; W. Belson, 1975; David Downes, 1966). In fact, the overall decrease of lawbreaking with age fits badly with social and economic deprivation models, since these cannot explain why it is just a passing attribute of the young, particularly young males. If it is due to these things, why does it not persist?

> . . . [if] their unseemly behaviour was constrained through compulsion or commitment, then involvement in delinquency would be more permanent and less transient, more pervasive and less intermittent than is apparently the case. Theories of delinquency yield an embarrassment of riches which seemingly go unmatched in the real world. (D. Matza 1964)

More instrumental adult crime is for the rational piece-meal and opportunist self-enrichment *in addition* to legitimate means. The professional criminal is out to rub shoulders with the legitimately rich and famous, not to publicise the evils of society. In contrast to this, it is usual for those whose crimes are in the interests of a cause to seek to proclaim this as loudly and widely as possible. Yet, it appears, our juvenile delinquent is exceptionally shy and inarticulate, leaving it entirely to the expert to tell the world the pressing reasons why he acts as he does. So deep is his deprivation, that he lacks even the key to his own code which others are left to crack.

Where once popular psychoanalysis looked for all manner of emotional traumas in his anti-social behaviour, now a whole intellectual industry specialises in peering into the socio-economic-political crystal ball, at every squirt of the vandal's aerosol. A writer (Stan Cohen 1973) speaks of the killing of swans on ornamental lakes as being due to not having a worthwhile job, or the opportunity for one, and elsewhere, in an essay entitled *In Defence of Hooliganism* (1976), Geoffrey Pearson (Lecturer in Sociology, University of Bradford), has set himself the task of re-casting delinquency as the 'unbearable alienation and social situation of the working class'.

Apparently, black crime with white victims is a 'symbolic representation of a history of oppression which reaches back to the slave ships'. And white crime against blacks? This is no fault of either group's history or attitudes, but instead, the fault of the 'violent and brutalising economic relationships' which are imposed upon them both. Attacks on homosexuals are, in turn, made because their lack of toughness reminds assailants of the middle class (who are, presumably, too formidable to attack openly?) And football violence? Pearson may be more candid than he intends when he claims that an 'awkward fact about hooliganism and rowdyism is that they can sometimes be fun'. However, he asserts that the fun wouldn't be necessary if it wasn't for 'the experience of marginality and worthlessness among young, particularly lower working-class men in an advanced industrial society'. It is a 'release from the drudgery of the working week . . . becoming like a human machine through the repetitious movements of factory labour'.

Forever virtuous and eternally martyred, without blame or blemish, even the warts on the working class are, for Pearson, due to their oppressors' treatment, and can be shaken off and laid at the oppressors' door. That the oppressed should be warped into carrying them is a double indignity. Indeed, if the working class (God forbid) were goose-stepping behind National Front banners, Pearson—if he were still around —could probably cite this as even greater evidence of the depth and barbarity of their oppression. Pearson's theory is compatible with any state of affairs: unfalsifiable and useless.

Many make the mistaken assumption that anyone who denies a connection between social deprivation and law-breaking must somehow be condoning such deprivation. This is not so: social ills are evils in themselves. But these people must in turn ask themselves whether they really think it is right or acceptable that one citizen should harm another, often no better or worse placed than himself, because of his own misfortune. (This is, of course, if they regard the delinquent as a protester acting deliberately, rather than a sick individual.) Consider this example:

> One of the girls told me that she had beaten a teacher unconscious with a chair because the teacher had called her a 'black bastard' and advised her to 'go home'. (*Social Services Paper* 1 February 1975)

The writer does not question the reaction, or, for that matter, the initial connection. There may be other ways to react to name-calling than beating someone unconscious with a chair. Is the teacher in this tale allowed to go one better and bash that girl's brains out? 'Horrible lot', said an official of these girls. This, concludes the writer, 'proves their [the girls'] point about prejudice'—but not the official's—about *their* conduct?

This is extremely important, since the automatic assumption

that insult or deprivation must naturally or justifiably lead to violence must be seen in the light of the fact that ideas about society have a habit of becoming ideas *in* society. Experiments with the frustration-aggression hypothesis reveal that neither verbal nor physical aggressiveness is an inevitable result of frustration. (People can cry with frustration, or flee from it, and so forth.) But on the other hand, the evidence suggests that how people do behave in frustrating circumstances is heavily dependent on the suggestions and examples given by others. If this is true, the utterances both of Enoch Powell and black activists, of the reformer as well as the thug, may well reduce inhibitions about street violence by seeming to give authoritative support to it, or simply by suggesting it as a viable possibility.

If, as a result of the misfortunes of life, we are entitled to take it out on others, where is the mutual carnage supposed to stop? Some of the arguments we have seen here appear to apply the principle of guilt by association to the nth degree. Even the ancient principle of guilt through blood-ties is wildly outstripped when an attack is committed, *because one's great grandfather was a slave* (Pearson), on any member of the white community (whose grandmother may have fared even worse), or simply because the victim otherwise reminds one remotely of something else. Add to this the observation that 'deprivation' is allowed to mean any suffering, disappointment and unhappiness in life. For the individual is *never* the victim, even of the unintended consequences of his own actions, but always a result of society's failure, where society could not hope to save all the people all the time, unless it were omnipotent and omnipresent. (We know, for example from Michael Rutter's and Nicola Madge's analysis of the cycle of deprivation (1976), that over half the people who are 'disadvantaged' at any particular time did not come from disadvantaged backgrounds: illness, death, the vacillations and clashes of personalities, and just plain bad luck, take their toll as we move through life.) In the end, the accusations made against 'society' appear to dissolve into some kind of generalised, inchoate rage:

> The trouble of young people up against the law had to be seen as a red flag indicating the rottenness of society—and the violence of vengeance which discarded youth would

wreak on the community would increase. . . . Young offenders were the rejects of a corrupt society. They come from the
dispossessed bottom rung. (*The Guardian* 17 April 1974, on
the report of the Young Offenders Group of Radical Alternatives to Prison)

Fine words. But who has dispossessed them, and of what? What
precisely has the community done? Whose corruption? What
rottenness? What does an uncorrupt alternative look like? Few
except the doctrinaire Marxist can give much sustained
defence of this position. Yet so many educated people vaguely
accept that violence is inevitable, or excusably directed against
'society'; that when violence erupts the police and authorities
'had it coming to them' in return for some ill-defined evil of
which they have been considered guilty. The increasingly blasé
acceptance of violence in the name of revolt against society is
almost as common as it once was in the name of patriotism.

Needless to say, a carnival riot which involved blacks against
police is pure elixir to this persuasion: it is just what the
prophets ordered. That black pickpockets had converged on
Notting Hill after the easy pickings of the previous year, and
were robbing other blacks, is neither here nor there. Nor is the
amount of thieving which goes on at other black events. The
battles between white youths and police at football matches,
motor-cycle events and so forth, do not give rise to half the
rhetoric, presumably because here the oracles of strife have
been less clear.

Objective reality doesn't count for very much. Does it matter
that it is difficult to demonstrate, with proper comparisons and
evidence, that Britain is a fearful, cruel despotism, which
relentlessly crushes the worker, the black, the dispossessed?
Where is unbiased truth? The answer is given that such
required objectivity is a myth. Doesn't society itself manufacture the rising crime rate in order to have an excuse for its
oppression; and isn't the structure of British society a sham,
and isn't the subtlest sham of all the pretence that it is fair and
democratic, and that it can justify itself by an appeal to 'facts'?
Thus fiction becomes documentary which becomes evidence
for theory:

Among the people who were not surprised by the riots at the
Notting Hill Carnival were the happy few who have seen the

film *Pressure*. Shot over two years ago, *Pressure* is a vivid
portrait of the problems of a young black school-leaver in
Notting Hill. One scene in which a Black Power meeting is
raided by the police is almost prophetic of the bitter atmosphere at the carnival. And yet so far the film has been shown
only to audiences at the London Film Festival.

'We didn't want to make a picture just for social workers
who already know what's going on', says Buckler [producer],
'we wanted to make a picture in which black kids see people
like themselves as heroes.' ('Observations', *New Society*, 9
September 1977)

Logically, this line of argument cuts the ground from under
everybody's feet, since once any pretence of objectivity is
dropped, we have no more reason to believe the alternative
fantasy than the official one. Morally, it has associations with
those despotisms and inquisitions which try to abolish the
distinctions between truth and falsehood, guilt and innocence,
myth and reality, to suit the manipulative purposes of the
rulers.

If we have to talk about society through the veils of class
categorisation, then we could be said to suffer, not from
'middle-class' oppression, but from middle-class sado-
masochism. Vicariously delighting in the thud of boot and
bullet, as excited as children round a bonfire, they are also ever
watchful for the sin of pride; ever wary of success, satisfaction
and self-congratulation. It is as if over forty years or so, the
burden of indefinable guilt, both domestic and foreign (the
latter centring mainly on Empire), and the corresponding
necessity for self-flagellation, is in a geometric progression. The
stance has Evangelistic overtones in the shape of a great, con-
trite mission to the dispossessed (who alone are capable of
wielding the sword of righteousness), and in the purism which
refuses to compromise with the sordid world. While society
contains a single wrong, it stands absolutely condemned. So
long as even one of its members is injured, it is rotten through
and through. If you can't have learning without rules and
impositions, then you don't have it at all. If you can't abolish
force totally from human affairs—then why not a free-for-all?
And what begins as an earnest critique of society has a habit of
ending in the screech of the spoilt child who wants everything

and wants it now. Frustrated in this desire, the answer is to destroy everything, so that someone will be sorry.*

* Writing of punk rock, whose appeal lies in the whipping up of the crudest aggressive arousal in children and adolescents, Peter Marsh enthusiastically tells us that '. . . punks are trying to do something radically different' about the problems of modern society, because they 'attack much more' than other activists. 'They attack everything—even themselves', and he quotes lyrics such as 'Don't know what I want/But I know how to get it/I wanna destroy' (Peter Marsh, 'Dole-queue rock', *New Society*, 20 January 1977)

11 New Jerusalem

The world is awaiting transformation into one where the necessity to 'criminalise' will completely pass away, and present crime, delinquency and violence are, in fact, providing the creative impulse that will bring into being this society, the like of which has not been seen on this globe before. The delinquent is the only one who sees the world aright, and is capable of taking, not merely an active part, but the correct stance towards it. The tables are turned completely on any notion of the offender as sick, nor is he simply the passive creature of much deviance theory, who is acted upon as he drifts into areas defined by others' rules. He is the golden revolutionary. His acts are no longer 'cries for help'; they are acts of 'authentic rebellion'. And so the arguments shift and turn over the public's head.

Confused renderings of this Neo-Marxist view of the offender are to be found in the genre of ultra-left literature, social science publications, and of course, from the lips of community workers, offender pressure groups, the new generation of probation officers and so forth. The central text and the seminal work is probably a book entitled *The New Criminology* (Taylor, Walton and Young 1973). This operates on several levels and its wide impact on students and reformers is easy to understand. In good Marxist fashion, it is both a sociological critique of past and present criminology and a call to action. Anything less than the revolutionary change to a classless society which will no longer 'criminalise people' is taken as an evasion of the real problems of criminology. However sincere, it will degenerate into mere 'correctionalism', which takes the existing framework for granted and is therefore forced to view the criminal deviant as abnormal in some way.

> For us, as for Marx and for the other new criminologists, *deviance* is normal—in the sense that men are now consciously involved (in the prisons that are contemporary human society, and in the real prisons) in asserting their human diversity. . . . The task is to create a society in which the facts of human diversity, whether personal, organic or social, are not subject to the power to criminalise.

The great bulk of *New Criminology* is at the level of academic social theory, and the critical analyses are interesting and forceful in their own right, irrespective of whether one adopts a Marxist theoretical position. There is, for example, sustained criticism of traditional theories which have sought to explain crime either in terms of biological abnormalities, or failures of psychological conditioning. A central theme, developed in the course of this encyclopaedic review, is that genuine criminology cannot be insulated from larger social theory. Explanation of crime is only an instance of the explanation of deviance generally, which belongs to Sociology in the grand manner (in this respect Emile Durkheim is quoted with approval). Of course, this view does not prejudice *which* grand sociological theory is to be adopted. Indeed, some of the recent theorists who are dealt with (notably Dahrendorf and Turk) presumably do accept that the existence of order and deviance in societies, and the forms which they take, have to be explained, but they offer accounts within non-Marxist frameworks.

But, having examined virtually all other available theories, and found them wanting, the authors insist that the only successful theory would be built on the assumptions that criminality results *solely* from society's power to criminalise which, in turn (going further than many deviance theorists), *arises from inequalities of wealth and power*. Crime, it is explicitly asserted, would be irrelevant in a society after a revolution which would 'precipitate moral and social consensus'. In such arrangements—briefly, the classless society preached by Karl Marx—authority would be merely an 'administrative instrument' in the interests of men as a whole, and would therefore be 'divorced from the domination of men by men'. Alternative theories are condemned, not for failing always to do justice to the facts, but for failing to 'confront the possibility' of a society which does not criminalise. Their fatal blemish is that they implicitly acknowledge that law, authority, and hence criminal acts of some kind, will always be with us. But, equally, the New Criminologists could stand condemned for quite failing to define or elaborate their exciting concepts. In an otherwise critical argument these concepts stand out conspicuously as naive, bald challenges, or mere slogans. With their *Critical Criminology* (1975), which followed *New Criminology*, and promised to tie up deviance theory with ideas about class and wealth, we still have little but Neo-Marxist doctrine bridging the gap between the existence of deviance and the system which is supposed to manufacture it. (It is not necessarily the Utopianism which is at fault specifically with Neo-Marxists, as this is shared by all the reforming Left's beliefs about crime and violence.)

What is interesting is how the *traditional* Marxist views of crime are criticised here. Marx himself saw the criminal classes as the *lumpenproletariat,* products of brutalising capitalism, merely parasitical on the organised working class, and without a historical mission. They might be used occasionally by the exploiters (Church and King mobs, strike breakers etcetera) but essentially they were unproductive flotsam which would disappear when the real proletariat captured the means of production.

However, in common with most neo-Marxists, these authors stress the libertarian, against the 'deterministic' aspects of Marx, and insist that deviant and criminal behaviour is meaningful rebellion, involving conscious choices by the deviant and by the agencies of social control who classify his act as 'criminal', and to which he in turn reacts. His own beliefs and actions—however inarticulate—are to be seen as essentially *rational* responses to the realities of inequality and domination, from his particular position in the system. They stem from such facts as the thwarting of opportunities, the frustration of instilled expectations, low status labelling, and other forms of alienation in a class society. The deviant may not, of course, understand the social forces against him, and his action may be quite ineffective as a response to them. But none the less criminal action—from vandalism and property crime to rape—is to be explained as making sense only within an overall *political* framework; as reaction within an antagonistic social structure, and as an attempt to resolve those antagonisms. In this sense, crime is always to be subsumed under the general phenomenon of humans struggling for liberation within a coercive social order. And *any* social order built around inequality will be coercive, since there will not be complete voluntary acceptance of its norms, and hence compliance will always have to be enforced, to a certain extent, through the physical and psychological processes of 'criminalisation'.

It is important to see just how radical and idealistic this view is, even compared with conventional kinds of Marxist outlook. Taylor, Walton and Young are emphatically not arguing that criminal behaviour is an anti-social product of brutalising conditions, or manifest poverty, or the acquisitive competition ethos brought about by capitalism. Indeed, they take to task the traditional Marxist criminologist William Bonger, who related crime to the injustices of capitalism in this way. Bonger did not believe all egoistic, anti-social dispositions could be made to disappear, but he did believe they could be minimised by removing the incentives which exist under capitalism, by social education, and by legal sanctions which reflect an equitable moral and social order instead of an oppressive and corrupt one. He is accordingly derided for his belief that criminal Man, even under socialism, will still be in need of *some* social controls. On the contrary, it is proclaimed, there are no intrinsic anti-social dispositions: criminal action is simply one response by alienated Man attempting to resolve class antagonisms. To suppose, like Bonger, that it might still persist in a truly classless society is to betray an un-Marxist fear of the unruly, and a belief in 'order for its own sake'. A Socialism which requires law-enforcing agencies *at all*, however superior its social institutions, will still be a divided, coercive society in which man dominates man. (Among other things, poor old Bonger is criticised as 'idealist'!)

Where these authors enter into the mundane empirical world of actual physical offences in our society, their position is preserved by a crude unfalsifiability—again, exactly parallel with that found for psychoanalysis. If an action occurs as predicted by the theory of rebellion against coercive capitalism, it corroborates the theory, but if it does not—it still corroborates! Appeal is made to the Marxist analogue of the unconscious mind—where any evidence can be magically transformed into what the theorist wants it to be—the concept of

'False Consciousness'. For example, they use this device to dismiss the arguments of the criminologist Matza. He said that it is hardly possible to believe that delinquents hold values that are an inversion of the values of respectable society, since they do not actually view their behaviour as morally correct. If they ever go beyond the self-explanatory admission that it was 'for a laugh' for example (*and* they know of a forbidding norm), they are likely to give *ad hoc* 'neutralisations' (that is, excuses) for why the moral rule did not apply—'insurance pays'; 'they can afford it'; 'nobody suffers'; 'they asked for it', and so on. For this, Matza is accused by the New Criminologists of denying 'any possibility of self-conscious and oppositional meaning from deviant action'. But where is the self-conscious oppositional *statement* from the delinquent to be found, as it clearly is in the overt rebel such as the IRA man?

Researchers have always been at a loss to find any set of *alternative values* among delinquents to those of the wider society, as much as they have been at a loss to find that they are protestors against injustice. David Downes in the 'sixties found his delinquents as loyal to the monarchy and the government as anyone else: hatred of coppers '. . . was not a manifestation of "withdrawal of attributions of legitimacy from conventional norms", but rather a particularistic aversion to the kind of control enforced by the police.' In other words, they disliked the police simply because they got in the way of their gratifications—as much as they might also resent their mothers for doing the same—and not because they represented some hated authority or symbolised oppression. And Downes' boys were drawn from the least qualified, lowest-status minority in the working class. Their attitude to both middle and skilled-working-class work life was not at all consistent, where admiration as much as resentment might be expressed towards those who had done 'better' than they, when, indeed, they identified with them at all.

It appears that the whole thing is so 'self' conscious that—according to the New Criminologists—the delinquent himself is not aware of it! Apparently, 'it is possible that the vocabulary of motives utilised by the actor may represent a false account of the realities of his predicament'. Only the New Criminologists are qualified to tell the delinquent what he really thinks. And what he thinks is an implicit critique of the system, whether he knows it or not, however incoherent he may be. Indeed, his very incoherence is evidence of a hidden sense which needs interpretation. What justifies this conclusion? Nothing, except that 'even in the most extreme cases of verbal disorder where linguistic utterances are hardly possible by the deviant (for example, schizophrenia), it has been strongly argued by Laing and others that non-communication itself[sic] can be understood as political attack upon the double-bind concentration camp of the nuclear family.' There is the minor consideration that Laing's ideas on the causation of psychosis are totally bereft of any evidence, and he has never seen fit to attempt to offer any. But this does not bother those writers, who in effect support their method of fantasy by appealing to even bolder and wilder fantasies.

A further level of absurdity is reached in their claim that the reason why the utterances and acts of delinquents do not seem to bear out their Marxist analysis, is that the capitalist system is *even keeping from delinquents* the realisation that their actions are authentic rebellion against the oppression of the ruling classes. 'Most of the cultural options available to those who are oppressed in a divided class society serve to minimise the possibility of their choosing an alternative system of culture.'

The *coup de grâce* for Matza is given by the statement that

> Matza's delinquent, moreover, is largely concerned to negate his society in a neutral fashion: a peculiar observation to make about delinquency in societies where the mass of delinquents are literally involved in the practice of redistributing private property. (Taylor, Walton and Young 1973)

The rationale of redistribution is presumably why vandals are more likely to destroy the immediate environment of neighbours in the same boat as they are: presumably why (outside commercial areas) offence and offender rates are highly correlated in residential areas (see J. Baldwin and A.E. Bottoms 1976; A.E. Bottoms 1976); and it is presumably why the statistics for the Metropolitan area in 1975 record that 6,000 of the 7,959 robberies were against individual people, with 70 per cent for amounts under £25 (well under a week's wages for virtually *any* job in this society). This property is being 'distributed' away from women and old people, among the lowest wage-earners and the poorest in our society. (One notices in the

New Criminology that misogyny common in the far left—
women are doing well out of the 'system', while young males
suffer its constraints. The similarity is with the far right
stances—that women are a corrupting or softening influence on
the noble expression of masculinity). Iron bars, pickaxes and
chair-legs have been used against the elderly, often by smartly
dressed boys, to 'redistribute' a few shillings. Of the burglaries
in that same year, 57 per cent were in residential houses and
flats; with 18,000 involving goods worth less than £5, and
61,000 involving goods worth less than £100. Screwing the rich?
Or banditry against the weak and vulnerable?

Not surprisingly, these neo-Marxists hold no brief for existing Communist societies. Unlike their predecessors, they are
not one whit embarrassed by the empirical realities of the
actual historical societies—from China to Yugoslavia—which
have consciously attempted to reconstruct themselves along
lines inspired by Marx and Lenin. All these societies have, of
course, recreated and greatly strengthened a state and police
structure. Many of them have also abolished a great deal of
poverty and inequality, and have sometimes succeeded—at
least at the beginning—in replacing a corrupt and acquisitive
set of social relations with an undeniably fairer one; this has
encouraged and rewarded work, community and cooperation.
Where this has been achieved, it has, of course, depended
heavily on new and vigorous social controls, formal or informal,
to secure compliance with the new norms which the leaders and
the party are determined will be taken seriously; the lazy, the
thieving, the aggressive, are indeed labelled, stigmatised and
criminalised; a very definite idea of 'deviance' is deliberately
established. Indeed, from Vietnam to Cuba, the existence of
crime is regarded as a residue of the decadence and moral
squalor of capitalism, which permits such squandering of vital
resources. This is of course in total opposition to the view
expounded by the New Criminologists, that the Krays and the
foul-mouthed vandal up the street are somehow brothers in
arms in the vanguard of the revolution. In actual Marxist-
inspired revolutions, one of the first tasks has been to sweep
such riffraff away.

However, none of these facts cause any hesitation to the
neo-Marxist theorist of deviance, who claims to be interested
primarily in *advanced* capitalist society, and even then at a level

of theoretical models which revolve round the *possibility* of abolishing all coercive power of men over men. Curiously, these sociologists—who are all theory—bear striking kinship, not to early Marxists who felt some obligation to defend Soviet or Chinese society, but to the simple, moral Socialists, innocent of theory, whose 'pure' Socialism is not the least disturbed for not being manifest anywhere on earth.

Since they expound their own positive ideas so provisionally and laconically, we may well be sceptical of what appears to be, for the most part, acts of faith. How, for example, is that eventual, classless 'genuine consensus', in which there is no need to criminalise actions, going to accommodate all that assertion of 'human diversity'? If men are indeed free actors and not simply the passive putty of good or bad economic environments, how is this moral and social consensus even to define itself, unless it deliberately attaches sanctions to its norms? Such sanctions might perhaps be symbolic rather than physically punitive—group ostracism, shaming etcetera and whether they are called 'criminal sanctions' is perhaps arguable, but their very essence would be to uphold norms by labelling and discriminating against the actor who violates them: that is, by defining an area of deviance however large or small, and thereby creating the people who occupy it. How could authority even be efficacious as an 'administrative instrument in the interests of men as a whole' if it were wholly divorced from any exercise of power?

Perhaps we are not supposed to ask these crude questions. Perhaps all such implicit conflicts in the future classless society are just part of the eternal Dialectics of Liberation. Or perhaps only limited sense can be given to arguments about the structure and problems of a radically different society which does not exist. At all events, what is so strenuously insisted on is that social theory continually confront the radical *possibility* of a society without criminalisation and without controls. And in a sense, this exhortation can never finally be invalidated. Whatever the fortunes of actual societies in the next century, or ten centuries, one could still, presumably, confront the 'possibility'.

But what, finally, do these New Criminologists prescribe in the face of actual crime in this society—assuming that they acknowledge its existence under some description? Certainly, as theoretical sociologists they may quite reasonably say that the practical problems of social administration are not their concern: their concern is to explain why crime, deviance and control take the different forms they do in different imperfect and inequitable societies. But in fact, they repudiate such value-neutral status, and insist boldly that their theory is normative. And so, on their own admission, this is a perfectly legitimate question to ask.

The answer is a sobering one. The upshot of their expert advice—and presumably this extends beyond academic criminologists to the present generation of sociologically trained administrators, community workers, teachers and probation officers (and also, one assumes, to the wave of far left, sociologically minded councillors increasingly being returned under a Labour ticket in urban areas)—is to break completely with the system, politicise the whole issue of crime, and work for the revolution.

However, since Marxism is both a creed and a theory deeply involved with violence, it might be logical in one sense to link the delinquent and criminal whose ways are already violent, with the furtherance of this. Marxism considers ethics and law simply as a reflection of the apparatus of domination of one class over another. Class power is the only reality, and anything which furthers the historic mission of the 'workers' against the rest is justified. In turn, where Marxism has helped to make 'middle class' an expression of contempt this is used to denigrate and dismiss the rule of law, while force becomes sanctified and acceptable by being held aloft as an attribute of the semi-sacred 'working class'. Social change is, in this theory, furthered, not by any democratic process, only by violent upheaval. In this country the progress of Marxism has been marked by a trail of violent incidents—stormtrooper politics—whether we look at the events at North London Polytechnic (C. Cox, K. Jacka and J. Marks 1975), the beating up of University guest speakers, the charge on the police in Red Lion Square when Kevin Gately died, the smashing up of a church to prevent a radio broadcast, and the now numerous incidences of concerted mob violence against the police. The actions of camp followers aroused to rioting and looting are, in turn, taken as exhilarating confirmation of Marx's prediction about the social holocaust to come. To many it might have an attraction for the mundane reason that delinquency and violence appeal to the hooligan—it is a quick means to get your way—moreover, like the football hooligan, you have group support and a justification which might allay any residual liberal qualms. However, as modern Communist states and parties near power demonstrate, not even they can tolerate street violence for long. This is incompatible with any stable society. What human social systems are fundamentally about is order. Whatever form this takes, human social life is impossible without elementary predictability and reciprocity.

When you have freed yourself from the last bourgeois fetishes, such as respect for the rule of law, and control of force by legitimate authority, revolutionary Marxism is not the only tradition from which these things can be attacked. Thomas Mann described Nazism as 'vulgar barbarism', and Fascist squads are certainly a more obvious choice for lawbreakers. Once the gloves are off it has usually been the Marxists who have found themselves up against a wall.

But then, such timid, layman's considerations should not ruffle neo-Marxist theorists: what is important is less the real, historical world, than the 'permanent possibility' of a state of affairs where there is no need to enforce norms.

In effect—pie in the sky. The vision is apocalyptic—a future state of being, where the conditions and constraints which we have hitherto always had to contend with, have evaporated or metamorphosed; a world where the lion lies down with the lamb, and has presumably turned vegetarian. Since, for obvious reasons, it is difficult to give maps of the Kingdom after the Last Judgement (as well as it being indicative of bad faith to ask), it is no wonder that some neo-Marxists are apt to take refuge in that fervour which claims that 'the revolution will make its own solution'.

Historically, millennial movements have a habit of ending in gory, sordid and sorry mundaneness. Norman Cohn documents, in his *Pursuit of the Millennium*, how, on the promise of visionaries that they would find the New Jerusalem—a paradise where all mortal constraints and the contemporary social and economic order would be negated—hordes of medieval men left their homes and headed for plague, starvation, slaughter, cannibalism and slavery. Are we, accordingly, to regard a masochistic enthusiasm in the rising rates of crime and violence as a token of the higher freedom to come? God appeared to have asked less of Job, and shown a better hand, than the dialectic asks of, and gives us.

The working class in Britain, however one wishes to characterise it, gives abundant evidence of preferring the devil it knows to the one it doesn't. Union cooperation with government and industry in the face of the economic crisis of the mid-'seventies has been almost exemplary, and there is little sign of a widespread desire for massive upheavals, or an end to this society as we know it—rather the contrary. Those who do want to be rid of it are quite unrepresentative, but unfortunately they cannot be ignored just by being placed on a par with Jehovah's Witnesses, where they really belong.

The influence of such opinions is grossly out of proportion to the attractions of explicit Marxist parties as demonstrated by the ballot box. This itself accounts largely for the fact that just as Marcuse had to look to students, coloured minorities and the unemployed as the last reservoir of revolutionary energy, so the British neo-Marxist seems driven to look to the criminal and the undersocialised to deliver the revolution which the organised working-class has failed to deliver. The actual power bases of Neo-Marxism are in the control of so many social science departments at Universities, further education colleges and other institutions of higher education, as well as educational media and literature. Some institutions, like the Centre for Cultural Studies at the University of Birmingham, seem to be in the nature of latter-day diviners, interpreting every fad and fashion of youth—legal or otherwise—in terms of the inter-generational response to the class struggle, with texts like *Rituals of Resistance*. In turn these academic institutions now have more control of the training of people like social workers and probation officers (The National Association of Probation Officers' Conference is now Marxist dominated). Within academic institutions domination is frequently acquired and maintained, as I and many others have seen, by the gross bullying and shaming of students into acquiescence.

In the way in which its orientations have percolated through the discussion of social problems and the framing of social issues, it has fuelled—in no small way—that incoherent revulsion with society and the urge to tear it down, described in the last chapter. It has made the term 'middle class' one of abuse, yet we owe much of what we enjoy in the way of civil liberties and social welfare to the 'middle class'. The overwhelming majority of whom the word is used have no more share in the ownership of wealth in the nation (barring the roofs over their heads), than the 'workers' who have assumed that sacred status. Furthermore, despite Marx's ideas on social 'polarisation'—supposedly marked by a dramatic increase in the numbers and wretchedness of the 'working class'—it is the 'middle-classes' who have grown to constitute at the present time nearly half the working population. Presumably all of these are to be eliminated in one or more senses of that word. Ironically, it is the 'workers' who are often puzzled, dispirited, and not a little dismayed by the constant denigration of British society from an *intellectual* 'middle class', so apparent in media and policy-making.

In community work, the emphasis on the powerless who must be championed and identified with in order to solve their problems, has neo-Marxists blurring this laudable intention with the need for the 'client' to fulfil an historical mission already cast for him. It becomes increasingly common to find that what the 'community' want or says is what the community social workers want and say, and it often reads uncannily like a far-left text. Even if the voice is in the name of a specific minority, it may be quite misleading to build a picture of any social situations on their claims. For all the complaints of neo-Marxists about a massive reactionary conspiracy on the part of the establishment, we seem to be faced frequently in education and social services with the strange phenomenon of revolution on the rates.

Part Four

The Lessons of Life

12 Parents and the Leisure Child

I have considered many of the explanations which have been given for the considerable rise in lawbreaking, particularly among the young, over the last couple of decades, and the success or otherwise of policies built upon these explanations. As we have seen, the theories themselves have shown a development which, although beginning with the good intention of alleviating the problem of lawbreaking—even solving it completely—has taken a course where this end has not only been dropped, but in some cases has given way to an active sponsorship of the delinquent and the violent themselves.

In this section I am going back to the premiss that the growth in delinquency and violence is inherently undesirable, and I am going to look more closely at those aspects of the environment of youth which may encourage and permit, or discourage and check this behaviour. In looking at the factors which surround the child in the family, the school and the community, I shall cover more fully other explanations for the rise in delinquency than those criticised in the previous sections. From this, I hope finally to outline some of the reasons for the modern boom in violence and delinquency, and some steps that might be taken to reverse this tendency.

In modern society, the effect of the sum total of attitudes to childrearing and the child's 'nature' has been to remove adult involvement from children in those two areas primarily responsible for upbringing and education: the family and the school. I believe that this has been the logical outcome of the theory and practice of the past couple of decades.

It is a commonplace observation that since man comes into the world with no inbuilt instinctual means for living, he has to acquire this from those who already possess it; he is entirely dependent on cultural transmission. Yet the new knowledge in child psychology appears to have cast culture as man's enemy, rather than his only lifeline. The adult is envisaged simply as the grown up result of his own pre-cultural childhood, which was nurtured or thwarted during a period of essentially self-regulated growth, where the child 'knows' what he wants in a quasi-instinctual way. The attempt to shape the child in accordance with adult expectations interferes, imposes its own form, and thus almost declares war upon the child's 'needs'. Yet culturally, if the traffic is from those who do know to those who don't, there is no getting away from the fact that this has to be an adult-centred and controlled business. Yet adult-centred child-rearing environments, characteristic of the past, tradi- tional societies, and also of present Communist societies, have been constantly represented as asking a 'price' of the child in mental suffering and distortion.

Teaching is the pivotal function in cultural transmission, via the medium of language. If we insist on starting from scratch and discovering the world anew each generation (like monkeys), it is clear that this central function of teaching is largely redun- dant. The Plowden report, which has changed the face of primary education, insists that 'The curriculum is to be thought of in terms of activity and experience rather than knowledge to be gained and facts to be stored.' Somehow, miraculously, these raw experiences all add up to a viable picture of the world without any need of correction or interpre- tation. 'Any practice which predetermines the pattern and imposes it on all is to be discouraged.' So fluid, structureless educational environments have been in vogue, even down to the wall-less classroom and the lineless paper; and 'finding out' replaces the rapid communication and dissemination of infor- mation and skills by instruction. The key has been *stimulation*, to nourish the mind with novel experiences and enable it to create its own individual thing.

On the other hand, an upbringing concerned with the transmission of cultural understanding and skills is out to *restrict* stimulation rather than multiply it. The educator does not seek to develop all the random moves his pupil makes, all those flickerings of attention from stimulus to stimulus: he is only liable to pick out a tiny number of moves which might have meaning for him, name them, encourage or discourage them.

Meaning and communication can be established only by some items being deliberately selected as stable tokens, and others, which surround them, being suppressed. If every item in every experience was equally 'meaningful', nothing could occupy the invariant role which carries the same meaning from one situation to a different one: there could be no formation of stable concepts. Also, while the child is learning, he might be able to envisage the goal at the end of the journey, but he is unfamiliar with the path to it. Therefore he is open to distractions and false leads all along the route. The adult therefore has to filter stimuli and prevent the child from chasing after them, in order to enable his attention and grasp of skills to have a chance to extend and establish themselves (see Jerome Bruner's comments on the educational process 'The Styles of Teaching' *New Society* 1976).

Of course, children, like all mammals, are drawn to those objects and events which provide perceptually 'interesting spectacles'. This observation that the infant is pleasurably aroused or alerted by novel stimuli has led to claims that this *search for excitement* is what has previously been seen as the innate need for love or mothering (see A.R. Schaffer 1971). The mother is feeding-in stimulation and protecting from it, since at a certain point it ceases to be exciting and becomes confusing and anxiety-making. Sensorily overwhelmed, the organism withdraws to lower its arousal and assimilate the 'newness' at a slower rate. So, we are told, the adult modulates the child's arousal, increasing and warding off stimulation 'on demand', beginning with bouncing the baby up and down to heighten his arousal and hugging him when he gets upset. *The adult role, in this story, is not to educate, but to excite and protect.*

However, raising and lowering arousal, thrills and comfort, is hardly a way in which a child could acquire any inkling of social situations (except to the extent that the adult might communicate to the child what he thinks his attention is caught by and what he thinks will next please). But, as there is no doubt that as children are excited by all manner of things, adults do often take this to be the spontaneous 'need' that they must satisfy; gratifying, but not interfering in the amoral vagaries of the child's attention.

In contrast with the role of exciter, protector and source of emotional satisfaction, an adult-centred, cultural view of human development gives the adult the function of involving the child in some goal or task. When Jerome Bruner (1975) speaks of culture being 'symbolism in action', he points out that the emergence of language, both in our species and in each child's development, is almost inseparable from the organisation, pursuit and proliferation of tasks. Human evolutionary survival and success have been dependent on joint action, on cooperation to attain goals, and obviously the development of symbols to pass on information, coordinate activity and plan ahead brings an enormous bonus to the group. That there are other, perhaps more important, reasons to come together, than simply a search for sensation or emotion has gone unnoticed. In any society, at any stage of development, what people are 'doing together' (or proposing to do together), is not exclusively, or even usually, expressing love or seeking high sensory arousal—nor is it necessarily what keeps people together, or interested in each other. Observation of adults with children suggests that the use and development of language are particularly involved with the direction of the child in a goal-orientated pursuit, a shared task; he learns the rules of this inseparably with the rules of language—even if it be simply a game. (Games, with their constitutive rules, are to be distinguished from free-play.)

It should be apparent that, where the environment is adult-centred, for all that it has been condemned as bad for children, the adult as an active, deliberate educator must be lengthily and closely involved with the child. The relationship is hierarchical, because the adult must assume leadership (and, in the beginning, 'speak for the child'). In many societies, of course, this has meant that children are physically brought into the range of the day-to-day activities of their community as soon as they are able to master them.

The child-centred environment, paradoxically, while ostensibly making the child the focus and pivot of attention, has largely rendered the adult, not merely passive, but actually superfluous. This can be illustrated by the studied withdrawal one encounters so much in modern parental behaviour, particularly in the vanguard of the new child-rearing expertise. Determined to follow the best advice and make no mistakes, the educated parent frequently worries and cares desperately—in a way which his father and grandfather never did. He believes that children must be self-motivated in anything they do, and reach it self-sustained. *The children* are the initiators, maintainers and terminators of their own activity: they cannot go to bed because they haven't 'chosen' to go yet—however young they may be. They may choose midnight, when they stop prodding, poking and throwing, and collapse onto the floor. If they want the television on full volume, how can they be stopped? The parent avoids all the 'dos', 'don'ts', 'nos', 'wrongs', even definite answers and instructions, for his biggest headache is the assault on their security and expression, the cramping of their confidence by rules and restrictions. Where the children might harm themselves or others, he distracts their attention—from the power socket, the vase, from masturbating in front of guests—and hopes they never know that what they have just avoided is dangerous or forbidden. Sometimes he is exasperated as the child pummels into visitors or tips up the table—he shouts, and is soon overcome by guilt at what he nearly did. He tries urgently to compensate. He is pleased that his child's very dependent days are nearly over. At about five the child doesn't have to be at home with adults to amuse him: he can be out with other children. According to the theory, the adult has little left to do once the crucial first five years of emotional life are gone. This is in sharpest possible contrast with the fifteen, twenty, and five-and-twenty-year preparation for life in earlier and other cultures.

However, concern over the child's academic attainments often sets in with our well-read parent as his offspring gets older and accordingly the child is taken up with more academic pursuits. Large sections of the professional and white-collar classes have reservations about the new expertise, or have accepted only a modified form in which the child is still heavily obliged to acquire intellectual skills. It is perhaps the working class who have taken it really literally, even if they may be accused of failing to grasp its subtleties. From being regarded as more authoritarian with their children, in the space of a remarkably short time 'working-class' parents are now found to be the most permissive in many respects and the most child-centred of all (J. and E. Newson 1968). Well-intentioned passivity is widely manifest in the absence of any attempts to control what a child does, and frequently there is even a conviction that the parent is in fact powerless to do anything. 'How

can I stop her?' asks the mother of a three-year-old who insists
on going into the street: 'He's out, playing on the railway', says
the mother of a six-year-old—she is happy, since the child is;
it's what he wants to do.

Above all, what the ordinary parent feels he has been told
is—*stop interfering*. Hardly anyone could be unaware of all those
things it is so easy to do wrong. There is a parent behind every
case of murder, suicide, psychosis, depression, unhappiness,
and it is always a meddlesome parent who did not give enough.
With all the damage that rejection, denial or deprivation may
do, a thousand perils lie in anything that might be interpreted
as a lack of love, or in an upset or a confrontation. Clearly, when
it comes to weighing up the interests of others against the
interests of one's child, then it is not difficult to see that the first
fence to fall to parental paralysis is the serious teaching of social
norms. It is true that recently child-care advice has spoken
guardedly of limits on child behaviour, but it tends to leave its
realisation to the nebulous hopes of 'right' love alone; vague
and impossible contradictory prescriptions are given for discipline without thwarting and imposition, disincentives without
disappointment, and conformity without guilt, loss of face or
privilege. For example,

> if the child complies willingly, of course (even if his willing-
> ness has been engineered by offering him the illusion of
> choice), his self-esteem can be kept intact; but whenever he is
> forced into an unwilling compliance by the threat of sanc-
> tions, whether these be pain inflicted or approval with-
> drawn, he will inevitably suffer in some degree feelings of
> powerlessness and humiliation. (J. and E. Newson, *Seven
> Years Old in the Home Environment*, 1976)

All of it tries desperately to square the normative circle, and it is
all very puzzling and bamboozling. It is no small wonder that
the response of many a parent is to leave well alone. The choice
is the child's: the kid knows best. To this one must add the
media's continual emphasis on 'youth culture': the young know
it all, they have the bright ideas and set the trends that their
elders would be wise to emulate. In business and public service
too, employers who buy youth believe that they buy 'fresh'
ideas, new creations, because they are carried by new people;
ideas that owe nothing to the dead hand of the past.

If love is the first need at home, when the child moves out into the world, the community's duty is mainly represented as the provision of play. Children are, indeed, held to become juvenile delinquents if they have nowhere to play. Even bishops launch campaigns for play with threats of a holocaust of violence, vandalism and crime if we don't provide enough of it.

At the top of the road where I used to live, the council bulldozers wiped a couple of streets of terraces off the map. There was nothing wrong with the houses; they were well-maintained and constituted a reasonably contented, quiet neighbourhood, and the residents resented the enforced move. The land was needed to build a little annexe to the primary school on the corner, which itself would have required only the demolition of one or two houses. Ah, but you see, said the council, the children of the area have nowhere to play. This is a matter of urgency, with the Borough's escalating crime and vandalism; can't the selfish residents understand that every penny spent on play is more than recouped in savings on destruction? So they pushed ahead with this scheme and others. The pattern has been similar across the country. Play is particularly a priority on new housing developments. Play is the councillors' answer to delinquency. But near the new playground which has emerged on the demolished streets, the vandalism relentlessly goes on increasing.

Why play? When children are seen, no longer as immature adults or small, untutored human beings, but special creatures with their own needs, then they require a specially-designed world better suited to their precise requirements. In this stimulating world they can work out their own destiny untrammelled by adult order and demands. Other societies didn't have our knowledge, and involved their children in practical work, but now we know that 'Play is children's work'.

Of course, children have always played, play is enjoyable and there is no reason why life shouldn't be enjoyable in the here and now. However, the new attitude is that Play is *the* serious business of life for children. It is not something for when you have finished your tasks and are not interfering with anybody else. The tenant who complains about the children's noise and behaviour when they play gets short shrift these days: their development is at stake, not his headache. The campaign for Fair Play for Children claims, predictably, that children will 'get back at society' if it denies their (natural?) 'rights' to play-space, much as an oppressed group will do if its civil rights are denied.

As mentioned elsewhere (Jack Tizard, Jane Perry and Peter Moss 1976), Play as Work has two sources. One is the Rousseauesque tradition emanating from Froebel in 1826 of the 'good gardener' approach to education, where the child provided with the right soil constructs his world and discovers the skills he needs, at his own pace, via play. In the education colleges a garbled version of Piaget's theory of sequences of sensori-motor and cognitive development seemed to reinforce these ideas of an internally unfolding, biological growth of human intellect. As Plowden (1967) says,

> At the heart of the educational process lies the child. . . . Adults who criticise teachers for allowing children to play are unaware that play is the principal means of learning. . . . The child is the agent in his own learning . . .

and in Marianne Parry and Hilda Archer's 1974 Report of their survey of 'good practice' in pre-school education:

> through play the child finds opportunities to explore materials, to create, to destroy and discover. . . . The child learns how to mix with other children by sharing experiences with them, discovering how friendships occur, witnessing how other children behave, particularly when their wishes are opposed to his.

However, in educational literature one can read indefinitely about how vital play is, but fail to find any concrete evidence to substantiate it. Claims that play 'furthers development' or 'maturation' have never been put to any assessment, and indeed, they are so vague that it is difficult to see how they ever could be.

The second source, acknowledged or not, lies in the psychoanalysis of Melanie Klein (1932) and the Tavistock Clinic. Here, play is therapeutic. It is the way the hidden, unconscious mind acts out its fears and fantasies (in disguise). The struggles in the infant mind project themselves through play, the Oedipal lusts, the conflict of the Good and Bad mothers, and so forth. All objects are utilised for their symbolism: they might represent father, mother, faeces, penis, intercourse, separation anxiety and virtually anything else. On this model it would be dangerous to make children do things adults wanted, since it would restrict the internal mechanism's freedom to work out its destiny in free-play. However, we only have the believer's word.

So is 'play as work' just an empty cliché, with a few dubious speculations about human development trailing along behind? There is certainly no evidence that children in societies where they work alongside adults—and this has been in most societies—suffer mentally from this; nor do they seem to suffer from having to play within the tolerance and surveillance of adults. Nor do these societies appear to suffer the aggression of children deprived of play. One society, exhaustively described by Margaret Mead many years ago, appears to have a child-rearing pattern unusual for a primitive people, a pattern which greatly resembled the emerging one in America at the time the book was written, and the one which we have in Britain now. In Manus, children can play all the time:

> Here in Manus are a group of children, some forty in all with nothing to do but have a good time all day long. The physical surroundings are ideal, a safe shallow lagoon. . . . They are free to play in every house in the village, indeed the reception section of the house is often hung with children's swings. They have plenty of materials at hand . . . (Margaret Mead 1930, *Growing Up in New Guinea*)

And where 'the only convention of the child's world is a play convention', to expect a child to undertake a small task is felt to be 'a terrible intrusion upon the child's leisure which must be avoided at all cost'. Adults comply with the child's demands as and when they are made, for 'The whole adult scheme is phased in terms of children's claims upon it'. The children bitterly resent growing up and have an 'habitual contempt for adult life' and wish to know nothing of it. Another result is that the child's play itself is 'the most matter-of-fact, rough and tumble, non-imaginative activity imaginable'; they have no dances, no games, no puzzles, no legends, no folklore, no clubs or societies, no use for art, and their language is limited and deplete of imagery. The adults are only intent on instilling in the child at an early stage the property rules which keep the society together. Otherwise adult interaction is hostile and impoverished;

the only value of anybody is in their monetary worth, which is not surprising since this is all that the child is taught.

Of course, the very mention of 'child labour' triggers such reflexes of indignation that it is difficult to remind ourselves that work done by children does not necessarily correspond to sending little boys down mines or up chimneys. There is in fact a strong tendency to regard *any* child work as a sign of low status, of poverty and backwardness, both in the family and the nation—even if it is making a bed, washing up or minding a baby. For children to do a paper round, help the milkman or help in the house (for all that they seem to enjoy it), is on a par with their having to share a bed, or a room. As society moves forward it tightens its child-labour laws and raises the school leaving age. Families, as they become more affluent, *should not need* to depend on children's help, just as, until recently, it was felt they should not need to depend upon a wife working. They can now afford to give the child 'the best'—in effect, to make an article of conspicuous consumption, displaying the family prosperity with his expensive toys, the latest bike and idle hands.

Indeed, the booming economy of the 'sixties created a climate which was extremely receptive to the new child-rearing. Very many new families were started, or new babies added to an earlier brood and child perfection was the ideal. Parents were never so concerned to do well by their children, now that for the first time it seemed that, freed from pre- and post-war austerity, they could give them a really good start in life. They were eager to spend big money and eager for advice. Thus child-centredness was in one sense already a part of family consumption and expectations, and the dubious psychology (whose foundations were laid years before), found fertile ground. (None the less, the *particular* emphasis of the psychology must not be regarded simply as a manifestation of family prosperity. Victorian prosperity built for the child a frilly world of innocence, where he was subjected to a very intense moral and educational training.) The tendency of local authorities and Government to 'spend on the children', and of reformers to envisage a carefree world of exploration and excitement, may owe a lot to changes in consumption patterns where nothing was too good for the child. Indeed, he was in the vanguard of the move to unlimited leisure for all in a future where work was to be replaced by automation. The worry was not how he might fit into the world of work after the world of play, but how we were going to fill all the free-time. Even if it was conceded that the child might have to work when he grew up, not only was this regarded as relatively unimportant, but a 'water-tank' picture of learning-potential prevailed: the mind had a fixed capacity. It was no use teaching specific skills, since skills rapidly became redundant in the modern world; they just cluttered up the brain. As Tizard and colleagues mention in *All Our Children* (1976), the emphasis on play in this century owes nothing to any advance in scientific development psychology, but a lot to our notions of the role of the child.

There is no evidence to suggest that the provision of play facilities diminishes delinquency. On the contrary, surveys of vandalism have shown that the most heavily vandalised places are parks and playgrounds.

An article on delinquents on Hackney estates, 'The Young Criminals' (*New Society* 24 April 1975), has Paul Harrison running through the various causes for lawbreaking, and proposing that:

> Perhaps the easiest factor of all to change is facilities for play. If anyone is looking for more causes for urban aid to go to, then this should take a very high priority.

Yet beforehand he had mentioned that

> Perhaps the saddest aspect of the more serious delinquency is the way it can undermine all efforts to provide something for the kids to do. The bare and dilapidated flat used for a youth club at Haggerston had to close down for three months after it got flooded out when someone turned the water on in one of the empty flats upstairs. Just before this happened, some boys broke into the club, smashed up the juke-box, and stole some records and sweets belonging to the club. A similar club on Stonebridge bought a slide and a swing with a small grant from the council. The slide was stolen and the swing busted. On Holly Street, the adventure playground was closed for a year after some boys smashed all the windows and fittings.

In contrast, the preventative conclusion of Tony Marshall in 'Vandalism: the Seeds of Destruction' (*New Society* 17 June

1976) was for the integration of children's and adolescents' activities into the same areas as those used by adults. In other words, a reversal of the play-space programme. This logic would bring the children back into the front-room, the back-yard, onto the door-step—with all the resulting restrictions.

The reason that surveys show parks and playgrounds to be the worst vandalised areas is a simple and obvious one, *the law of vandalism is that it rises with increasing numbers of children and decreasing adult supervision*.

Having grown up in East London after the war, when life was spartan and dull, but delinquency rare and vandalism virtually unknown, I have often pondered on what exactly is meant when it is said that children are delinquent because they are 'bored', or have 'nothing to do'. I stood at a bus-stop in Richmond not long ago and was told that a conductor had recently been stabbed on the route by a group of older children. The educated young woman concluded her evidence with '. . . but they haven't got much to do, you see'. Now these children had been coming from an ice-rink and a discotheque, in an area where there are abundant facilities for all sports, societies for many interests, plenty of parks, and an open and pleasant country landscape with all urban advantages. Did she recommend non-stop movies on the upper deck to tide them over the tedium of the bus-journey? And what if the action ever flagged?

In Laurie Taylor's *Signs of Trouble: Aspects of Delinquency* (1976), the children who were free to roam at any hour of the day and night, and had reduced much of their estate to a ruined shell, complained that they had 'nothing to do' (they had 'consumed' the play facilities long ago)—in a world which was one big playground where they might do exactly as they liked. One tries in vain to envisage something for them with such an elemental, overwhelming attraction far outweighing in excitement the thrill of destroying it, that would hold them mesmerised and their attention totally held for ever. (Taylor sympathised with the children in such a wasteland, and seemed to incline to the social deprivation theory, even when it was the children who were largely depriving themselves.)

The question of whether or not children enjoy or are bored in their spare time was put to 14,000 eleven-year-olds in the National Child Development Study (Ken Fogelman 'Bored Children' 1976). Overall 3.6 per cent of the children said that they were often bored; girls, who are about ten times *less* delinquent than boys, were more likely to be frequently bored. Children who often felt bored were less likely than other children to borrow library books, read books, meet friends, read comics, make models, collect stamps, go to the cinema, listen to serious music or play games. Bored children were more likely to come from large, unskilled families, to have poor educational attainment, and to be less involved with their fathers. The child's boredom level bore no relation to the availability of facilities for children in the area, whether parks, play centres, recreation grounds, societies, cinemas and so forth. There was no relation between self-reported boredom levels and self-reported stealing and damage to property.

In one sense, the child who is more likely to commit offences—particularly vandalism—may have far more 'leisure' and freedom to play than others. If delinquency is higher in working-class groups compared with middle-class groups, the amount of supervision also goes down and the amount of pocket-money up. The Home Office studies found that the peak age for vandals brought to the notice of the police was under ten. Tony Marshall and Gordon Rose speak of the vandalism characteristic of different ages from the observations of the Blackburn and Liverpool studies. A third of damage could be described as 'play vandalism' as children left to themselves break things, throw stones and deface walls. Another third is accounted for by adolescents for whom it now carries prestige among their companions. It drops off with age and involvement with jobs and girl-friends, except for those who drift the other way—deeper into malicious damage, grosser forms of hooliganism and burglary. Vandalism as a means to another end (robbing vending machines, stripping lead) accounts for a very small amount of child vandalism. The vandalism of children and adolescents is for the intrinsic enjoyment of the act, it is stimulating, exciting, and there its purpose ends: it's 'fun', as the children say. If there is a natural propensity for the child to be drawn to stimulating objects and events, he soon discovers that many can be initiated by himself. However, the child does not consider the animal he is tormenting, the people he is stoning, or the value of the object he breaks, unless he is taught to, and unless those around him make it advantageous to abide by this. As the criminologists G. Sykes and D. Matza say

(1961), the delinquent is far less deviant than he is often thought to be: it is all too 'normal' for children to seek thrills. It is so mundane, in fact, that this is why we are left with so many theories of delinquency—with that 'embarrassment of riches which seemingly goes unmatched in the real world'.

It is, in fact, the very lack of any reason, any socially intelligible goals or 'meaning' in the hedonistic behaviour of children and adolescents, its 'moral randomness', which so often prompts so many urgent attempts to 'explain it'. The expert might be said to be the prey of the same factors which make the delinquent especially fearful to others—the human necessity to give meaning and therefore order to life. You just don't go around putting a life out here, a lamp out there, as if they were all one; you don't set light to a tramp for a giggle as you do to a waste-bin. So the task becomes like the naming of Rumpelstiltskin, where that which is given meaning loses its terror and its non-social, non-human aspect. What cannot be faced is that it has no meaning, no 'motive'. The unsocialised child is capable of doing anything in his search for thrills; the attractions of excitement for him are not sifted or constrained by moral rules. This is essentially all there is to it, and anybody who wants a motive, a meaning to it beyond titillation is going to be disappointed, search as they may.

> A boy, aged seven, started a house fire in Hull in which an invalid woman, aged 35, died, and another woman, aged 23, was badly burned. (*The Times* 20 May 1975).

Refusal to face what children—indeed, what anybody—is capable of 'naturally' doing for excitement in the absence of normative constraints, particularly sustained the idea that delinquents were mentally sick. After three five-year-olds wrecked a school (and killed pets), the caretaker said that he felt '. . . concern and sadness for the boys that did it. Think of the dreadful state they must be in to want to do this'. The boys' comment of 'What have we done wrong?' is probably a more helpful guide to their condition (*Daily Mail* 29 November 1976). This probably was no different from that of another boy who flung a girl to death from a building and was found 'sane and fit to plead and suffering from no mental disorder. Psychiatric examination casts no light on the motive for this meaningless crime' (*Guardian* 10 December 1975).

Sykes and Matza realise what many criminologists are slow to grasp, and planners even slower, that play is not in conflict or competition with delinquency, but merges into it if it is allowed to. Those who attribute delinquency to 'boredom' do not consistently mean that delinquents have unusually drab lives, which can be cured by finding interests and being provided with recreational facilities. Rather, they mean, in effect, that there is a search for maximum excitement, and they equate 'boredom' with anything less than this. If that is so, then to provide alternative thrills which will displace delinquent behaviour by being even more exciting, seems an impossible task; it has simply to be stopped.

Schools accused of failing to compete in interest with delinquent activities are trapped in a blind alley. If schools are to be places of education and not 'pure' entertainment, it is difficult to see how they could ever compete, since the pursuits of untrammelled stimulation and learning are not—strictly speaking—compatible. Learning cannot proceed while the individual's attention is constantly distracted by stimuli. I have known teachers willing to provide virtually anything that would stop the pupils breaking up the furniture, throwing fireworks, and fighting. They manifested some passing wish to know about Nazi death camps and sexual murders, but attempts to use these interests as a springboard to literacy, historical or political knowledge, moral discussion, etcetera, foundered at the first hurdle beyond the gory details—and back came the protests of boredom. Teachers who appeal to their charges to think of their long-term future, treat their pupils as more controlled and competent than they are. The youths may even complain that they are getting no qualifications. They are, by themselves, incapable of suspending their pursuit of any passing gratification, whether at two or fifteen years of age, unless the adult first prevents this pursuit. If he does not, the child is being given an empty choice, because he simply has not got the ability to exercise it. Education can, of course, create vast new opportunities for enjoyment, but if he is to acquire these, the individual's concentration still has to be trained and his attention focused.

Historically, the hedonistic pursuit of excitement *per se*, and the correlative complaint of boredom, is associated with those classes enjoying plentiful leisure. These have sometimes been aristocracies or élites, but by no means always. Sometimes their pursuit of thrills could be kept within the bounds of law (if not morality), sometimes not: feudal knights rode down the peasants for sport, and the drunken aristocrats in *War and Peace* tie a policeman to a bear and throw them both into the Neva. (That some pursuits of excitement have been contained within the bounds of law and morality leads Matza to speak of the juvenile delinquent suffering from 'bad timing', due to his ignorant lack of control, his inability to wait for the right times and places.)

The existence of so much spare time is, almost invariably, an indication of poor integration into the surrounding culture in the sense of low participation in its everyday tasks and goals. The Roman mob lived on doles; an idle but privileged proletariat, voting for those consuls who would provide the grandest and goriest spectacles. Similarly, some aristocracies have had few direct economic, governmental or ritual functions. These general descriptions clearly apply to the modern child and the adolescent, whom Sykes and Matza term members of the 'last leisure class'. Indeed, they share with some dominant élites of the past a relative immunity from the law, as well as exemption from economic tasks and social obligations.

The lack of integration of child and adolescent with the rest of society is likely to be pushed further by the mounting emphasis on the importance of the play world. This is because low involvement with others in mutual tasks and goals means low identification and insensitivity to them as people, and thus even lower commitment to norms which inhibit using other people as means to the pursuit of excitement. Also play time is spent with peers, and today in Western society the peer-group appears to be connected with both internal aggressiveness and anti-social behaviour. In a study by Bronfenbrenner, Siman and Condry (1968), predominantly 'peer-orientated' children were reported to be engaging in more anti-social behaviour, more truancy and more baiting of other children, than were 'adult-orientated' children.

In a series of experiments carried out in different countries (Urie Bronfenbrenner 1964, 1967), children were placed in situations where researchers could test their readiness to engage in morally disapproved behaviour, such as cheating, lying, damaging property etcetera. There were three different conditions where the children thought that (a) only the scientists would know how they responded, and then only as a whole, not as individuals; (b) parents and teachers would see the results on charts; and (c) only their peers would see the results. American children were even more inclined than usual to engage in misconduct if their peers knew. The opposite was true of Soviet children, with the peer group just as effective as parents and teachers in decreasing such behaviour. But in the Soviet Union, the child is not left for long in his peer group unsupervised by adults. Under the direction of adults, the Soviet peer group acts to support behaviour consistent with the values of adult society, and succeeds in inducing its members to take personal responsibility for maintaining and creating such behaviour in others.

Other experiments involved children in Soviet boarding schools who were compared with those in Swiss children's homes (which reject the Soviet emphasis on the intensive teaching of social standards). They were asked what they would do if they knew that a classmate had indulged in a range of twenty-one incidents of anti-social conduct. In the majority of cases, the Soviet youngsters were willing to talk to the offender and try and stop him doing it; invoking the aid of other children in doing so. No clear consensus emerged for the Swiss children, with 20 per cent opting to do nothing, compared with only 1 per cent of Soviet children.

The anti-social peer group is a comparatively recent phenomenon in what must now be a considerable part of Western society. I recall both at my primary and secondary schools how horrified one's peers would have been if any of their number was found stealing—or was even suspected of it. Certainly if any had been, their future existence among other children in that school would hardly have been worth living. Now the pupils combine for shop-lifting sprees and girls compare the rings their boyfriends have stolen and boast about the number he has beaten up. Recently, when the harmless, backward Enrico Sidoli was drowned in a Hampstead swimming pool, the tremendous social pressure of the peer group did not manifest itself in any communal expression of horror at killing, any hunting out and persecution of those who might have been involved—on the contrary, it closed ranks to protect its members from parents and police.

The child cannot normally envisage socially good goals if he is not taught them. Even if he can, he is scarcely capable of reaching them on his own, by his own personal, individual decision. Nor can he see their relevance to himself—unless the adult actively involves him first. (It is not that instruction does not go on in Playland. Far from it, the adult who has abdicated his right to impose his choices is now replaced by the older child one sees carefully instructing a younger one on the precise moment to throw a half-brick at a car window. His pupil has all the nervous concentration of others when they first form a letter or cast a fishing line.) If the child knows that the surrounding society of adults—or some of them, or the police, disapprove, or might try to prevent some activities, then he will treat them merely as obstacles to be circumvented. Otherwise their existence might add spice to the exciting adventure—that is all:

> He told the sergeant that he and the other boy were kidding on if we had the guts to kill somebody—and it got serious. He continued: 'Mrs Finlayson opened the door and when she did so, I stabbed her. She cried: "Oh, my God, what have I done to deserve this?" I could nae stop myself after this'.
>
> He added that the other boy 'got the knife next and stabbed her'.
>
> Dr William McClay said Mrs Finlayson had been stabbed more than twenty times. (*The Times* 8 July 1975)

[*It was stated in court that the boys might have done it because they were bored at school.*]

Unlike his age-peers, the adults who have withdrawn are no longer in a position to utilise the range of potent social pressures which make human beings conform anywhere—disapproval, punishment, ostracism and the terror of being outcast or rejected. Adults have deliberately made the child independent of their instruction, their lore, their company and their favours; they have not made their interests, concerns and tasks, *his* interests, concerns and tasks. Accordingly their anger and condemnation mean nothing to him: having little that he values, they have little to withdraw. The most effective models for a child are those which are the major support and control in his environment. And now these models are older children, not adults. The potency of others as models increases as the model is seen to possess high competence, status and control over resources (Albert Bandura, Dorothea Ross and Sheila A. Ross 1963). But the adult as a perpetual 'giver', lacking in power because he must never withhold, may be ineffective in many ways—however loving he tries to be in shaping the child's outlook and controlling his behaviour.

A vicious circle has been set up. Adults—whoever they are and whatever they stand for—have withdrawn from any instrumental role in the lives of children. The effect of a shallow psychology with the most kind-hearted of motives has conspired with the good intentions of parents to get adults off children's backs. (Or, at the very best, it makes them subservient to an utterly vague concept of child need, where it is unclear what their function is at all, apart from pleasing.) By the same token, the adult ceases to be part of the child's immediate human reference group and, being irrelevant and ineffective in so many ways to the child, he becomes ill-placed to use social pressures to gain the child's compliance. In such a situation, belated and clumsy attempts at control by the adult often only serve to make matters worse (L.D. Eron, Leopold O. Walder and Monroe M. Lefkowitz 1971). The sporadic 'good hiding' or threat simply turns the adult into another noxious object to be further avoided and outwitted, and confirms solidarity to peers. Anyway, a possible 'belting' at the end of the rainbow when he gets home is rather irrelevant to the child among all the temptations of the adult-free here and now. Evidence suggests that the more a child identifies with his parents, the more does their punishment (including physical punishment), inhibit his aggression; but the less he identifies, the more does their punishment *increase* his aggression. Parents of delinquents seem to emerge as more passive than usual in the face of misbehaviour as well as poorer supervisors—even if they desire the same standards from their children as the parents of non-delinquents—but they have a tendency to 'lash out' at the last minute (David Herbert 1977).

Child-centred rearing made the child primary, and playland completes the process of dissociation from the dethroned adults. But we do have emotional satisfaction *per se* and it all leads to a blind alley. And, irony on irony, more provision for the special world of children—more play, more interest, like more love—is urged to solve the problems. In the last analysis, isn't even all the talk about caring, of significant relationships, just so much hypocrisy, when children have been, in effect, left to bring themselves up?

In Bogotá, Latin America, thousands of parentless children live on the streets, orphaned and abandoned. They live mainly by crime. The older ones teach the younger ones and these in turn teach even younger ones the tricks of the trade. Might is right, and the smaller child's obedience is usually punished by acts of sadistic cruelty (see Serita Kendall 1975). In Russia in the chaos after the Civil War a similar situation existed, when groups of orphaned children of different ages roamed the countryside.

In the television series *Signs of Trouble,* already mentioned, delinquency started as soon as the child was out of nappies, and older children passed to younger ones the techniques of offending. The police reckoned that they had reached the lower age limit for car-stealing, since the feet of anyone under about nine or ten could not reach the pedals. However, this did not stop even younger children riding around with their older peers throughout the night. The police were driven to admit that there was little they could do as they struggled to hold down the lid. The difference between this and Bogotá, as between many areas of Britain and Bogotá, is that these children were neither orphaned nor (officially) abandoned.

13 School and the Leisure Child

Education has never been represented as so broad, ambitious and influential as it has been in the last decade: 'we now have the job of preparing the child for life', or 'we develop the kind of person he is' and so forth, are common claims of the teaching profession. Harold Silver speaks of

> . . . the existing recruitment of more 'socially idealistic' students. Teaching has been so much talked about in recent years as a kind of social work, and in a detailed social content, that the colleges and departments have recruited students who want to use the schools as their sphere of social involvement (1976).

Certainly, never has so much money been spent on education, with expenditure doubling as a percentage of GNP since the 1950s. Yet, at the same time, never, in practice, have schools felt that they could achieve so little.

Their particular paralysis is derived from a mixture of the same popular psychology that affects the home: a determinism of the early years and intimate relationships, which set a course the school is powerless to alter later. And on top of the dead hand of family determinism, there is also one of class. Contributions from economic determinism create the attitude that it is the working-class child particularly that the school cannot help.

One of the strands was contributed by Jenck's work *Inequality*, whose American thesis held that the composition of classes and occupational groups owes itself to macro-economic forces in society, and not the educational system. It is these forces which decide how many vacancies there will be for clerks and butchers, managers and dustmen, and what they should be paid. So, it was concluded, if schools cannot end inequality, what is their point? Indeed, they may be worse than useless. It has also been continually repeated that all the schools do for the working-class child is confirm him in his own inferiority —schools are an instrument of an unequal society; as the children come through the door, the selectors are almost supposed to say from on high 'that one for the boardroom and that one for the barrow'. The children are left to act out the roles that they have been given in this quasi-deliberate manner and if they fail, it is because it is planned so.

Basil Bernstein (1971) pointed out that the working class were linguistically impoverished; or anyway, impoverished in terms of the middle-class cognitive curriculum which pertained at school. They employed a 'restricted code', which made the use of abstract concepts difficult. There was a wringing of hands over this (supposed) irremediable incapacity. There was a double unfairness, even sadism, in putting hacks over courses intended only for thoroughbreds. Indeed, the educational system seemed nothing but a mechanism built for and by the middle class. This imposed itself on those of an alien culture.

But why? It became part of sociological wisdom that schooling emerged in the nineteenth century to defuse the socially innovatory potential of the working class. In short—it was a middle-class plot to keep the noses of the poor to the grindstone.

In such a climate, any suggestion that the school's task was partly its traditional one of imparting socially desirable behaviour, was met with a variation on the reply that it could do little in the face of familial and socio-economic forces, and would be very presumptuous to try. It was 'out there', in society, that the answers lay.

This tendency to remove the school from the cultural initiation of the working-class child is, in reality, much at odds with the traditional expectations of many working-class parents, that the school should take a large share in rearing their children. It is the parents of those children whom the schools have thought that they could do least for, who often expect the institution actively to 'make something' of their children. They expect not just instruction in basic literacy and numeracy—but social skills and norms—'getting on with others', 'good manners', 'behaving themselves', 'thinking of other people' and so forth.

As much as it has been proclaimed that there exists a sepa-

rate working-class culture, equally valid and worthwhile, complex and evolved as that described as 'middle-class', there
seems to be great difficulty finding it. (Other than a 'twee'
section for teachers in the *Times Educational Supplement* 5 October
1973 on *'that other culture'*, which covered things like dog-racing,
'pop' and Bingo.) As Martha Vicinus describes, the development of the pre-industrial peasantry into the urban working
class meant that the old dialect folk-culture was extinguished.
As a result, the working classes have been more dependent
upon what they have acquired from others (and are still more
dependent on professional educators like teachers to transmit
this), and just as expressive of 'mainstream' culture as any
other group. In Britain, regional differences are probably as
great as or greater than class ones. For example, higher
academic education, which the English working-class has
never had a great fancy for, is far more greatly respected and
desired by its Welsh and Scottish counterparts. The mass
media probably have a greater impact on the working class
compared with other groups, and what the *Times Educational
Supplement* described as unique features of that other culture
were largely limited to the offerings of the mass entertainment
industry. Whether this and pop can constitute some kind of
neglected indigenous folk-culture, I am not too sure.

Nor, it appears, are working-class parents. Disquiet over
what is happening in schools over the past couple of decades
has come as much from working-class parents as from middle-
class traditionalists. Attempts to preserve the cultural integrity
of the working class by shielding them from the contributions of
others, may take away a very large portion of that culture on
which they have hitherto been dependent. The parents may not
be aware of the reasons, but as far as modern education goes,
they have been very worried by the results.

Far from schooling being an attempt by the middle classes to
eradicate working-class culture and tame the workforce, in the
nineteenth century trade unionists and self-educated working
people were in the forefront of the drive for educational opportunities. The urban poor of the previous century, having lost
their rural heritage, became renowned instead for a cruel
hedonism. The violent, gin-soaked existence they led made up
a lifestyle that was indeed, nasty, brutish and short. It might
have been conducive to rioting, but certainly not to any

planned insurrection; and the only proletarian alternative it offered to the system, when it briefly held sway, was to drink its way through the distilleries.

In his *Religion and Respectability: Sunday schools and English working class culture* (1977), Thomas W. Laqueur traces how Sunday schools became, during the nineteenth century, 'relatively autonomous working-class institutions'. (By 1850 two million working-class children were enrolled in Sunday Schools, managed by working-class people and being taught primarily by working-class teachers.) More than religion, the sheer pressure from below was due to the fact that the poor saw the *secular* education and socialisation which Sunday schools provided for their children as the surest path to self-improvement, when many could not afford the day school. Also Harold Silver writes of nineteenth-century elementary day school teachers as mostly coming from the same lower classes as their pupils.

That short-term hedonism has perhaps been more a feature of the working class than other groups, does not mean that this is to be favoured as some kind of authentic expression of their values or culture, over and above those values they share with other groups. Nor does it mean that the working class even find this very congenial themselves; the conflict between the 'rough' and the 'respectable' in the working class has been a perennial observation of sociologists, as Dennis Marsden outlines (1976). If high delinquency areas are the ones with strong working-class values, then those living in them do not seem to enjoy it very much. They are usually anxious to leave for places where 'middle-class', or 'respectable' working-class, values prevail. This has been the aspiration of people throughout this century living in 'rough areas' where social relationships are not governed by clear rules, and frequent disputes are settled *ad hoc* with aggression and counter-aggression.

> Those delinquencies which are not illegal, and which would be kept in check by the informal pressure of public opinion in a middle-class neighbourhood are integrated within a normative cultural pattern, [in which] the only control being exerted is by an adaptation of the *lex talionis*. . . . the principle of 'giving as good as you take' operates, so that abuse over the garden fence must be met by further abuse, slanders by

counter slanders and so on. Such a way of life is essentially unsatisfying and frequently mentally unhealthy. It is not surprising that almost all those individuals who can, seek to abandon it and adopt the norms of the middle class. (Terence Morris 1957)

(It was the working-class parents and the non-teaching staff in the affair of the William Tyndale school in London who objected to the schoolchildren's language and behaviour which the progressive, quasi-Marxist teachers were permitting as 'working-class culture'.)

The gulf that has opened up between parents and schools in recent years is often explained by the claim that the parent has yet to catch up with innovations in method since his own schooldays. This is, strictly speaking, untrue. It is the parents' understanding of *aims* that has been lost; and the history and philosophy of the progressive revolution suggest that the schools are none too sure of their aims either. But trends in the schools feed back into, and reinforce, the changes in parental behaviour at home. It is not just that the working-class (or West Indian) parent has taken the criticisms of the school to heart and eased up a bit on discipline; they feel that they cannot hope to ask things of children at home when different standards prevail at school, and far more simply, they can observe without necessarily comprehending that 'they don't think that matters these days'. In view of the evidence which we possess on parental imitation of educational methods elsewhere, it would be strange if the school's relinquishing of its socialisation functions to the home did not see them more accepted there, but further diminished.

Is there not a contradiction between the parental withdrawal at home and parental criticism of the passivity of the school? In some ways there is. People's knowledge and behaviour are neither complete nor thoroughly consistent. Parents want to follow the best advice, and they want to give their children the best start. This start usually meant (and still does) better acquisition of traditional knowledge, skills and behaviour, and here they still expected the schools to do what they had always done, or do it even better. Thus the parents put into practice the new expertise at home, but seeing it from the outside in operation at school, they fear for their children's future. (At the

extreme of incongruity, a parent may defend his child's misbehaviour unconditionally against outsiders, and vociferously
side with his child against teachers. Yet he complains about
delinquency in children generally and even about the standards in the school!) Again, the evidence suggests that parents
of delinquents have much the same expectations about their
behaviour as parents of non-delinquents, but they either use
ineffective methods of control, or remain passive and indulgent
in the face of actual misbehaviour.

But is the parent, or anybody for that matter, justified in
believing that the school can critically affect his child's
behaviour? Or is the school right in pointing to the 'environment' or the 'society' which is to blame for failure? A series of
studies suggest that schools have been unduly modest about
their influence.

A study by Michael Power, published in 1967, showed large
differences in the delinquency rates for schools in the London
Borough of Tower Hamlets, which could not be explained by
the differences in the delinquency rates of the areas from which
the schools drew their pupils. The findings echoed other work
by Michael Rutter. However, in spite of their importance—and
some said it was the most important new angle on delinquency
for decades—permission to conduct further research was
refused by the Inner London Education Authority and the
teachers' unions.

But later research was carried out in another homogeneous
working-class area, by David Reynolds, Dee Jones and Selwyn
St Leger (1976), where stringent checks were none the less
made to see if any resultant differences in pupils at different
schools were the result of initial differences in intake (social
class, ability etcetcra), parental choice of school, or variations
in the catchment areas. Within nine schools, attention was
focused on three measures: school attendance; academic success, and delinquency (defined as being found guilty before a
court or officially cautioned by the age of fifteen). It was found
that on all three measures there were '. . . nine schools producing children who appear to be very different on three separate
indicators'. One school, for example, had a 10.5 per cent delinquency rate, and another had a 3.8 per cent delinquency rate
per year; one sent over half its pupils into the local technical
school (regarded locally as the key to a craft or apprenticeship),

and another sent only 8.4 per cent per year; one school achieved an examination success of 85 per cent, and another (even when pupils were entered for a more limited range of examinations), only 47 per cent. The researchers concluded: 'In our opinion, and even on the basis of our analysis so far, the belief that a school can only be as good or bad as the character and ability of the children entering it, is simply wrong. . . . What goes on in school between nine and five *is* an important determinant of the type of child that emerges at the end of the process.'

With this in mind, one must consider the demand from teachers and others for resources and facilities to deal with a growing number of children who are disruptive in classrooms. 'Sanctuaries for children who can't cope' were not found necessary before the introduction of so many progressive innovations. The question has neither been raised nor considered, whether these are not in fact simply mopping up the mess that would not have been created in the first place if certain choices had not been made.

The forty to fifty suspensions per year quoted by the National Association of Schoolmasters as supported by them, is small fry compared with the rate of school suspension in America described by Thomas Cottle (1976). There, of the two million children listed as being regular absentees from school, about 11 per cent have been suspended. It results in many poor and black children missing education. In some cases it appears to be used to *avoid* taking disciplinary action over bad behaviour and infringements of rules which the schools have coped with without much difficulty in the past. The situation seems to have come about whereby the schools have to deny educational benefits to those most in need of them, because these children do not already have the appropriate attitudes and behaviour which the school was partly instituted to develop in the first place.

In fact, in America over the last couple of decades similar movements have occurred in education as in Britain. Expenditure doubled as a percentage of the gross national product between 1955 and 1970, and in the far better equipped schools the trend was to choice and freedom for the child, discovery and activity methods; a change from assessment and competitiveness to the integration of children of all abilities and levels of attainment in unselective schools and unstreamed classrooms, and a sensitivity to the child's own 'culture'. But in April 1975 Senator Bahy was to compare the killing rate in American schools between 1970 and 1973 with American losses in the first three years of the Vietnam war, with 277 pupils dying in the 'combat zones' of the nation's schools. Between these years, rapes were up 41 per cent, assaults on pupils 85 per cent and on teachers 77 per cent. Investigation by a US Senate committee has shown violence to be a very serious and growing problem (with, for example, threequarters of a sample of high school students saying that children were too frightened to use the lavatories, and the numbers of Chicago school police increasing from two in 1966 to 600 in 1973). But several studies also show illiteracy to be growing. A recent study showed that millions of American youth were unable to perform even the most basic tasks required in a complex society. And, with children frightened to attend school because of violence, or just truanting, the demand has grown for an end to compulsory schooling by liberals and progressives, since youth was 'choosing' to have nothing to do with it at all. Thinking that the error lay in the residual rules and impositions that remained, another move has been to call for, and set up, 'free-schools' where the children alone were the arbiters of whether they attended or what they did. On a smaller scale, the pattern has, of course, been duplicated in Britain.

Yet, at the same time the children attending *voluntary* schools in America increased from 3.2 million in 1960 to 7.5 million in 1970; and during the three years from 1969 to 1972, the total number of adults in all kinds of schools jumped 21 per cent. In some cases minority groups such as blacks and Puerto Ricans have set up their own segregated schools in disgust with the results of white liberal policies; they were certainly not amused by the suggestion that their children's impoverished speech, incompetence and resultant unemployability, were an expression of their own 'culture'. Overall, the evidence (see article by David B. Tyack 1977) suggests no *rejection per se* of education by Americans, only rejection of the type of schooling given in recent years. (Polls show over half the citizens asking for schools where the 'three Rs' and strict discipline are the central features.)

And in Britain? The very poor attainment, for example, of West Indian children in inner city comprehensives, and their accumulating behaviour problems, have prompted the similar response that it might be better if these children dropped out altogether from our attempts to impose 'middle-class white culture' upon them. The large numbers of blacks pronounced educationally subnormal are also deemed to be manifesting a different culture: there is a world somewhere where stupidity is handy! All this seems to presuppose that they might find employment in a totally viable, separate society of their own, so that they have no need to acquire the tools essential for ours. However, their backwardness may be just what it seems and is due to the failure to acquire the basics needed to participate adequately, and be of use in any culture. (Human culture is not composed of items which cancel each other; but is ever cumulative and diverse. It has not hurt Jewish culture one whit that Jews have also taken full advantage of the Gentile educational system. We do not say that we must refrain from educating Jewish children because it destroys their own culture, we leave that to the good sense of the people to preserve if they find it worthwhile.)

West Indian parents in Britain are even more dependent than native working-class parents on the wider society taking over child-rearing, educational and socialising functions. The extended family network and the community involvement in child-rearing common to the West Indies are absent here. There is little to fill the void. The child may acquire little more than fragmentary rudiments of linguistic and social skills from a minder, and when he gets to school he encounters an environment which can only be of use if he is already competent. He also comes from a tradition which develops the intellectual and social capacities of the child at a later age than ours; much of what an English child, particularly a middle-class child, acquires before five, he is meant to acquire after this age. A recent report by the Commons Select Committee found that West Indian children in Britain are academically poorer and have worse behaviour than their peers in Jamaica. Children returning to Jamaica sometimes had difficulty 'settling down' because of the differences in the school systems, where orderly Caribbean schools stressed skills and good behaviour.

If what goes on in the two areas which share between them the major task of child-rearing in modern society—the family and the school—*does* affect what children are, then the radical

changes introduced over the last couple of decades may have a
lot to answer for. The tragedy is that so much was done with the
best of intentions. When, for the first time historically, there
was an enormous concerted effort and an immense amount of
good will and money available to give a generation of children a
really good start, the results are not only pitiable, they might
also be disastrous. We may soon be asking, if we are not doing
so already, not what benefits these innovations have bestowed,
but 'how much harm have they done?' Accumulating evidence
shows that 'traditional' adult-centred child-rearing environments come out well compared with child-centred ones. The
boot is on the other foot, it seems to be the latter which are
'asking a price'.

In China, all child activity is adult-initiated, maintained and
terminated, with the emphasis on rule-governed, language
mediated and task-based behaviour (see W. Kessen 1975). But
although the American delegation of psychologists engaged on
a detailed observation of Chinese kindergarten and schools
found the children sociable and expressive, they failed to pick
up much in the way of '. . . disorders of behaviour we have
come to expect . . . in American schools—hyperactivity, impul-
siveness, isolated withdrawal and neurotic symptoms.'

It was noticed that Chinese adults quickly intervene if children's behaviour starts to become chaotic or aggressive in tone;
they rapidly introduce the children to calmer, coordinated
alternatives. It might have a lot to do with the comparison the
delegation made between the 'relaxed quality' and social atten-
tiveness of Chinese children, compared with the edgy, easily
distracted and aggressive nature of so many American ones.
The tendency to cultivate and tolerate high arousal states in
children in the West with 'free-play' and 'expression' might
have something to do with its corresponding epidemic of
'hyperactivity'. In our past children were similarly not allowed
to get 'over-excited'.

Through example, explanation, encouragement, exhortation, repetition and reasoning, socially correct and responsible
behaviour and the principles which govern this are carefully
and explicitly transmitted to the Chinese child. Use is not only
made of simple drama where children 'practise' what is, for
example, an unselfish act, but also of the 'moral tale', where
heroes the children can model themselves on do good deeds.

This feature of our past, too, is now heavily frowned upon in the West, since it is supposed to undermine the child's individuality and self-confidence by suggesting that perhaps he could be a little different, or better than he is. Emphasis is instead on 'identification', not emulation: the model must share all the child's problems, and be no better in any respect:

> Carol Bergman, a young American who taught remedial reading classes for the Inner London Education Authority from 1968 until last year, believes that the lack of material to appeal directly to black students is part of the reason many of them need remedial reading at secondary level.
>
> She has therefore written three short books . . . in which the heroes are black children in situations which will be familiar to many black pupils. Although weak on plot in the conventional sense, the books are packed with incident. In one a schoolgirl runs away from home when she discovers she is pregnant. In another the hero, a teenager who cannot read, is suspended from school for pushing a teacher over.
>
> Mrs Bergman thinks realism and honesty are important if the books are to fulfil their purpose. (*The Times* 10 June 1975)

In schools the dogma which says that for the teacher to transmit, rather than simply develop what emerges from the 'child's own experience', is both somehow demeaning and incomprehensible to the pupil, can simply lead to the practice and reinforcement of socially undesirable and personally unhelpful attitudes and behaviour. When the teacher throws the ball back to the child and asks him to make up his *own* compositions and dramas about the world he knows, this often results in the pupils presenting a hammed-up version of 'sitcom' Television Shows, since the TV is often all he has left as a source of ideas and inspiration. When we know how strife-ridden homes are correlated with delinquency (probably because of the poor models of interpersonal behaviour they present, and the hostile attitudes they cultivate), the wisdom of allowing children who have undeveloped social skills to practise social situations where mother, father and the children shout, swear and mutually insult each other as both expression and preparation for their 'working-class culture', perhaps needs to be questioned.

In Soviet schools great attention is paid to good behaviour, procedures are very formal, but the children are themselves involved in the mutual reinforcement of adult norms and values. These are particularly concerned with the performance of civic duties.

> The overall status of each pupil is evaluated by his peers, following standards and procedures taught by the upbringers. Since each child's status depends in part on the standing of the collective of which he is a member, it is to each pupil's enlightened self-interest to watch over his neighbour, encourage the other's good performance and behaviour, and help him when he is in difficulty. In this system the children's collective becomes the agent of adult society and the major source of reward and punishment. The latter typically takes the form of group sanctions expressed through public criticism and, ultimately, the threat of exclusion from membership. (Urie Bronfenbrenner 1971)

Overall, Soviet youngsters were

> . . . well mannered, attentive and industrious. In informal conversations, they reveal a strong motivation to learn, a readiness to serve their society, and—in general—ironically enough for a culture committed to a materialistic philosophy, what can only be described as an idealistic attitude towards life. In keeping with this general orientation, relationships with parents, teachers, and upbringers are those of respectful but affectionate friendship . . . it is apparent that instances of aggressiveness, violation of rules, or other anti-social behaviour are genuinely rare.

This is not to say that delinquency is unknown in Russia—far from it—observation of the proceedings of local committees and the informal 'comrades' courts' reports the usual procession of thieves, drunks and vandals. But on the other hand, one cannot dismiss all this with the cynicism which says that delinquency is just as bad in Russia, but the statistics are simply suppressed. Statistics apart, whether one is a casual visitor or part of a team studying child-rearing—like Urie Bronfenbrenner— observational evidence is against the amount of damage from vandalism accepted almost as a normal part of the urban scene in Britain, or the number of hostile incidents. It is easy to conclude that the price paid for this security is the oppressiveness of the Russian political system. It is doubtful whether the liberty of the Russian people would be increased by a rise in street crime. Our surfeit of crime often works to undermine our claims to be a defender of individual freedom.

Turning from modern Communist to very traditional groups, a recent comparative study was made in this country of Asian immigrant children chosen at random from schools in Leicester and matched for age, sex and classroom with English children (A.M. Kallarackal and Martin Herbert 1976). The English children were rated as three times more maladjusted than the Asian children on symptom scales for problems that obviously distressed the child, or those around him, markedly, for long periods. Family size, social class and maternal employment did not seem to be involved with the difference. However, there were no broken homes in the Indian sample, whereas in the English sample, 22 per cent of the children came from one-parent families, and 40 per cent of the English maladjusted children came from homes where there was either only one parent or severely impaired relations between parents. (But 60 per cent were in apparently stable families, or at least, intact ones.) If the behaviour of the husband and wife was freer in the English homes, so too were the 'children freer, more independent and had less supervision and discipline than their Indian counterparts'. There was, however, a tendency for maladjustment to rise in Indian children with length of residence of the family in this country.

A full-scale study of the emerging association between child-centred 'permissive' rearing and maladjustment has not been undertaken yet. But the 'accidental' findings in a detailed study and follow-up of hospitalised children by M. Stacey, Rosemary Dearden, Roisin Pill and Daniel Robinson 1970, found that those most upset in hospitals and those most maladjusted beforehand overlapped. One of the distinguishing features of this group was that they came from homes which were generally characterised as 'permissive' or 'child-orientated', compared with those who had lower rates for maladjustment, and who coped better outside their homes. Yet the authors of this intensive study of children and hospitalisation are clearly committed to the child-rearing methods which they found associated with these problems; a fact which their conclusions reflect. 'If, therefore, our suspicions that there may be an association between the permissive home and disturbance are confirmed, it may have important consequences for future policy', which requires that the children need to be 'cushioned by the continual presence of parents and/or playleaders'. Despite claims that it is the more timid or introverted child who is particularly harmed by adult-centred and controlled environments, the Bennett research (1976) on informal versus formal teaching methods found that the nervous child did four times as well in formal settings. Informal classrooms raised anxiety levels and such children 'dithered' more, finding it difficult to coordinate and focus their attention on the tasks in hand.

It appears that countries with child-centred methods of child-rearing are experiencing a general growth in 'maladjustment' as well as outright delinquency. Instead of equipping the child with the tools to make his way in the world, enabling him to control his attentions and direct his actions to some constructive end, the child is left either fearful in the corner, or chaotically and offensively blundering about the place, sometimes with a motley collection of accidentally acquired habits in tow. More children are having difficulties coping with social life, are unhappy and confused, at the same time as more are becoming a nuisance and threat to others. On the face of it, this could look like evidence for 'emotional damage' on a wide scale; but it could as much, or more, point to a problem of the great untaught. In the past there might not have been so much maladjustment for the same reason that there was not so much delinquency—it was not allowed. Adding all this to the corresponding growing lack of basic intellectual skills and—in a society which is bigger and better in everything, and has gone farthest down the child-centred road—a report to the President of the United States from the White House Conference on Children was driven to assert that 'America's families and their children are in trouble, trouble so deep as to threaten the future of the nation'. Urie Bronfenbrenner, who served on that committee, had this to say:

. . . what I have referred to elsewhere as the 'unmaking of the American child' is the product of many disintegrative forces operating simultaneously to undermine the effectiveness of the family, the school, and other agencies charged with responsibility for child-rearing. In some segments of American society, notably among the economically disadvantaged, the social disorganisation has been so extreme as to impair psychological functioning and development to a point that countermeasures have had to be introduced on a national scale. Among the well-to-do, the effects are not so extreme, but are nevertheless perceptible primarily in the spheres of motivation and social behaviour. (Urie Bronfenbrenner 1973)

But adult-centred upbringing is represented as a weary, difficult struggle with resentful, unhappy children. However, this is not commonly borne out by experience. In most circumstances there is no question that the child will not follow and meet what the adult requires; that is, after all, how you take part in your immediate group, where the human interest and benefits lie. So often the educated 'liberal' adult simply projects his own doubts onto the child as he does onto the general public. But, although we may be fearful to ask anything of our children, and certainly to *make* them do anything—we must remember that, paradoxically, over the last few years, we have never locked up so many, and we are being asked by some to resign ourselves to locking up more in the future. Boston has had to impose a curfew on those under eighteen in the evening, and in Britain cages are proposed for young football fans between train and football ground. The withdrawal is complete; unable to live with our young, we must segregate them from our society for our own safety.

Another very sad aspect of the child-centred aftermath is the way in which the normative breakdown and social inadequacies which it has caused are taken to be that very 'working-class culture' we are called upon to preserve. Its creators would not usually consider living in the social environment which they have so helped to bring about; as Oscar Newman, author of *Defensible Space*, comments: 'It is strange to find the enlightened middle classes fleeing to suburbia, fleeing the liberated atmosphere they have worked at creating in the cities; stranger still to observe their flight and their apparent content with leaving behind an immobile population far more vulnerable to the ravages of criminals, addicts and abusive agents of authority'.

Part of the solution—it should be most obvious—is to help the adult and restore his primacy, so that he may do more for the child. A rebuilding of his eroded confidence is imperative, particularly in relation to the schools; not only should they have a duty to prescribe, but a duty to give to the young many of the skills to enable them to participate in the life and work of the community. We can perhaps take a leaf out of the book of the old vocationally orientated Approved Schools, who had a lower recidivism rate than the recent therapeutic homes because they provided a speedier introduction to adult social life and adult employment. The most ironic aftermath of the economic determinism which decreed that the schools could do nothing to alter the occupational distribution of the population, is that many pupils cannot fill the vacancies the 'system' is offering them because they are quite unequipped with the most elementary social, numerical and verbal skills.

It must be considered whether it is possible to guarantee that pupils at school gain some elementary standards of intellectual and social competence in concrete and comprehensible skills that both teacher and taught can clearly understand and aim for. Research indicates that, for example despite initial preferences for 'interest'-based approaches to the teaching of literacy, both teacher and taught achieved more with, and came to like better, 'skill'-based sessions (Carole Striker 1976). I have known schools where large numbers of the children perform badly in most spheres and where heads are shaken over the intractable problems supposedly posed by so much 'disturbance' or 'deprivation'. Yet teachers who take the initiative and who go to the pupil with clearly defined and limited goals, and a precise focus on developing skill, find their charges not unamenable. In fact, they improve vastly, not only in the task at hand, but in their general control and competence—they were, after all, quite normal young people. It might also be considered whether it is possible to guarantee job experience to pupils who meet certain specific standards and want to work; job experience where they can increase their skills and contribute towards the community. It is interesting that the supportive and paternalistic environment of the craft apprenticeship has produced both responsible, independent citizens as well as conscientious and skilled workmen. Perhaps this is because it involves that relationship which is at the heart of the cultural process—the collaboration of teacher and taught in the pursuit of a mutual task. At all costs, the young must be welcomed and *expected* to participate in the activities, aims, responsibilities and relationships of society, not discouraged and sent off to play.

14 Setting an Example

If I have just talked of the lack of example and instruction, this chapter is concerned with a plethora of it. At a time when other values and other examples remain unasserted and undemonstrated, the possibilities and the glories of violence are held ever more variously and ever more enticingly before the child.

Before the new expertise appeared to dethrone the adult as teacher and model, before the necessity to transmit and uphold a moral code was decried, there was already present in society a factor which deviously worked to foster more delinquency than would perhaps have occurred without it. It was reflected in the differential rates of lawbreaking for boys and girls. In a society making distinctions between people, and evaluations of their conduct on ground of sex, it was traditional that males had the privilege of both freedoms denied to the female—the indulgence to be, comparatively, unreasonable and irresponsible, and the licence, if not positive encouragement, to be aggressive.

The appeal of aggression goes deep: it has its own psychology. And in entertainment, it is as if the media have become the repository of that tacit 'subterranean' blessing granted to the male's less-socially constructive propensities. In becoming the 'church' of violence, and having made it all its own, the media increasingly gives us new dimensions and variations on the theme.

'He described our society as "a desert of a place" for young people to let off their violent feelings, and said that we ought to be looking at producing acceptable outlets for them' (Dr W.A. Beson at the British Association. Report in *The Guardian* 24 August 1973). Another justification apt to be frequently heard for the Play-way out of delinquency is that children—particularly boys—need provision to 'let out' energies, or even be specifically aggressive. Society stands accused of stifling its young males by not giving enough opportunities for 'healthy' aggression, and it deserves what it gets when their instincts turn sour. However, there is some confusion about whether the youth or child *converts* aggression into something less destructive, or directly discharges it, given the right facilities. Thus we find the provision of facilities for children to smash things, so that they won't have any energies left to 'let out' smashing up other things:

> A gang of schoolchildren armed with hammers and saws began tearing down part of a £30,000 council development scheme seconds after it was opened today.
>
> As council officials and a Government Minister looked on the children began hammering and sawing away unhampered.
>
> For the hammers and saws were provided by the council. It was all part of a plan to let the children work their destructive instincts off before they ruined their brand new playground. (*Evening Standard* 22 April 1971)

Notions of letting out aggression or energies have been described as 'ventilationist' by Professor Leonard Berkowitz (1973), and they have been specifically associated with Conrad Lorenz and his popularisers. Notable volumes are Robert Ardrey's *African Genesis* and *Territorial Imperative*; Desmond Morris's *Naked Ape* and *Human Zoo*, and Anthony Storr's *Human Aggression*.

The belief is that aggression is unlearnt; it does not occur because it is encouraged, rewarded, or imitated. Nor is it an inherent disposition to behave in a certain way which still has to be triggered off by some outside stimulus. Aggression is represented as a wholly internal energy which accumulates in the nervous system like water in a cistern, and which has to be periodically discharged. Lorenz emphasises that aggression can 'explode' without demonstrable external stimulation. Aggressiveness is totally unmodifiable: we must recognise, not evade, our unchangeable animal nature. The trouble with modern society is that there are not enough opportunities for aggression: '. . . present civilised man suffers from insufficient discharge of his aggressive drive', says Lorenz, and Storr believes that as modern democracies have moved away from a

hierarchical society based on brute force 'they have set themselves a problem in the disposal of aggression'.

Attempts to suppress all this spontaneous aggression do
harm. In childhood 'If there is no one person to oppose, the
child's aggression tends to become turned inwards against the
self so that he pulls his own hair, bites his nails, or becomes
depressed and self-reproachful' (Storr). In addition to this
aggression that is building up all the time, there also appears to
be a second reservoir, a sort of long-term account '. . . within us
all who have been brought up in Western civilisation . . . there
must be reserves of repressed, and therefore dangerous, aggression which originates from the restrictions of early childhood'.

Well beyond the readership of the 'Lorenzian' books, there is
the belief that children who are expected to behave well at
home or school must therefore be the very devil outside. Pat
Barrett in 'Are You Sitting Quietly?' for *The Guardian* (30
January 1973) said about a school that she admitted to be
highly esteemed locally: 'I suspect that the rigid discipline . . .
drove the pupils into a dual code of behaviour, demure and
submissive in the classroom and all hell let loose outside'.

However, it is not apparent that modern Americans have a
far lower rate of mental illness than other peoples because they
live in a society which 'directly expresses' its aggression in,
among other things, a high murder rate. Anyway, there seems
to be a very thin line between 'direct' and 're-directed' aggression. Opportunities for the latter soon begin to look indistinguishable from the former. When the Roman mob demanded
more and more torture and death in the arena, was it a harmless release, or the real thing? Did it diminish the sum total of
aggression in that society, or simply add to it? Societies which
are neither internally violent nor particularly warlike have no
more mental troubles than anyone else—they just have fewer
broken heads.

Lorenzian aggression is indeed a miraculous substance. It is
claimed to be the basis of society: we come together because we
hate each other so much and would annihilate our species if we
didn't. Our social relationships are conceived in the model of
the stereotyped territorial posturings of birds, which constantly
ward off the tendency to lash out, and which signal 'No, not me,
let's get the fellow over there instead'.

An energy which has to emerge, yet has the astonishing

metamorphic properties to become all we hold dear—it is Love or Libido over again; the tired old mystical energies of the pseudo-sciences. In fact, Freud in his later years postulated Thanatos as well as Eros, or Libido. And if the devotees of his heretic disciple Melanie Klein have allowed Love to conquer and become all and forget the aggression, the Lorenzians have taken in the other half of the washing and founded a universe of Hate instead. (That our social relationships and culture can be boiled down to something like the automatic, programmed territorial responses of birds, is exactly parallel to claims that they somehow derive from the compulsion to suck or cling.)

It being only males who are commonly credited with this aggressive energy—or have sufficient quantities of it—the implication frequently is that women are not really fitted for social or cultural existence! Broadmoor and football hooligans are a small price to pay for the male propensity for mayhem to which we owe so much. One author, following in this tradition, waxes almost lyrical over the groups of violent young football fans: such male 'bonding' is pure society in the making (Peter Marsh 1975). (This cluster of attitudes emphasising exclusively the instinctual, the territorial and the holy community of male aggression, is unfortunately too familiar in recent European history.)

If the theoretical basis for 'getting it out of the system' does not look promising what is the state of evidence on catharsis? Catharsis can be construed in two ways: either the individual has aggression *à la* Lorenz, which builds up all the time and has to come out somewhere, or it is only when he is actually aggressively aroused that it has to be discharged. The classic study on the subject, which is sometimes used to support a catharsis argument, is that of Feshbach and Singer (1971), who studied 400 boys from seven institutions; three were private schools catering for boys from middle-class homes, and the other four were institutions for those from inadequate, mainly lower-class, homes. Divided into two groups, the boys watched six hours of either violent or non-violent TV for six weeks. Their respective behaviour was rated each day for physical and verbal aggression, provoked and unprovoked. The findings showed that the non-violent TV boys had been the more aggressive. However, this applied only to the boys from the institutions; the reverse was true for private school boys. The

institution boys were used to seeing a great deal of violent TV
and when denied it (and faced with 'lousy shows' like 'Petticoat
Junction'!) reacted with threats and disobedience. Another
researcher along the same lines (W.D. Wells 1972), found that,
in a sample of six hundred schoolchildren, those who watched
highly violent television programmes were the ones rated most
aggressive by their classmates. Nothing is being discharged. In
laboratory experiments where subjects were allowed to make
hurtful responses towards others, the adolescents who had
more opportunities than other groups to 'discharge aggression'
in delinquent peer-group activities, and by watching violent
movies and TV were, for example, the *most* willing, not the
least, to pull shock levers to the highest intensities (L.D. Eron
1963). Many other examples can be quoted where exposure to
violent material makes the subjects more violent afterwards if
they are given opportunities for aggression, than if they had
seen non-violent material. Angering, or frustrating a person
first, then exposing him to violent material, still makes him
more, not less, likely to attack verbally or physically (R.H.
Walters and E. Llewellyn-Thomas 1963).

What about children 'acting out' or expressing their aggression in play or fantasy, to stop it coming out elsewhere? Feshbach, for example (1956), studied three groups of boys and girls
which met for 50-minute sessions over four weeks. Records,
stories and then free play on aggressive themes resulted in more
subsequent aggression on the part of the children towards each
other outside the context of the play themes, than did more
neutral themes. This rose with age. The same researcher later
found (1966) that aggressive play following frustration had no
cathartic effect—rather the opposite. Permitting children to
make verbal expressions of hostility towards the frustrator in
aggression experiments similarly increased, rather than
decreased, the subsequent aggressive behaviour.

But re-direction? Here the evidence suggests that sports, for
example, do not drain away aggression, but become the
instigator of it *once the observer of any game starts to construe its
meaning as violent.* Aggression spreads to a previously non-
aggression area instead of vice-versa, when subjects in experiments are encouraged to see a sports event in terms of vengeful
aggression or retaliation (Leonard Berkowitz). All this should
make people think twice about getting children or youths to see

sport in terms of aggressive battles. Only a few years ago, apart from Rangers and Celtic with their religious rivalries, hooliganism and football enthusiasm were distinct, but now the two have been indissolubly linked. The cues for violence are now so numerous and so strongly established that the atmosphere of football—crowd, noise, team-symbol, precipitates violence straight away among many younger spectators before the game even starts. Commentators who seek to make sport more exciting by talking of annihilations and massacres had perhaps better watch their language, before cricket and rugby go the same way. Sport is a particularly sensitive area, since evidence suggests that a person already in an excited state due to *any* cause, is easier to precipitate into aggression than someone in emotional equilibrium (Leonard Berkowitz 1962 and D. Zillman 1971).

The pairing of aggressive suggestions with pleasantly heightened emotional states, or socially desired and approved images and activities, serves to break down any anxiety or aversion that person may originally have about enjoying his own or another's aggression. With experimental audiences who were shown *A Clockwork Orange* (*British Medical Journal* August 1973), the music and sex sweetened the gratuitous violence which—on its own—tended to frighten and revolt many adults with strong inhibitions against such spectacles.

As there is nothing intrinsic to an object or event which marks it off as an aggressive cue, but only its connection with something which already has this function, the list of items capable of causing the incitement of aggression by association is depressingly endless. Hostility can be generated simply from a pairing of negative expressions with personal names (Leonard Berkowitz and Russell G. Geen 1966). Perhaps it is this ease of learning which has made many people believe in an 'instinctual aggression' bubbling away and waiting to burst, completely independent of the environment. However, if there has been this misunderstanding, it is a dangerous one. Demands for facilities to 're-direct' aggression are in themselves a call to proliferate it further rather than reduce it.

The film industry, with growing pretensions to seriousness, occasionally finds it necessary to justify its increasingly violent fare in more high-minded terms than box-office returns. Here it finds the 'catharsis' argument very serviceable indeed—in effect, it is doing just what the psychologist is supposed to have ordered. The celluloid version of the Roman circus displays ever more breathtaking butchery of man and animal, and is really doing society a therapeutic service. Thus *Rollerball* and *Death Race 2000*.

The atmosphere in Britain over the possibly harmful effects of media violence—especially on children—is uneasy, but still inclined to a timid agnosticism. The mere existence of rival 'catharsis' and 'learning' hypotheses, invariably creates the superficially fair-minded impression that nothing is proven. And where some barriers are set up against the tide, this is usually more to placate outraged public opinion, than out of any conviction from the evidence.

There are, however, a large number of experiments on the effects of the observation of violence, including media violence, and I have room to mention only some of them here.

The experimental design of Professor Albert Bandura and his colleagues at Stanford University (1965) is usually to place children in a familiar playroom, where, as if by chance, somebody (whether another child, an adult or teacher) plays with toys. He may strike inflatable dolls, throw objects, mutilate animal toys and dolls, use hostile language, and so forth. Later the children who accidentally observed this behaviour are allowed into a room similarly equipped. Quite normal, middle-class children invariably engage in the aggressive acts they have witnessed, adding their own variations on the theme; the behaviour often indicating high emotional arousal as well as simple 'cold' copying. Films are as effective as live performers in teaching the children. Numerous other studies with children show a repetition of aggressive acts after watching them live or on film, and each time it is clear that the children not only imitate specific aggressive behaviours, but *generally* behave more aggressively, improvising and utilising aggressive responses they have seen in other contexts. As Urie Bronfenbrenner says, the child who witnesses aggressive behaviour not only mimics but 'takes on their expressed motivations as a model for his own, and then adapts his concrete actions to the conditions of the new and different situations presented by the fictional experiment' (1971). The training of persons in verbal hostility also leads them to acquire this presented interpersonal 'mood' (Leonard Berkowitz 1973, Clemens A. Loew

1967 and I.O. Lovaas 1961). (In connection with this, one might question the modern practice of permitting children the free use of obscene expletives as a token of 'broadmindedness'. They were strongly discouraged in the past, not simply because they were naughty words of the same class as penis and bum which might offend Aunt Maude, but because they were felt to cultivate in the child a vicious orientation to other people).

But is the imitative aggressiveness of children 'for real'? One well-known study tested not simply children's readiness to attack objects, or each other, but strangers. Here young boys observed on film an adult male model attacking a life-size clown (including shooting at it with a toy machine-gun, beating it with plastic mallets and verbally abusing it). Half the experimental group and half the controls then went to play in a room where there was a real human being dressed as a clown standing by, while the other half played in a room with a plastic doll. None of the children who had not seen the film showed aggression towards the real clown, whereas those who had witnessed it imitated the assaults sufficiently to leave bruising (M.A. Hanratty, R.M. Liekert, L.W. Morris and L.E. Fernandez 1969). The limitations placed on the children's copying seemed due more to the innocuousness of the weapons than any lack of motivation.

As to the reality or otherwise to children of fictional episodes involving violence, an American survey gives 46 per cent of adolescents saying that crime shows were likely to 'tell about life the way it really is'. Many boys perceived TV violence as realistic, and these boys tended to be the more delinquent. About two-thirds of the respondents thought that both the situations and characters on their favourite programmes were true to life, with highly violent programmes as likely to be considered as realistic as low to moderately violent shows. Data suggest that the position is little different in this country (J.M. Mcleod, G.K. Atkins and S.H. Chaffee 1972).

It can be argued that the effects of witnessing aggression are very ephemeral. Yet studies all point to an opposite conclusion—that there is a permanent, or semi-permanent addition to the individual's repertoire. One study of children made eight months after they had seen a violent film found that they could still perform 40 per cent of the TV models' hostile actions (D.J. Hicks 1965 and 1968).

Two objections are made by the 'non-proven' school to studies of aggression like those I have been talking about. One is that in real life the situation is more complex, with perhaps countervailing factors. The other is that the experimental situation fails to isolate the factor of exposure to violent stimuli, and is therefore picking up something else which makes people more violent after they have seen violent material. The last one was put by Enid Wistrich (former Chairman of the GLC Film Viewing Board) in a way which leaves open whether her demonstration of scientific ignorance is wanton, or genuine. She dismisses the evidence from studies of imitative aggression simply by asserting that there are correlations between many things, including European stork populations and the birthrate. However, there is a host of uncontrolled variables in her example, which the aggression experimenters have not allowed to flood their laboratories. The whole point of controlled experiments is that all factors but the one under test are, as far as possible, eliminated. The control group is matched, except for not being exposed to this one factor, so that any differences which emerge between it and the experimental groups are clearly associated non-randomly with this. When results become repeatable over a series of tests, and appear to be corroborated by other designs of experiment, a causal connection becomes increasingly probable. If there is a third factor at work which is unknown or has been overlooked then it would need to be something which always accompanies the antecedent conditions—in this case the presentation of violence—and the onus is on critics to suggest what it is.

Overall, ten thousand children and adolescents from every kind of background and in different countries have taken part in the studies reviewed by Liebert, Neale and Davidson in their *The Early Window: Effects of Television on Children and Youth,* and the evidence all pointed one way, to the conclusion that 'the watching of violence produces increased aggressive behaviour in the young', with the progression from imitative practice to a 'lasting addition to the repertoire of behaviour'. (On Wistrich's criterion, all laboratory experiments with drugs, carcinogens and pollutants tell us nothing because they merely show 'correlations' of arbitrary factors.) Judged by the criteria which educational psychologists find useful in predicting the effectiveness of teaching programmes, the characters in violent TV

and cinema shows would seem to rate high in teaching effectiveness. Surely, by all very well demonstrated learning
criteria, are we to believe that attractive, powerful and admired
characters, demonstrating techniques of violence and a ready
acceptance of brutality as a solution to problems and an enjoyable adventure, will fail to be successful as teachers to those
children, youths and even adults, who are regularly exposed
to them? (See, for example, O.J. Harvey and J. Rutherford
1960.)

Such an assumption runs directly counter to what is known
about learning and about the best employment of audio-visual
aids to teach specific skills and behaviour. The denial of harm
in media violence is puzzling in an age so finicky over the
possible effects of minute amounts of substances in our diet on a
minute number of people. The extremely tenuous claims that
petrol lead in the atmosphere is leading to delinquency in
children—via hyperactivity—appear to be taken more seriously than all the pile of research papers filled with imitative
aggression.

'But most people do not come away from violent entertainment and instantly enact it.' This objection is essentially saying
that many other considerations and countervailing factors exist
in real life to shape the person's behaviour and attitudes which
do not operate in the artificially restrictive conditions of the
laboratory. This is correct, but it also focuses attention on the
actual presence and strength of those countervailing factors. As
we have already seen, once a delinquent act becomes part of the
individual's repertoire, the weight is thrown onto normative
and social controls to prevent him repeating it. The vigilance
has to be accepted as permanent—as long as these techniques
are remembered, transmitted, *and* possible. The trend in film
violence has been away from the historical context, where the
relevance to present day life may be tenuous and the techniques
impractical, to modern contexts using familiar objects. Things
are very different from the days when Errol Flynn swung from
the rigging.

The more that ways and means to commit crimes and
aggression are suggested, the stronger and more complex must
social control mechanisms be. Formally and informally, these
are at an all-time low for juveniles. And if anti-social techniques
and inhumane attitudes are disseminated, it is largely in the

absence of rivals. The child in the peer group is ideally placed to receive the heartless message of the 'fun' violence industry:

> The vacuum, moral and emotional, created by this state of affairs [the withdrawal of the adult from the child's life] is then filled—by default—on the one hand by the daily message of commercialism and violence, and on the other, by the socially isolated, age-segregated peer group, with its limited capacities as a humanising agent (Urie Bronfenbrenner 1971).

The sociologist Andreski might well claim that:

> Now, for the first time in recorded history, Western liberalism offers us the spectacle of a system which not only has given up the task of moral education, but actually employs vast resources and means of persuasion of unprecedented power to extirpate the customs, norms and ideals indispensable for its survival (*Telegraph Magazine* 1972).

However, perhaps the media simply reflect—neutrally—the rottenness of society, its growing violence and toleration of violence? This is often *factually* nonsense when we come to the multitude of shows and films crammed with more slaughter than any American cop might find in his lifetime in the inner city. We are all—by virtue of being social, communicating beings—adding something to the chain of reinforcements and the nature of standards. Whenever we look at the modern rise in crime we encounter that resignation which says that we are all to blame, and therefore, conveniently—no one is responsible. It is difficult to see how those who play back the viciousness of 'rotten' society for its delectation, cannot help but make society more readily accept what they want it to enjoy. There is now a dawning awareness in this country of television and film as a 'school for violence',* a phrase coined by Fredric Wertham. For the first time in a major public document, the Committee on the Future of Broadcasting (1977) cast its vote against the

---

* Whether crime and violence programmes arouse a lust for violence, reinforce it when it is present, show a way to carry it out, teach the child the best method to get away with it or merely blunt the child's (and adult's) awareness of its wrongness, television has become a school for violence (*The New York Times* 5 July 1964).

cathartic party. It stressed instead that evidence was on the side of the view that violence in the media did harm: having a particular impact on people whose attitudes and values are unformed and whose alternative sources of influence and information are meagre. Reports to the United States Government (where most research has been carried out) have long stressed such conclusions.* Even if we leave the whole matter of imitation or attitude-changes aside, we must ask ourselves whether or not the brutal smashing-up and torture of other human beings, like the baiting of animals or the battering of babies, is a fit subject to serve up as entertainment. The market is morally blind, and in all sorts of areas, limitations on profit maximisation for ethical reasons have had to be applied. In the area of entertainment, entrepreneurs will always push in the direction of maximising gain by maximising simple aggressive arousal. All that matters to them is that it should excite.

But not that, in one sense, the media do not 'reflect' some aspects of our society. The criminologists Sykes and Matza mention how there are pervasive attitudes running through our society, what they term 'subterranean values', which are tolerant, even admiring of hedonistic pursuits which are otherwise in conflict with widely held values. These centre not only on a male pursuit of thrills, but particularly, on an indulgence shown specifically to male aggression as both a means of gratification and getting one's way. Ambiguity exists in the condemnation of violence against the person, side by side with anxiety over boys who do not fight, and are 'cissy'. The dilemma is particularly developed in lower working-class groups, where sexual differentiation and inequality are most marked:

> The delinquent is the rogue male. His conduct may be viewed not only negatively . . . positively it may be viewed as the exploitation of modes of behaviour which are tradition-

* In Britain, William Belson's longitudinal study of boys' aggression (not yet published) has now clearly indicted the media as a significant contributor to violence. An American longitudinal study of the development of aggression, *Growing Up To Be Violent*, by Monroe M. Lefkowitz, Leonard D. Eron, Leopold O. Walder and L. Rowell Huesmann (Pergamon 1977), pinpoints violence in the media and low identification and interaction with parents transmitting alternative values as the major environmental cause of violence in children and adolescents.

ally symbolic of untrammelled masculinity . . . (G. Sykes and D. Matza 1961).

A strong repository for this particular subterranean value has, of course, been the cinema for many a long year. Traditionally, there was extreme sexual stereotyping, with the classic Western man whose natural red-bloodedness was properly turned against the outlaws, while a simpering pale girl, prone to fainting, slowed up the action and pleaded with him to settle down to peaceful family life—which, in the last reel, he eventually did. These stereotypes, and the simplified moralities associated with them, have indeed changed; but from the point of view of any effect on undersocialised juveniles, hardly for the better. The portrayal of male violence has become infinitely worse, an image of sadism and domination, ungraced by chivalry and without any framework of moral justification (occasionally a woman has her fun too by cutting out the tripes of her rapist). Indeed, recognition of rules is a token of degeneracy, and the male cleanses the world by snuffing out the weak and vulnerable in the Peckinpah genre of fantasies:

> To be able to hit hard and to strike terror in the hearts of one's opponents—that makes one count when the chips are down. . . . Hurting is a test of virtue and killing is the ultimate measure of man. Loss of life, limb, or mind, any diminution of the freedom of action, are the wages of weakness or sin in the symbolic shorthand of ritual drama. (C. Gerbner 1972)

Clearly, the manufacture of excitement by the entertainment industry in hating and hurting has now gone beyond the permission of the 'subterranean values' described by Sykes and Matza. The standard expression of these, in the pursuit of excitement and the demonstration of virility via aggression, was usually constrained by a minimum of rules about when, how and on whom. Notions of chivalry, correctness or fair play might rule out weapons other than fists, or 'real' harm without provocation, and so forth. What makes the old bruiser shake his head over the delinquent is his feeling that 'kids' have no style, no sense, no courage, and that they trivialise, degrade, even brutalise the manly virtues, with their group attacks on 'soft' targets—the old, women, younger children; their ready use of weapons, their kicking when down. But if Sykes and Matza claim that the delinquent oversteps the limits of the subterranean values and exists rather as their caricature, the values now suggested by the entertainment industry not only match him, but frequently outdo him in viciousness. Shouldn't we cease to buy?

And shouldn't we, in an era of greater sexual equality, stop buying the entire double-standard over male aggression and law-breaking, as we have stopped buying his licence for sexual gratification from women sworn to chastity? It is nothing less than extraordinary how the most striking feature of all delinquency samples, the ratio of males to females, usually escapes comment, let alone investigation. Virtually the only times the ratio itself is a matter of interest is when the gap appears to be narrowing, when terrible consequences are held out for society if the female rate of delinquency and violence reaches that of the male. I agree; seeing the recent fruits, largely of male labours, it *is* terrifying, and what's more, the gap *is* narrowing. In 1965 31,011 women appeared in court for indictable crime. In 1975 this had risen to 86,304. In 1965, 22 girls under 14 were charged with wounding. In 1975 there were 99 girls under 14 charged with that offence. Up to 17 the number has risen from 86 to 555 (Home Office Statistics, England and Wales 1975).

The lack of comment and investigation of the sex gap in offences owes a lot to the notion that, like sexuality in the past (and some would say over rape today), aggression and recklessness are supposed to be harder for boys to control, while female controls are taken for granted. There might be a tendency, noted by researchers, for boys to be more 'naturally' active and pursue (or not to be put off by) heavy stimulation, compared with girls, who are held to be more sensitive to language and social signals. However, both are disputed, as are the average levels of the difference (see, for example, discussion of John Archer and Barbara Lloyd 1974). But, even if it were true, does greater difficulty with the socialisation of boys compared with girls mean that this should be pursued *less* intensely? If the difference exists we seem to be responding to it in the wrong manner. Child-centred rearing, on top of the traditionally greater freedom accorded the male child, does not appear to be doing boys much good, as they are also more affected by the resultant hyperactivity, maladjustment and educational

handicaps. Even if the same amount of supervision and upholding of norms was practised with boys as for girls, this would
probably go some way to narrow the gap in comparative
offence rates. In modern China, in fact (Kessen 1975), observers reported that the educators mention that boys are first
inclined to be 'naughtier', but the response is to intensify the
process of socialisation and cultural induction. Under such a
regime, sex differences in behaviour are greatly diminished.

We certainly have no excuse to exacerbate male aggressiveness by specifically providing instruction and cues for it. (In
experiments with the *learning* of aggressive responses and hostile attitudes, it has been found that girls will pick these up as
readily as boys if they are given appropriate examples to copy,
or if they are reinforced. Particularly when they think that they
are undetected, girls can become quite as aggressive as boys.
The relative constraint on female repetition of violent acts that
they have observed, may depend on the serious deterrent represented by the acute shock and social rejection which is likely
to be the reaction of the surrounding community.)

A concerted effort to reverse the rates of violence and delinquency must involve a long, hard, critical look at what is
probably the last bastion of male privilege, and what form we
want the irreversible move to greater equality to take.

15 Opportunities and Repercussions

The 'management' of delinquency is also a matter of the informal and formal controls which apply in the wider society. These, of course, can and do feed back into the home and school. The controls operating in the wider community can roughly be divided into controls on the opportunities to commit offences and the repercussions which follow on the individual's behaviour. There are also those more subtle, involved social policies or circumstances which, usually unintentionally, either exacerbate or discourage tendencies to lawbreaking.

First of all, it has always been a truism that crime is opportunity, or alternatively, that virtue is a lack of it. In the Home Office report of that name illustrations were given of the reductions and increases in the rate of certain types of offence in relation to certain specific changes in the individual's access to the setting in which they might be perpetrated. For example, since 1971 all new cars have been fitted with steering column locks. The proportion of new cars stolen, or taken without authority, in a Metropolitan Police sample, fell from 20.9 per cent in 1969 to 5.1 per cent in 1973. However, total car thefts rose, as thieves diverted their attentions to older models. (In West Germany, where all cars have been fitted with anti-theft devices since 1963, all car thefts have decreased sharply.) On double-decker buses in Britain (there is always more damage on the upper deck), there was five times as much damage on rear-staircase buses, and twenty times as much on one-man operated types.

Other restrictions on opportunity involve, for example, the familiar one of limiting access to guns, knives, or other offensive weapons. The astonishingly high murder rate in America is partly due to the ready availability of fire-arms to a population steeped in lessons on when and how to use them. In this country the use of air-guns in a record 2,518 serious crimes in 1975 (with 1,795 cases of serious violence and two deaths), is partly due to the ease of availability to children and young persons (unsupervised use is legally allowed at fourteen and anyone who *looks* over seventeen can get an air-gun over the counter). It is intended that the law should now be changed to limit availability.

Reduction in opportunity can also mean more locks and bars, guard dogs, fences, and wired glass. But many things that come under the heading of restriction of access to the law-breaker, mean restriction of access for everybody. Urban civilised life is steadily being squeezed until it ceases to exist—no civic architecture, no gardens, no trees, no memorials, no sculpture, no shops displaying wares, and no safety in being out in the rubble of the boarded-up wilderness. Nothing remotely stealable or destructible can be left unguarded; the victim restricts access by staying at home. Some of our inner cities and housing developments may be rather like this already. But this kind of cure looks surprisingly like the illness: people want to be rid of delinquents, not more circumscribed by them. They are not an impersonal natural force like the earthquakes or tornadoes that some communities have to adapt to. Surely, then, there should be restrictions on what the individual himself may do, instead of keeping things out of his way?

What works against everyday surveillance and willingness to uphold norms? Why is adult supervision and control so *difficult*? A lot has been made of Oscar Newman's *Defensible Space* about the impact of architecture on crime and delinquency. It has now become a cliché of the 'broken home' variety, that tower blocks, for example, are the villains of the piece. Change your housing and you won't have such high delinquency (particularly vandalism). Councils have tried hard to comply with this demand—at least in recent housing developments—and have generally removed families with children from high-rise flats for this and other reasons. Newman believed that many estates failed to encourage residents to protect the areas around them, because they were too 'public' for anybody to regard them as their own territory: they were simply thoroughfares for strangers.

A promising theory. To test Newman's hypothesis, a Home Office research project on vandalism was conducted by comparing rates of vandalism on fifty inner London public housing estates of differing designs, but all blocks of various kinds (see Tony Marshall's summary). Results showed that the damage on such estates tends to be concentrated in public areas, especially the more secluded, like underground garages, and predictably damage was helped by the use of easily destructible materials, such as glass. The same results were found for Blackburn. Yet the much-publicised connection between vandalism and high-rise dwellings failed to materialise. It was true that the higher the buildings, the more the public areas suffered damage, but tenure type was more important. Private dwellings in high blocks suffered less than public dwellings in lower-rise accommodation. The Sheffield study similarly found connections between tenure and crime rate (see A.E. Bottoms 1976; A.E. Bottoms and J. Baldwin 1976).

In the light of this finding it is not surprising that councils who had hoped to reduce vandalism with nice low-rise dwellings with gardens have been disappointed; and despite a nation-wide policy of removing children from tower blocks, the rate of vandalism continues to rise:

> Vandalism in high-rise blocks in north London has become so bad that housing officials are considering a plan to 'seal them off'.
>
> Intercom systems may be installed to restrict access to stairways and lifts to visitors approved by families living in the flats.
>
> The council is seeking the cooperation of tenants in a big drive against vandalism on housing estates which is estimated to cost ratepayers more than £20,000 a year. A special party has been set up to consider the problem.
>
> Hopes that vandalism would be drastically reduced when families moved into new homes with gardens have been dashed by the experience at Surrey Street, where 500 new homes built three years ago are, according to the council 'slowly going downhill under a relentless wave of minor vandalism'. (*Evening Standard* 5 October 1976)

If children do not vandalise their housing in private developments this is presumably because there is the closest possible relationship between the destruction and the payer; a household which destroys its own goods fines itself heavily. Variations on the theme of owner-occupation, in place of council housing in as many cases as possible, would also seem desirable from a number of other points of view: for instance, it is cheaper, it is preferred. Similar considerations of directness might apply to vandalism in schools, where children are (supposedly) under fairly continuous adult supervision. Would alteration of the accounting and financing system in education lead to more care at classroom level? Suppose payment for damage came out of the allocations spent directly by staff, rather than being automatically covered by the authorities from the general maintenance funds? That it doesn't at the moment, might partly explain the phenomenon where, at the point of occurrence in the schools, vandalism and violence are played down or ignored, while at the spending end, they are admitted by Ministry, Local Authority, and Insurer to be vast and expanding. (At least, it *enables* this stance to be adopted.)

Most significant of the correlates of vandalism found by the Home Office in its studies was the type of household composition found on estates. The most important predictor of vandalism was the number of children per household in the block. Where there were large numbers of children, all estates tended to have a vandalism problem, only moderately affected by the design of the buildings. But if the numbers of children were kept within a certain limit, only those buildings which were 'indefensible' in the Newman term, with poor possibilities for surveillance, had high vandalism rates. Thus the ratio of children to adults is important for policy-makers. The study concludes that the 'potential for normal social control within a community is severely restricted if larger-than-average families are concentrated together, thus causing an unmanageably high ratio of children to adults'.

Indeed, the rate of vandalism as a function of the ratio of the presence of children to adults is illustrated by the findings already mentioned: those facilities where children are likely to be most alone with each other—playgrounds, parks, open spaces and empty property—are the most vandalised. As far as repercussions on housing go, policy is more important than architecture. The present policies of councils in allocating council housing concentrate together large families, and families at their peak child-bearing years. In fact, public housing policies may contribute to the development of 'delinquent estates' and in an extended sense increase 'deprivation', by their very policy of allocation on the basis of need, particularly with regard to the numbers of children in the family:

> . . . striking is the way teenage wives respond to their housing situation and prospects. Many teenagers start their married life living with relatives. Their aim is to achieve a council tenancy. But the workings of the public sector of the housing market are based on quite different principles to those of other sectors . . . those most in need have priority over those who can provide adequately for the present. If they are to share with relatives, it is in their best interests (from a housing point of view) to share with those relatives who can afford the least room, not the most. Similarly, if they rent a flat privately, it is best to rent somewhere bad enough to merit a closure order, rather than somewhere spacious, healthy and self-contained. And if they have one child it is best to produce another as quickly as possible. (*Teenage Brides* Bernard Ineichen 1975)

The younger father finds that parenthood rules out apprenticeship or training. Trying to keep a family on an unskilled teenager's or young adult's wages may be as difficult as on benefit, or more so. Work may only be worthwhile if benefits can be drawn as well. Thus one sees a drift from working on the sly in a variety of casual, shady jobs, to direct participation in adult criminal activities—receiving, fraud, stripping houses, and so on. Again, the 'polarisation' of estates might mean that such life-styles become common. The person does not feel himself under pressure or scrutiny from his neighbours to change his behaviour. Thus, in a more extenuated way, housing simply on a need-criterion can exacerbate those factors which prevent a youth from acquiring the training and the job which would counteract lawbreaking, and it might cultivate a cynical attitude to the authorities—nobody gets anything by right or merit, only by subterfuge and pretence.

If children will damage things when given the opportunity to do it, adult *proximity* is as important as the ratio to children, or more important. Tony Marshall speaks of the need to integrate the activities of children and adolescents into the same areas as those used by adults. A reduction in areas where children may go alone, for example, parks, football matches, and so on, would seem to be indicated. But first, advocates of the need to create 'community' in housing developments might consider some American research on the much-lauded public life of the 'slum' which planners have been so desperate to re-create in modern developments. Charles Holahan looked at three adjacent housing areas with comparable populations in New York, but of contrasting environments, that is tenement slum and remodelled estate (with 'creative play' facilities). Despite very good facilities, 'community life' often failed to get off the ground on the remodelled estates. One factor which he found might be relevant is that in contrast to traditional public settings, their modern counterparts are heavily geared to children. Instead of the adults getting together over the swings and sandpits, they only serve to drive them away. (Allotments might be better, where the adults can take the initiative and bring the children into their activities instead.) If one considers the community areas in, say, a traditional Mediterranean town—cafés, squares, steps—the striking thing is that they are primarily public places for adult relaxation, to which children have to adapt, and not purpose-built playgrounds where children dominate.

In connection with these observations, one must consider the growth—not of child and adolescent drinking *per se* (discussed in Clive Jones Davies and Ronald G. Cave's *The Disruptive Pupil in the Secondary School*)—but the consumption of alcohol by the young without adult supervision. The sale to the young at supermarkets needs to be examined, and so does the growth of what can only be described as the 'children's pub': premises which cater almost exclusively for teenagers (and attract those even younger), where there is no more place for adults than there was for women in the Glasgow dram shops of a generation ago. Commercially, here, as elsewhere, it is more profitable to concentrate upon one section of the market and monopolise it, than to diffuse and diversify your efforts to bring in small slices of several. And aspiring entrepreneurs here, as elsewhere, represent this as a great social gain. There is 'something for everybody', and if 'the old regulars don't want loud pop music' they can always find somewhere which will cater for them—and so the age groups are again segregated. This development makes the notion of the nice family outing to the local, beloved by the would-be reformers of the licensing laws, rather quaint. An alternative development which might be more beneficial is a hard look before licences are issued, at the sort of clientele the premises aim to attract, and a stronger line taken over under-age drinking, perhaps by ending the over fourteen 'entry-without-drinking' rule which can result in the *under* fourteens entering *and* drinking on licensed premises.

Adult proximity has been reduced by the acceptance of the child as arbiter of his own movements. 'Bedtime', which used to remove children from the streets in late evening, is virtually extinct, as is any insistence on the young person being at home by a specified time. The law of neglect is not used against parents who permit even a young child to wander the streets at night, even if he be on premises like railways. More police checks on the return home of children on the streets late at night might provoke an outcry about liberty from a vocal and influential minority; but if things get much worse in some areas, we may have that curfew yet.

But beyond surveillance and proximity is intervention. The environment can only make it easier to stop offences being committed; there has also to be the willingness and ability to do so. I recall one landscaped venture into communal intimacy, which must have allowed for maximum surveillance from the houses which opened into walled gardens. The children were busily engaged in knocking the walls down and smashing the plant pots with hammers. Why are the public so passive? They, after all, are supposed to have tougher attitudes to delinquency than the 'experts' so why don't they intervene? The simple answer is that they know to their cost that if they do, they will get no support whatever from the law and the authorities, and may even be in trouble themselves. To blame the public for passivity when they observe offences being committed is like blaming a man for not fighting when both hands are tied behind his back. Even the attempt to create 'defensible space' backfires—the children use it to screen and control the adults instead. In the housing development I have just mentioned, on my visit a boy drove his bike into me asking 'What the fucking hell do you want here?' The adult residents hated the place, they just wanted to be out of it as much as possible. Similarly, a Rotherhithe case I came across involved a woman who called the police as the children put out the windows on the ground floor. The police arrived under a hail of stones, and gave the children a 'ticking off' which was treated with derision. The woman could not afterwards go out, as she was kicked and punched; had lighted paper pushed through the door and her flat broken into. She fled to her daughter.

In the face of this kind of situation, appeals for the manifestation of 'community control' (spoken of as the 'missing link' in the containment of delinquency) are just more of those fine-sounding nothings. There is a marked reluctance to spell out the implications, and a vague hope that 'the community' can exercise its influence without any of the concrete instruments for doing so.

> People are often afraid to intervene in any vandalism they see, or if they do they are abused by the children. A common reason given by tenants on the Manchester estate was 'fear of reprisals'. Lacking in many city areas is informal social control—the kind exerted purely by the fact that people are continually around and by integrating children's and adolescents' activities into the same areas used by the adult community. Police and 'anti-vandal patrols' cannot be everywhere at once. (Tony Marshall)

Purely by people being around—but people *are* around, and vandals often completely disregard the presence of adults as a contingency to be reckoned with. Children, for example, aim their balls at the windows of offices I know of, and simply go in and ask for them back if they go through. The citizen reads of the policeman off duty who encountered boys ransacking his mother's flat, and made them clean up—his career hardly benefited as a result. A farmer came home to find children riding a tractor through crops and fences; she lashed out with a riding crop and was heavily fined. The citizen is duly warned and duly cautious. Even if the press exaggerated, the accused perhaps over-reacted and a jury is sympathetic—it is no consolation:

> ... farmer Mr Maggs—tired of vandals damaging his land—took the law into his own hands when he saw two 16-year-old youths running riot in a field of seed potatoes.

He boxed their ears and sent them packing, confident that right was on his side.

He could scarcely believe it when police told him he would be prosecuted for assaulting two boys and causing them actual bodily harm.

But Mr Maggs, who claims that the police have done nothing to stop vandals causing hundreds of pounds worth of damage at his 70 acre farm . . . has been cleared by a jury at Bedford Crown Court. (*Sunday Express* 31 October 1976)

So how is the community to exercise its control? Resident patrols and security rotas are felt to be distasteful in the extreme. A conference delegate from Bromley describes how the Borough had set up a twelve-man, mobile, citizens anti-vandal force led by an ex-superintendent, which in a year had tackled 144 incidents (but made only five arrests) and cut the public cost of vandalism from £30,000 to £2,300 per annum. This was condemned as 'obscene' and 'fascist' by the Coventry delegate (the Chairman of Coventry Education Committee), with the rejoinder from another delegate that 'vandalism must be kept away from those who did not understand the real nature of the problem or its causes' (*Times Educational Supplement* 6 October 1972).

'Vigilantes' conjures up stereotyped pictures of personal vengeance, quasi-legal mobs, bullies, B-Specials, or worse. But collective grass-roots action against delinquency would reaffirm the nature and necessity of law by people in the community, as a living force within that community, more than it would express arbitrariness and disregard for law. In an article entitled *Vigilantes—why not?* Laurie Taylor acknowledges that ordinary people are very worried about delinquency even if he doesn't quite share their concern. He supports the idea of vigilantes, partly it seems for the same reasons that he has sympathy for the delinquent in his deprivation and frustration—it is freedom from the alien impositions of 'the system' outside.

The sordid basics of 'community control' require adults to stop delinquents forcibly in the act, confident that they will be broadly supported by the law: to be willing to grab the arm, cuff the ear and make the culprit clean up after him. The essence of community control of delinquency is what that policeman did.

The community would be able to exercise its functions of informal social controls, if the law recognised and delineated reasonable steps an adult may take to perform them. And there must be deliberate discrimination between the person who intervenes to stop theft, violence and vandalism, and the person who threatens or exacts reprisals because somebody else has tried to stop his child's delinquencies—discrimination between action to uphold the norms embodied in our laws, and action to protect the lawbreakers.

One sometimes hears the very existence of our juvenile courts and penal measures cited as evidence of our hard and punitive attitudes towards children, compared with the informalities of primitive and traditional communities. It seems to be fondly imagined that because these communities have no formal penal system they are cheerfully permissive towards childrens' misdemeanours, at any rate they secure cooperation without resorting to sanction or punishment, or ever frightening 'kids'. In reality, such communities are far closer to the stories still retailed by those brought up in communities of the past: what happened to them at home was nothing to what happened on the way there. That such communities have little child-delinquency is due not to some mysterious primitive influence over their children. It scarcely needs saying that legal provisions for informal community controls need not in any way constitute a charter to bully children: but simply the restoration of a balance between the rights of children and the claims of adults, both being subject to the law. Informal controls in themselves can never replace the latter, but must be subservient to it.

Romanticism about the people, to whom are attributed an aversion to the police, heavily affects the attitudes of those like Laurie Taylor. The belief appears to be that—if the people want them—informal controls can fully replace formal ones. However, the concept of law runs deep in English society as a stable framework to appeal to for justification, to which to relate one's own and others' actions. Attitudes to the seeming inaction of tenants on estates is often bedevilled by the notion that a sort of 'direct democracy' can spring complete from grass-roots level, requiring no official contrivance or backing. Yet leaving people to develop spontaneously their own community of interests can simply be another abdication of responsibility which leaves them in a condition essentially little different from the one they find themselves in at present. This is the very reason why they want help from above, some sanction backed by an authority beyond themselves. In this country people are simply not prepared to lay down—let alone enforce on their neighbours—rules which are not embedded in law. The withdrawal of formal controls from the streets of this country would leave a vacuum—not just for the most unscrupulous thug—but for the Krays and Mafias of this world. Laurie Taylor is so mesmerised by the piggies in blue that he would make a tasty supper for the Big Bad Wolf. Certainly, some areas of New York which are controlled by the Mafia also have some of the safest streets. Professional criminals no more like disorder and randomness than anyone else and their public relations are usually excellent.

If the adult community is at present prevented by restrictions and uncertainties from operating informal controls against delinquency, are the formal controls in any way compensating for this, or are there plans to fill this acknowledged gap? We have seen, depressingly enough, how far the results of the 1969 Act have differed from what was confidently promised. When the children in 'care' continue and even accelerate their anti-social adventures, the eventual exasperated response of the reformers is to demand *more* secure places in which to lock up *more* children at an astronomical cost. Unwilling to manipulate the use of traditional, everyday penalties and controls, our reformers either go on doing nothing, or swing to far heavier-handed measures under another name. Custody is used, disguised as therapy. As we saw, Clarke and Cornish found no therapeutic benefits in the Community Homes which they could recommend to the Home Office, and therefore requested that their custodial and deterrent functions be investigated. What about the second? Despite being officially repudiated as desirable to use against juveniles, is deterrence in fact functioning, or can it be made to function?

If the medical model of delinquency were correct, clearly the notion of deterrence would be ignorant primitivism, and punishment would be indistinguishable from pointless cruelty. But we have good reason to think that the medical model is wrong. Surprisingly, there has been little investigation of the deterrent effect, and no repudiation from evidence. It appears to be an *a priori* decision that there is no such effect, and therefore nothing of any interest to investigate. One sometimes hears defenders of the present policies concede that there might be some such effect, but they quickly scuttle to safety by their insistence that it would be quite impossible to measure. Yet there are many areas where deterrence is believed in. Heavy fines or imprisonment are urged against the dog smuggler, the drunken driver or the possessor of dangerous drugs, and whatever the actual effects, it is rarely argued that they have none at all. It appears to be in connection with those crimes where law intersects heavily with morality—violence against the person, theft, and so on—that deterrence is more likely to be denied, and claims made for the deep social or emotional, and thus uncontrollable, irrational origin of the crime. Yet rational consequence is mentioned, for example, by children and adolescents in studies of delinquency. When Wilmott asked 800 youths what was the main thing that put them off breaking the law, a substantial minority said that they were put off by the fear of being caught by the police. Belson's study of self-reported theft reported the boys as saying that the main, immediate reasons for thieving were that they thought that it was all right to steal; their friends stole, it was fun and they did not expect to get caught.

Some of those who argue the impossibility of investigating deterrent effects seem to think that it would entail identifying and interviewing all those who, for example, didn't steal but would have done. This is not so. Essentially, it would involve careful comparison of offence rates before and after specific, substantial changes in the penalties. Crucial factors would be things like the extent of public knowledge of the changes, an estimate of the likelihood of being caught, and public belief about the likelihood. A wide range of offences would need to be studied, and allowance made for generalisation from one kind of offence to another, possible replacement of one by another, social attitudes to the offence and many other variables. That some individual offenders are quite unaffected by consequences is doubtless true, but beside the point. What is being sought is a mass effect. No one denies that such research would be difficult, but it is possible.

The dismissal of the deterrent effect draws a lot on the ideal of the final solution. Any proposal that will not eradicate crime and delinquency once and for all is a shabby compromise or only a stop-gap, until we get at the *real, underlying* problem. Again, the essential normality of rule-breaking and rule-breakers and the permanence of rule-breaking in human societies is denied (with its implications that controls are always going to be with us). It is as if, in not being able to abolish law-breaking, we must not contain it. One objection is that when deterrent policies are applied, some offences still occur; and it is also felt that even if people have been deterred through fear of the consequences, their criminal dispositions have still not been cured. But deterrence is concerned with numbers, and crime prevention is not thought control. Success of deterrence consists in minimising those criminal inclinations that are translated into action. In Scotland, heavier penalties on older football hooligans in the higher Sheriffs' courts have been followed by a fall in the violence and damage at matches —whatever many of the fans might feel in their hearts. (This is not to say that deterrence alone could contain crime in society. I have emphasised the need for a minimal broad, moral underpinning to the law if it is to be enforceable, but this should not be confused with the conversion of every would-be offender.)

To function as a deterrent, penalties must be clearly and positively related to the offence, following as a consequence of this and nothing else. (In America, the uncertainities of the legal process have long been partially blamed for the high crime rate.) To the public, the old Approved School, like the Borstal for the older offender, was a punishment for young law-breakers, as much as prison was for adult ones. The philosophy of 'care' sought to break down the punitive associations and represent the junior penal establishments as places for mind-cures, where the young could sort out their personal problems. Any success in the aim of removing the stigma of being sent away must, by its very nature, undermine the deterrent function, in that it is no longer a loss of freedom consequent on law-breaking.

At the same time, because they are unrelated to the offence so considered, care orders, unlike sentences, are open-ended. It is possible to put a care order on a twelve-year-old and have it run until his eighteenth birthday. (What does an adult have to do to merit six years?) And this decision, committing someone to custody or not, is made by extra-legal agencies answerable to no one, whose criteria and aims are inaccessible even to the Law Lords. It is ironic that the enormous power the care order gives to the social services has only really been realised in an accidental way, when it was proposed by the recent Government paper on the workings of the 1969 Act, to give magistrates the power to specify what should happen to a child in care, (after so many reports of absconding offenders). It was suddenly understood that this would give the magistrates the right to confine an offender in a secure unit for up to six years and it is, accordingly, unlikely to be implemented. (The old Approved School sentence was for a fixed period.)

Part of the public's hostility towards the social services has been based not simply on ignorant prejudice, but on their very secrecy and idiosyncratic behaviour, compared with the formal, understood processes of law and punishment. There is little complaint or criticism of the multitude of day-to-day 'fixing' activities of social workers over housing, benefits, services to the aged, and the rest. But Orwellian language of 'client' and 'help', applied to delinquents and baby-batterers, attempts the impossible when it tries to convert matters of law and morality into those of care and services; the confusion it engenders is all too apparent. And, all too often, the arrogance of the professional social worker—an arrogance even in failure—does not help his standing and reputation. It is no use accusing the public of undue suspicion when the operations are hidden from its view. The public hears apocryphal stories of social workers telling children to steal from some shops rather than others: or complaining that their young client, with fifty-two offences to his name, wouldn't have such a bad record if the police didn't keep picking him up: or of cases such as the boy of fourteen who committed over sixty offences of theft while actually in care; and the boy of thirteen in care for burglary who ran away sixteen times and was arrested after committing a hundred offences during his latest period of freedom. These strongly suggest that care orders are not merely inept but create a sanctuary beyond the reach of the law, like that run by the medieval clergy. It is no use protesting that these are untypical, if they cannot publicly be shown to be so. Those who operate in secret have always been thought to have something to hide, and power without scrutiny is, rightly or wrongly, thought to be abused.

A parallel uncertainty prevails over the payment of fines. Government spokesmen are not sure what can be done—if anything—to get a fine paid, so it is hardly surprising that the public are in deepest ignorance. What cannot be done is clearer than what can. A juvenile is not liable for his debts because he cannot own property, nor can he stand in contempt of the court. Thus he cannot be served with an order for distraint. Can a parent or guardian be responsible for his debts? Not really, since the parent did not commit the offence. Actually, there are provisions in law—unused provisions—for the parent to compensate for the damage his child between the ages of 10 and 14 might do. It is difficult to see how these provisions would work out before precedents have been set, and the same difficulties arise as over the enforcement of fines. (Compensation has largely remained a dead letter, for the same reason that levels of fines have been allowed to atrophy—that is the 1969 promise to end punitive and deterrent measures for juveniles.)

In the light of both the measures open to the court and the steps actually taken against the juvenile offender, is the public necessarily mistaken and too defeatist, when it feels that 'nothing can be done'? To the delinquent the opportunity cost is negligible or very small. The police are likely to evaluate action in terms of time and effort against the outcome of a discharge or tiny fine; preliminary investigation by police liaison and social services may either rule out any further action, or terminate it with a caution: the court itself will hardly find that the average case of vandalism or theft (and a delinquent with a home no different from millions of other citizens), merits setting in motion the whole apparatus of care proceedings. Age puts most juveniles out of the reach of Borstal (and anyway, for many offences, it is a sledgehammer to crack a nut), just as age puts the under-tens completely out of reach of formal controls, while juveniles of any age are not amenable to informal controls. Our would-be reporter of offences is, on the other hand, likely to have to go on living near the juvenile offender. The only certain result might be that he will suffer more.

It is interesting that a more matter-of-fact, deterrent approach to offenders has recently been suggested in place of the therapeutic policy, on the grounds that it might be *less* heavy-handed in many instances. As Norman Tutt mentions, if

the role of the care order and treatment were changed to one of
deterrence, the 'sentence' would be more certain, and shorter
for many offenders: they would, in fact, be comparable to those
on adults for similar offences. He points out that, unlike the
judiciary, social services have no historical experience analog-
ous to case law, on which to draw in making their decisions; and
he sketches a possible policy of fixed court sentences, related to
the offence alone via a case law, with the provision for mitiga-
tion after sentence is passed. Certainly, fixed sentencing could
be defended as more equitable in relating the juvenile's offence
closely to the repercussions. Now the latter are related to vague
background factors over which the juvenile has no control; he
might end up in a community home because his family is
drunken and neglectful, a matter which is hardly his fault, and
which he can do little about. To argue in terms of fairness is
already to abandon the care and treatment vocabulary in
favour of the concepts of punishment and responsibility: the
offender becomes once again a rational agent, capable of choice
and control and part of the same moral community of rights
and obligations as his accusers.

Social workers themselves have frequently said that society
places an impossible burden upon them by asking that they
undertake social control functions. They cannot both 'help' the
client, yet also uphold the norms of society. A solution to their
dilemma as well as ours would be to remove them from 'front-
line' areas of social control (always bearing in mind that as
human beings none of us can completely get away from the
moral prescriptions and judgements which are part and parcel
of our everyday social interaction).

I have stressed the enormous empty gulf between doing
nothing at all and having to put children out of circulation for
long periods. Recently, an alternative called Intermediate
Treatment has come into the news. Great things are promised
for it. It is intended to be applied to the delinquent in his home
environment and constitutes a compromise between residential
care and unrestricted release, and overlaps into the alternatives
to prison advocated for adult offenders. It comes in the wake of
the failure of institutional rehabilitation and is advertised as far
cheaper.

However, present provision is patchy, and it depends very
much for its extent and content on the local borough social

services department. By June 1976, not more than eight London boroughs had any kind of comprehensive approach of this
type. Over the rest of the country there are apparently only to
date about twenty other well-developed programmes; elsewhere there may be piecemeal facilities that the social services
can use. Much of the provision is for activities of various kinds,
from football to car maintenance and canoeing, some of these
activities carried out in spells away from home. Therapies of
various kinds also exist—art therapy, drama therapy (see for
example Mary Priestley 1976), variations on group therapy
and so forth.

Other provisions are for remedial education in special units,
training schemes for work and skills, and work situation projects. One of the most well-developed projects is in Hammersmith. This 'experimental project' has now been in operation
for about a year, and takes about sixty teenagers, referred there
from the social service departments, courts, and juvenile liaison
bureaux. They are put into contact with 'linkers' who have
similar backgrounds, and, perhaps, similar offence-histories.
These 'linkers' work with the adolescent and his family and
friends on an informal basis. 'The development of relationships
and the learning of practical skills are the main goals of the
project; *it is hoped* that achievement in these respects will mean a
reduction in delinquent behaviour.' [Italics mine].

Such a project appears to envisage working entirely indirectly. Given the appropriate skills the delinquent is then better
equipped to take his place in society, fitted for the situations
where these skills might be demanded and which possibly
control his delinquency. Certainly, work may carry the person
into an environment which is incompatible with offending, just
as better interpersonal skills might, and often have done. So far
so good. But these provisions pass the tasks of prescription and
control along the line to others.

The main experiment in Intermediate Treatment (1977) has
been a five-year research study carried out by the National
Children's Bureau involving more than sixty field workers in
seven neighbourhoods. In these the Intermediate Treatment
was provided within the overall context of general community
work, based on Family Advice Centres, staffed by social workers, youth workers and play leaders. The community projects
aimed to give guidance and assistance to the people in the areas

they served, and to provide the kind of services the people required. They wanted to encourage the communities to help themselves, to improve their social competence through participation in community provision; and they wanted the young people as well as the adults to take an active interest in the activities and the problems of their own neighbourhoods. These projects have been heralded as a great success, or at least, as demonstrating a promising way to deal with delinquency.

However, although these are spoken of as 'research' and as 'experimental', they present no results on which they might be evaluated. There is only the subjective opinion of the workers on the projects, who naturally have a big investment in their success, and who feel that many of the delinquents covered by the projects have shown 'improvement'. They say it works, and this has been accepted as establishing that it does, and so the green light has been given for more Intermediate Treatment. In the judgement of those working on the projects, an 'improvement' was noted in 44 per cent of the children and youth 'in contact' with the projects; but 36 per cent were to appear in court during this period. We do not even know whether that 44 per cent who were said to have improved were delinquent in any definite way; nor, indeed, do we know how many were there on Intermediate Treatment, and how many were simply other neighbourhood children. The use of the Intermediate Treatment by the delinquents was voluntary, and the staff deliberately played down any suggestions to the contrary. They aimed at avoiding 'labelling' or distinguishing the delinquents from the other youths and children, which partly explains why they could not say whether or not the projects were a success as regards delinquency. One might wonder why the experiment was supposed to be applied to delinquents at all, if they were not to be recognised as such. One cannot run experiments on cancer cures if one is barred from evaluating the results because one doesn't wish to acknowledge the disease. When the public are being sold Intermediate Treatment as an alternative to custody, they usually assume that it is non-optional, rather than something the delinquent can decide if he wants to take up or not. What if he doesn't fancy it?

In these projects the delinquent's behaviour is not directly noticed or condemned, but facilities are offered in the hope of providing competing attractions to delinquency, which the young themselves can choose. In so far as children and youths have engaged in other activities, their 'offending time' has been reduced, and this might have an effect, but can it really be a substitute for some explicit assertion of social rules and moral standards; upheld by some direct controls? Certainly, it is highly desirable that the people in the community show an interest in their youth; set up facilities for them and with them, so that in turn these youth come to do things with and for others in their group. But within this framework, norms do have to be prescribed and some pressure applied to uphold them, particularly in the case of definite lawbreaking, which calls for very distinct 'labelling', prohibitions and sanctions. The contradictions created by trying to merge the containment of lawbreaking into the provision of services which the community wants, may not have been recognised by the social workers in this particular project, but they were certainly felt by the community itself. The community was otherwise satisfied with the provisions being made by the community workers, and was beginning to participate actively itself in providing them. But they resented the fact that in order to attract them away from misbehaviour, the delinquents were given the best. They obviously felt that those who break certain rules *should* be singled out, condemned, and obliged to make recompense in some way or other, rather than become more privileged as a result. A local mother:

> People generally have a favourable impression of the family advice centre but they lost sympathy when they let the older boys run around. This was especially hard for the people who lived on the square. They had to lock and bar the doors leading from the square. . . . I don't think they should plan anything for the older boys because they are just interested in smashing things up.

A man elected to the neighbourhood council:

> All the resources seem to go to those kids who are always getting into trouble. If we give too much to the bad ones, the ones who are on the borderline are likely to see the troublesome youngsters getting more facilities and join them. The

most delinquent youngsters get taken away on holidays whereas with the ones who don't get into trouble their parents have to take them on holiday.

Ironically, in a project whose long-term aims are to get the community itself to manage its affairs, help itself, and cope with its problems, this is one area where the social workers cannot relinquish their control to the layman. Their approaches can never be reconciled with his, and the social workers' attempts to treat delinquency in this way must be self-defeating because, unlike the layman, they refuse to recognise the nature of the problem and the solution that it demands at the level of informal and formal community control of lawbreaking. However much talk there is of community solutions to delinquency, the purveyors of these are standing in the way of the actual community taking and initiating the action which will produce the results.

The 1969 Act was superimposed upon an already complex and devious system of juvenile courts and penal establishments with responsibilities towards the young ranging far beyond their misdemeanours. It might be fruitful to consider a more simplified system of juvenile justice, one not remote, unknowable or unintelligible to the public; a system of tribunals or courts without conflicting or ambiguous briefs, to deal directly with delinquency *as* delinquency. It has already been pointed out in a pamphlet by the Society of Conservative Lawyers (*Apprentices in Crime*) that the direct tackling of delinquency need not mean unconcern with, or neglect of children who are in need of care (whether delinquent or not) since there are plenty of measures in existence which can be used directly to help these also. A simplified system need not even possess powers for deprivation of liberty; that could be a more serious matter for a different and higher court. Most societies have managed to control their young without locking them up. Evidence suggests that fining is very effective as a deterrent, because it functions as an everyday control on the person while he remains in the community. Where possible, this could be related to the cost of the damage done, the goods stolen, and the inconvenience caused. If the child cannot be sued for debt, then in the last analysis his parent or guardian must be obliged to pay, if necessary via the distraint order. This is not making people 'deprived', but telling them that if you harm others or are permissive towards harm being done to them, then you can hardly be allowed to enjoy the comforts and luxuries of that group which you wrong. The same reasons why vandals do not smash up their own home needs to apply to other property: you pay and go without. The very strange anomaly exists where a person is responsible for the damage caused by his dog, but not caused by his child under ten—this needs overhauling.

The law of neglect may also need more vigorous application to deal with unsupervised, unaccompanied young children. The notion of reparation for harm done to the individual or the community might be utilised by orders to make good damage, as well as pay for it; or for the offender to take part in socially constructive work rather than attend voluntary entertainments or courses on hobbies. Parks, gardens, buildings need to be cleaned, maintained and restored, not least because the ravages of vandalism over the past couple of decades have so greatly taken their toll. What we must beware of is a repeat of the expensive charade of the therapeutic institution with Intermediate Treatment. It already looks as if public bodies are being uncritically stampeded into implementing this by those anxious to safeguard their position after the failure of institutional treatments. As there appears to be little or no idea of what to do and what might work, aspiring Intermediate Treatment oganisers are asked to try anything they fancy. The only certainty is that the provisions will increase. An advertisement for such a vacancy for the London Borough of Newham in June 1977, offers £4836—£5142 plus various expenses and car loan to someone with 'a firm commitment to new initiatives' in Intermediate Treatment and who will play a 'central role in the planning of the expansion', obviously before there is any proper assessment of whether or not such 'new initiatives' do any good.

There are very recent proposals to raise the levels of fines for juveniles from ten to fifty pounds for the under fourteens, and from fifty to two hundred pounds for the under seventeens. Whether this will find its way through the 1976–7 session of Parliament, and in what form, remains to be seen.* Some local authorities are obtaining legal guidance on the possibilities of trying to establish precedents on parental responsibility and

* This has now (in late 1977) received the Royal Assent along with a number of other changes in the Criminal Law, but waits to be implemented.

payment for juvenile damage. There is some movement afoot to re-vitalise deterrent practices in dealing with juveniles. More certain, and more publicly known prosecutions following offences, in place of the secret sifting procedures of the liaison schemes, is not yet on the cards.

It is clear that something urgently needs to be done to reverse the invidious position of the public which suffers both from the delinquent's acts, and from his derision and retaliation if any attempts are made to do anything about them. To be both impotent and insulted is not a healthy state. Public morale is at a dangerously low ebb, and if Governments merely wait for the backlash it may be of a nature that is socially undesirable and unconstructive. (Very many people now express a loathing for 'kids' and reject them outright.) The breakdown of socialisation and social controls began with the adult's embarrassment at prescribing norms for children; their withdrawal from the children's world, and the parallel abdication of the schools. This vicious spiral is accelerated by the hamstringing of the community which can no longer act in that continuous, informal process of upholding rules, at a time when formal ones have been dismantled or withered. It is within the day-to-day community that the solutions to anti-social conduct lie—not in casework conferences, or therapy sessions, or social services departments. But those to whom the community has entrusted this part of its social well-being have not merely failed in this trust but, having failed, have widely denied that their job is to do anything about delinquency at all. The definition of ends which they now argue over is the one prerogative that must belong, *not* to the experts, but to the ordinary people.

16 Asking For It?

We do not need any adjustments to the Act or the provisions of
1969; they need dismantling. The last thing which will help us
is the full implementation of the Act; we need its repeal. What is
critically needed as a first step in dealing with the tide of
delinquency is for the law to implement some direct and simple,
unambiguous measures of social control. The community
needs to be encouraged and supported in complementing these.
As a more long-term policy there needs to be an educational
effect in the home and school to teach and maintain standards
which have no place for delinquency, vandalism and violence.
Channels of communication need to face frankly their unwit-
ting role in the proliferation of techniques of lawbreaking and
vicious attitudes; and entertainment should not be at the
expense of destroying or undermining the worth and dignity of
human life. The community itself needs to examine its traditional double-standard towards aggressive male behaviour, if
equality is not to assume the vicious form of increased female
aggression. It cannot condemn on the one hand and grant a
special indulgence to its sons on the other.

If violence and crime are the major concern of our citizens,
next to inflation, this is more than coincidence. Violence and
destruction are the social equivalents of economic inflation.
They are maladaptive and feed nothing but themselves—from
whatever angle we regard them. (Politically, in a democracy
our delicate social problems could never be solved by violence.
The lesson of Lebanon is that nothing was gained and nothing
was learnt. And if the endless and depressing catalogue of
experiments on the effects of violence on the onlooker suggest
anything, it is that violence leads to violence, which in turn
leads to more violence, and so on, into the vortex.)

But, before anything can be done, there will have to be

recognition by those of influence and authority that the rise in delinquency and violence *is* a major problem in itself, and not a symptom of other problems.

Two scapegoats have emerged at the end of this discussion. One is obvious—it is the law-enforcement agencies, particularly the police. When lawbreaking is an expression of deprivation, then the police are seen as an unfortunate relic of an ignorant, brutal past. When you have no right to impose anything on anybody, then they are like tarts at a Victorian at-home. When lawbreaking is rebellion against a rotten social order, then they are indistinguishable from fascists. When the lawbreaker becomes the standard bearer for the New Jerusalem, then they are the very hosts of the Anti-Christ.

The second scapegoat is the victim. When I recounted the experience of a friend of mine, beaten, robbed and left with head injuries at a railway station, the automatic response of a number of educated people was: 'What they must go through'—they were *not* referring to her, but to her attacker. When writing this book I found that an interest in delinquency and violence was taken axiomatically as an 'interest in the underdog'; which by definition did not mean the victim. Reference to the victim, as to the problem of rising delinquency and violence, is generally considered unseemly; it is, of course, merely 'emotional reaction'.

The popularisation of deviance and labelling theory leads to the invisibility, the unmentionability, even the fictionising of the victim. And when 'we' or 'society' are somehow responsible because of deprivation, discrimination, oppression and presumptuous judgements, this too has repercussions for the victim. 'Of course, we are not condoning violence, but . . .' And the big BUT is the insinuation that the victim's lot is not as serious or as worthy of interest as his attacker's. Indeed, a parallel assumption to the one that violence is the result of deprivation of some kind seems to be that the victim cannot therefore be among the deprived, and can even be blamed in some tenuous way for the anguish the lawbreaker must feel. We are *all* guilty.

These attitudes are associated with the most extravagant fancies about the differences between delinquents and non-delinquents, which leave so many laymen wondering if some experts and social commentators haven't taken leave of their

senses. When you inhabit an area where the majority of delinquents, like the non-delinquents, sleep one to a bed and one to a
room, have kitchens, bathrooms, WCs, hot and cold water, TV
and carpets; where the vandals ride the latest bikes and wear
the latest clothes, it is utterly bizarre to be told by the good
Bishop Mervyn Stockwood that his guess is that *we* would all
have ended up as 'vandals, shirkers, layabouts or psychological
misfits' if we had 'one lavatory and two gas stoves for more than
fifty people' (*Guardian* 23 October 1974).

This line of argument is infuriating to many people because it
is so deeply insulting. Elderly people who were born, reared,
and in turn had to cope with grinding poverty in a pre-welfare
society feel that they are being told they are lucky compared to
young people who have resources, comforts and opportunities
that they hardly dreamed of at the same age, and must expect to
be harassed and despoiled as a result. There are too the
unpleasant insinuations about the human status of those who
have endured adverse conditions, contained in assumption that
the outcome will be some kind of moral imbecility; or incapacity
to do other than evil things to one's fellows. That this will be
understood and forgiven makes it worse, not better.

The questions raised by ordinary people like Lillian W. are
as rude to ask as it is to notice the problem they refer to. Lillian
lives in a low-rise GLC estate, which has been broken into by
the local children, who smash her windows. She is almost
crippled by arthritis. Most of the time she is at her daughter's;
at home she is in a state of high anxiety. On one occasion, the
children injured her by running her down and over with their
bikes. Helpless on the ground and a figure of fun for a considerable time, she was eventually rescued by another pensioner.
Lillian herself was one of seventeen children, reared in a couple
of rooms, yet she emphasises that 'our mother taught us to
respect other people; to think of them too. We would not dream
of doing the wicked things these children around here do now.'
She is bemused by 'these social workers on television. I wish I
could get them here, to tell them a few things. They were going
on the other night about children not having enough to play
with, so that they have to do things for kicks. Why? Who ever
heard of such things?'

Sentimental? Emotional? Ignorant? None the less, Lillian's
words are not only echoed by a growing multitude of other

Londoners, they possess a crude empiricism and a historical perspective missing from so many an expert and favoured
commentator. Are the latter's theories any more viable? The
layman usually has not made that transition from factual
hypotheses to ideological commitment, or not to such an
extent. He treats these theories as still capable of falsification,
and his own experience appears to refute them.

In contrast to the development of numerous pressure groups
offering help, support and a voice for the homeless, fatherless,
disabled, suicidal, the offender and ex-offender, those ready to
further the interests of the victims of lawbreakers are conspicuous by their absence. Civil liberties groups have been the last to
be interested in preserving the most fundamental prerequisite
of any other liberties.

Certainly, the Criminal Injuries Board was set up by the
Government to provide monetary compensation for victims of
crime. Unfortunately, this humane action can become one
more wedge between anti-social action and the consequences.
We are invited to view criminal acts like any other accidents
when there is the firm feeling that this simply cannot be so in
the human social and moral order of intentional behaviour. It
can, in fact, even strengthen the hand of those who wish to
'decriminalise' society, by abolishing or ignoring offences. The
(ex) lawbreaker is not judged and penalised—diversity
rules—and the victim gets his pieces of silver. The logical end
would be universal *wergild* on the welfare.

But people still appear to be more in favour of justice than
accident compensation, as they were when the original
blood-money system gave way to law, responsibility and penalty. Many victims do not claim their cash, and an unusual
survey for the Home Office of personal victims of selected
indictable offences (chiefly theft, criminal damage and assault)
revealed a widespread disillusionment and dissatisfaction with
the seeming lack of concern shown for them by the legal process
(Julie Vennard 1976). More than money, what was wanted was
help, sympathy, and a firm reassertion of norms.

There are, however, some developments that might have a
bearing on the cause of the victim in future and, correspondingly, on the recognition that crime and violence are urgent,
primary problems in our society. The one schism in progressive
assumptions about offender and victim has been initiated by

recent feminist movements. With recent injections from psychoanalysis, the belief has persisted that raped women (and beaten wives) somehow deserved or 'asked for' what they got, and even liked it! (It has not yet been suggested that victims of mugging, for example, actually enjoy the experience.) On top of this, the progressive stance was, first, to extend to the rapist the sympathy shown to all lawbreakers as victims of deranged minds, and then (in the American Civil Rights context) to justify implicitly the raping of (white) women, because they somehow 'deserved' it from the oppressed. But, as Susan Brownmiller comments in *Against Our Will*, it came as a shock, and was taken as reaction, when these views were questioned. The victims of rape were identified as part of a social group more 'disadvantaged' economically, and more socially powerless than either black or white males: evidence suggested that in most instances rape was premeditated and the offender far from insane or 'out of control'. Moreover, such behaviour was condemned as morally wrong and hence impermissible. If the rapist acted from his own values—he might think that women deserved it—then his values were rotten. They would need to be changed by education and a social climate which made it reprehensible and heavily disadvantageous to act upon them.

If extended to other lawbreaking, the effect of such a stance would be devastating for the dominant progressive ethos, sections of which might now repudiate the idea that the delinquent and violent are necessarily sick, but will not accept that they are morally wrong in their presumed revenge against society.

If, at a more intellectual level, a problem such as rape or wife-beating might be analysed as part of more general social relationships and values, at the grass roots attention to the plight of the victim necessitates the focus of remedial action on measures to alleviate these as *immediate* priorities. Victim-orientated movements have the direct brief of relieving or changing factors facing the victim or potential victim in the most speedy, effective manner compatible with equity, humanity and justice. Victim movements have already been instrumental in getting something done for the battered wife and child, and have had no conflicting briefs about saving families as a whole, or a preoccupation with the secret psychic needs of their members—the child or woman is injured or in danger, and needs a way out of this. Such movements have—initially, at least—come essentially from *outside* the immensely cumbersome and expensive official welfare apparatus that was supposed to already cater for the problems they faced. (See Erin Pizzey 1974; John Howells 1974.)

If the women's movement, in its response to crime specifically against women, raises by implication some awkward questions about attitudes to lawbreaking and violence generally, so too must the rumbling discontent and fears of those who are exposed at work to the brunt of the tide of anti-social behaviour. This discontent flatly contradicts so many academic suggestions that violence is something to do with the revolutionary character of the working class. Unfortunately, the working class has been treated as pawns of other people's romantic aspirations. It is nothing short of extraordinary how, in a society where strikes over non-economic issues are still exceedingly rare, the widespread stoppages by public workers over the issue of violence have been so studiously ignored for so long by the New Establishment. The most tragic paradox of modern British society involves the demand for protection, even the plea for social survival, from just those who have been credited with a desire to overthrow the social order. The public are victims of lawbreakers partly because they are also victims of bad psychology and bad principles.

The vehicle for these was largely assembled in the 1960s, when complex issues of great scientific, moral and human significance were delivered into the hands of those with no theoretical clarity, empirical knowledge or practical experience to deal with them. None the less, they were to determine a great deal, from how we treat our children at home to what to do with our juvenile delinquents. For years now, the New Establishment has largely succeeded in ignoring or impugning the credibility of any views but those of its own distinctive spectrum. And, if its theory and methods have been at all evaluated, there has been nobody capable or willing to act on these evaluations.

Certainly, the New Establishment claims many politicians, many administrators and policy-makers, but there must be an increasing number who rue the day that they allowed themselves to be led by the nose. As the birds come home to roost, there must be many who are desperate to divest themselves of the policies they so enthusiastically espoused, if only it could be done without too great a loss of face and loss of position.

There are no excuses now for ignorant guesses over delinquency, to suppose it might be due to anything from lack of play to high-rise architecture. There is no excuse—in the light of the damning research on therapeutic rehabilitation regimes—for David Ennals, Secretary of State for Social Services, to claim as late as 1976 that 'Every pound invested in broad social programmes of reform and rehabilitation is an investment against crime'. Nor is there any excuse for him to speculate that delinquency may be due to factors like working mothers and living with in-laws. There is plenty of research in existence on possible causes of delinquency—if anybody wants to read it. That they don't wish to, is beginning to look like wanton neglect, rather than ignorance. The public deserve better.

They certainly deserve better than the easy substitutes for social controls and socialisation still being offered, whether it be more love, playgrounds or houses. They deserve better than the dreams of some reformers of a world without obligation, imposition, judgement, restraint and repercussion. If the goal of emotional satisfaction often looks like the substance of the psychology of the new expertise, it must be said that this psychology has given a very peculiar picture of man as profoundly asocial and acultural. Given this, it should hardly be remarkable that the children whose self-determined emotional development everybody has fretted over are now a threat to us. This has meant that many well-intentioned people, who sincerely want the best for the children's future and greatly desire their society to survive, are handing to those who really do wish to demolish it, a passable recipe to achieve this end. I have hardly been unique in stumbling on this conclusion. More than once I have had to meet those who have gleefully dwelt on the outcome of our child-rearing and educational theories as a substantial contribution to the 'collapse of the system'.

Andrew Sutton, of the Movement of Practising Psychologists, a group belatedly trying to get support for the proper evaluation of method in educational and social policies before they are thrust upon the public, had an apt metaphor for the state of the social sciences and services. He compared it with a garden where plants striving for air are choked by an abundance of dead wood and luxuriant weeds. As far as my particular concerns go, I could identify the dead wood as the philosophy and provisions of the 1969 Act, and the whole sorry psychology which has completely dominated our child-rearing. The luxuriant weeds are represented by that development of the notion that man and society are ill-mated, into ideas that delinquency represents some kind of revenge for the immense but usually indefinable wrongs perpetrated by society on its luckless inhabitants. Where first the means to the control of delinquency were rejected, now the ends are spurned, and neo-Marxism gives form to a nihilistic individualism, where the delinquent is the last of the just. His role is to deliver us to an Armageddon where there is nothing on the other side, since the discontent that is expressed with society is of such a nature that it could not be stilled by *any* society.

Whether in the psychology and the aspirations of those who promised to solve our problems; the moral confusions of those who wish society could be what it cannot be, and who prevent it becoming what it can; the politics of those so naively dangerous as to think that the delinquent and his violent act form some kind of argument for their programme and their ideals; the discontented intellectual chasing moonbeams; or those who dream of exchanging it all for a place in the void far, far away—the public are, above all, the victims of fantasies.

It is time we asked not only about the worth of what is being done in our name with our resources, but where we are being taken and for what. We might have very different opinions on the matter and make some very different choices.

Notes

1 *New Barbarism*
Greater London Council, 1975, Research Memorandum 443
The Inner City, 1975, London Council of Social Service
James Q. Wilson, 1976, *Thinking about Crime*, Basic Books, New York

2 *See No Evil*
W. Belson, 1975, *Juvenile Theft: the Causal Factors*, Harper and Row
K. Bottomley and C. Coleman, 1976, *International Journal of Criminology and Penology*, vol. 4, no. 1, p. 33
A.E. Bottoms and J. Baldwin, 1976, *The Urban Criminal*, Tavistock
A.E. Bottoms, 1976, 'Crime in a City', *New Society*, 8 April
Stan Cohen, 1967, 'Mods, Rockers and the Rest: Community Reactions to Juvenile Delinquency', *The Howard Journal* 12, pp. 121–30 and in W.G. Carson and Paul Wiles, Eds., 1971, *Crime and Delinquency in Britain*, Martin Robertson & Co.
Stan Cohen, 1972, *Folk Devils and Moral Panics*, MacGibbon and Kee
John Conklin, 1975, *The Impact of Crime*, Collier Macmillan
Stuart Hall, 1976, 'Violence and the Media' in Norman Tutt Ed., *Violence*, DHSS
L.F. Lowenstein, 1972, *Violence in Schools and its Treatment*, National Association of Schoolmasters
Murder, Manslaughter and Infanticide, Office of Home Economics Briefing no. 4
C. Pritchard and Richard Taylor, 1975, 'Classroom violence', *New Society*, 27 Nov.
Protection Against Vandalism, 1975, Home Office Standing Committee on Crime Prevention
Railway Accidents, 1974, HMSO
Report of HM Chief Inspector of Constabulary for the years 1974 and 1975, HMSO
Wesley G. Skogan, 1976, *Criminology*, vol. 13, no. 4, p. 535
Andy Sturman in Tony Marshall, 1976, 'Vandalism: the Seeds of Destruction' *New Society*, 17 June
Times Educational Supplement, 10 January 1975, *Fire! Fire!* Report on arson in schools
Paul Wiles, 1974, 'Explaining violence and social work practice' in *The Lawbreakers*, BBC

3 *The New Establishment*
Marcel Berlins and Geoffrey Wansell, 1974, *Caught in the Act, children, society and the law*, Penguin Books
The Child. the Family and the Young Offender, 1965, HMSO
Children and their Primary Schools, 1967, 'The Plowden Report', HMSO
Children in Trouble, 1968, HMSO
Crime—a Challenge to Us All, 1964, A Labour Party research pamphlet

Maurice Edelman MP, 'How the new system of patronage in government scatters the confetti of privilege', *The Times*, 14 October 1975

David Galloway, 1976, *The Public Prodigals*, Temple Smith

Ivan Illich, 1975, *Medical Nemesis* Calder

4 *Rights and Wrongs: Disease and Disadvantage*

W. Belson, 1975, *Juvenile Theft: the Causal Factors*, Harper & Row

Care and Treatment in a Planned Environment, A report on the Community Home Project, 1970, HMSO

H.J. Eysenck, 1964, *Crime and Personality*, Routledge & Kegan Paul, and Paladin, 1970

Robert D. Hare, 1970, *Psychopathy*, John Wiley & Sons Inc.

Mia Kellmer Pringle, 1974, *The Needs of Children*, Hutchinson, for Department of Health and Social Security

Austin T. Turk, 1964, 'Prospects for theories of criminal behaviour', *Journal of Criminal Law, Criminology and Police Science* 55, pp. 454–61

D.J. West and D.P. Farrington, 1973, *Who Becomes Delinquent?* Heinemann, for Cambridge Institute of Criminology

D.J. West and D.P. Farrington, 1977, *The Delinquent Way of Life*, Heinemann

Youth Treatment Centres, 1971, and Circular 26/1971, DHSS

5 *Those Vital Relationships*

W.A. Belson, 1975, *Juvenile Theft: the Causal Factors*, Harper & Row

John Bowlby, 1946, *Forty-four Juvenile Thieves, their Characters and Home Life*, Baillière, Tindall and Cox; part of this study first appeared in the *International J. Psycho-analysis* 1944, vol. XXV, pp. 19–53

John Bowlby and M.D. Ainsworth, 1954, 'Research strategy in the study of mother-child separation', *Courrier* 4, no. 3, p. 116

John Bowlby, M. Ainsworth, M. Boston and D. Rosenbluth, 1965, 'The effects of mother-child separation: a follow-up study,' *Brit. J. Medical Psychol*, vol. 29, p. 211

John Bowlby, 1952, *Maternal Care and Mental Health*, 2nd Edn, World Health Organisation, Monograph Series no. 2, Geneva, and as *Child Care and the Growth of Love*, 1965, Ed. Margery Fry, Penguin Books

John Bowlby, 1969, *Attachment*, Hogarth Press

A.M. Carr-Saunders, H. Mannheim and E.C. Rhodes, 1942, *Young Offenders*, Cambridge University Press

J. Cowie, V. Cowie and E. Slater, 1968, *Delinquency in Girls*, Heinemann

J.W.B. Douglas, J.M. Ross, W.A. Hammond and D.G. Mulligan, 1966, 'Delinquency and social class', *Brit. J. Crim.*, 6, pp. 294–302

J.W.B. Douglas, 1975, 'Early hospital admissions and later disturbances of behaviour and learning', *Developmental Medicine and Child Neurology* 17, pp. 456–80

J.G. Field, 1962, 'Two types of recidivist and maternal deprivation', *Brit. J. Crim.*, vol. 5, pp. 289–308

S. Glueck and E.T. Glueck, 1950, *Unravelling Juvenile Delinquency*, New York, Commonwealth Fund

William Goldfarb, 1943, 'Infant rearing and problem behaviour', *Amer. J. Orthopsychiat.* 13, p. 249

William Goldfarb, 1944, 'Effects of Early Institutional Care on Adolescent Personality', *Amer. J. Orthopsychiat.* 14, p. 441

J.F. Hooke, 1966, 'Correlates of adolescent delinquent behaviour: a multivariate approach', *Diss. Abstr.* 2136-B

Mia Kellmer Pringle, 1974, *The Needs of Children.* A personal perspective prepared for the DHSS

Mia Kellmer Pringle, 1975, letter to *Guardian*, Oct.

Melanie Klein, 1959, *Our Adult World and its Roots in Infancy*, Tavistock Pamphlet no. 2

Melanie Klein, 1936, 'Weaning' in *On the Bringing Up of Children* Ed. J. Rickman, Kegan Paul

Melanie Klein, 1932, *The Psychoanalysis of Children*, Hogarth Press 3rd edn, reprinted 1969

A. Little, 1965, 'Parental deprivation, separation and crime: a test on adolescent recidivists', *Brit. J. Crim.* 4, pp. 419–30

W. McCord and J. McCord, 1959, *Origins of Crime: a new evaluation of the Cambridge-Somerville Youth Study*, Columbia University Press, New York

H. Mannheim and L.T. Wilkins, 1955, *Prediction Methods in Relation to Borstal Training*, HMSO

Tony Marshall, 1976, 'Vandalism: the seeds of destruction', *New Society*, 17 June

Patricia Morgan, 1975, *Child Care: Sense and Fable*, Temple Smith

Siri Naess, 1959, 'Mother-child separation and delinquency', *Brit. J. Delinq.* 10, pp. 22–35

Siri Naess, 1962, 'Mother-child separation and delinquency: further evidence', *Brit. J. Crim.* 2, p. 361

Michael Rutter, 1971, 'Parent-child separation: psychological effects on the children', *J. Child Psychol. Psychiat.*, vol. 12, pp. 233–60, and Addendum, Dec. 1975, in Ann M. Clarke and A.D.B. Clarke, 1976, *Early Experience: Myth and Evidence*, Open Books

Michael Rutter, 1972, *Maternal Deprivation Reassessed*, Penguin

Rene Spitz, 1945, 'Hospitalism' in *Psychoanalytic Study of the Child*, vol. 1, p. 53, International Universities Press, New York

Rene Spitz, 1946, 'Hospitalism': A Follow-up Report, *Psychoanalytic Study of the Child*, vol. 2, p. 313, International Universities Press, New York

Rene Spitz and K.M. Wolf, 1949, 'Autoeroticism. Some empirical findings and hypotheses on three of the manifestations in the first year of life', *Psychoanalytic Study of the Child*, vol. 3/4, pp. 85–120.

Jack Tizard, Peter Moss and Jane Perry, 1976, *All Our Children*, Temple Smith

D.J. West and D.P. Farrington, 1973, *Who Becomes Delinquent?* Heinemann for Cambridge Institute of Criminology

S. Yudkin and A. Holme, 1969, *Working Mothers and their Children*, Sphere Books

6 *All You Need is Love?*

John Bowlby, 1952, *Maternal Care and Mental Health* 2nd edn, World Health Organisation, Monograph Series no. 2, Geneva, and as *Child Care and the Growth of Love* Ed. Margery Fry, Penguin Books, 1965

J. Cowie, V. Cowie and E. Slater, 1968, *Delinquency in Girls,* Heinemann

Susan Daresman and Frank Scarpatti, 1975, *Criminology,* vol. 13, no. 1, p. 33

S. Glueck and E.T. Glueck, 1950, *Unravelling Juvenile Delinquency,* New York: Commonwealth Fund

H.F. Harlow, 1961, 'The development of affectional patterns in infant monkeys', in B.M. Foss, Ed., *Determinants of Infant Behaviour,* vol. I, Methuen

H.F. Harlow, 1963, 'The Maternal Affectional System' in B.M. Foss, Ed., *Determinants of Infant Behaviour,* vol. II

H.F. Harlow and M.K. Harlow, 1965, 'Effects of various mother-infant relationships on rhesus monkey behaviours', in B.M. Foss Ed. *Determinants of Infant Behaviour,* vol. III

H.F. Harlow and S. Soumi, 1971, 'Social recovery by isolation-reared monkeys', *National Academy of Science,* vol. 68, no. 7

J. Kagan and H.A. Moss, 1962, *Birth to Maturity,* New York, John Wiley

J. Kagan and R.E. Klein, 1973, 'Cross-cultural perspectives in early development', *American Psychologist* 28, pp. 947–61

J. Kagan, 1976, 'Resilience and Continuity in Psychological Development', in Ann M. Clarke and A.D.B. Clarke, *Early Experience: Myth and Evidence,* Open Books

Mia Kellmer Pringle, 1974, *The Needs of Children.* A personal perspective prepared for the DHSS

W. Kessen, 1975, *Childhood in China,* Yale University Press

Lydia Lambert, 1976, 'Who needs a father?', *New Society,* 8 July

F. Leboyer, *Birth Without Violence,* Fontana

Jean Liedloft, 1975, *The Continuum Concept,* Duckworth

Patricia Morgan, 1974, 'Against clinging: mothers and monkeys', *New Society,* 29 Aug.

Patricia Morgan, 1975, *Child Care: Sense and Fable,* Temple Smith

H. Orlansky, 1949, 'Infant Care and Personality', *Psychol. Bull.* 46

Erin Pizzey, 1974, *Scream Quietly, or the neighbours will hear,* Penguin Books

Probationers in their Social Environment, HMSO

L.N. Robins, 1966, *Deviant Children Grown Up,* A sociological and psychological study of sociopathic personality, Williams & Wilkins, Baltimore

Michael Rutter, 1971, 'Parent-child separation: psychological effects on the children', *J. Child Psychol. Psychiat.,* vol. 12, pp. 233–60, and Addendum Dec. 1975, in Ann M. Clarke and A.D.B. Clarke, 1976, *Early Experience: Myth and Evidence,* Open Books

D.J. West and D.P. Farrington, 1973, *Who Becomes Delinquent?* Heinemann, for Cambridge Institute of Criminology

Harriette Wilson, 1962, *Delinquency and Child Neglect,* Allen & Unwin

7 Cures?

Marcel Berlins and Geoffrey Wansell, 1974, *Caught in the Act, children, society and the law,* Penguin Books

Children and Young Persons Act 1969, White Paper 1976, HMSO

B.D. Cornish and R.V.G. Clarke, 1975, *Residential Treatment and its Effects on Delinquency,* HMSO

Penny Cooper, 1975, *Social Services Department's Observation and Assessment*

Centres for Children, Movement of Practising Psychologists, Discussion Paper no. 3

Anne B. Dunlop, 1974, *The Approved School Experience*, HMSO

S. and E.T. Glueck, 1940, *Juvenile Delinquents Grown Up*, Commonwealth Fund

S. and E.T. Glueck, 1968, *Delinquents and Non-Delinquents in Perspective*, Oxford University Press

House of Commons Expenditure Committee on the Operation of the Children and Young Persons Act, Report vol. 1; *Minutes of Evidence*, vol. II, 1975, HMSO

C.H. Logan, 1972, 'Evaluation research in crime and delinquency: a reappraisal', *Journal of Criminal Law, Criminology and Police Science* 63, pp. 378–87

Joanna Mack, 1976, 'Disruptive Pupils', *New Society*, 5 Aug.

D. Martin, 1974, 'Disapproved Schools', *Humpty-Dumpty*, no. 5, p. 13

Prof. F.M. Martin, 1976, 'Children's Hearings', *New Society*, 12 Feb.

M.P. Righton (chairman), 1975, *Assessment of Children and their Families*, MIND

Glyn Roberts, Robin Lovelock, Elizabeth Reinach and Pat Gude, 1976, *First Year at Fairfield Lodge*, Social Services Research and Intelligence Unit, under the joint auspices of the Portsmouth Polytechnic and the Hampshire Social Services Department

The Sentence of the Courts, 1969, HMSO

Christopher Sherratt, 1974, 'Beyond the Playing', *New Society*, 18 April

I.A.C. Sinclair and R.V.G. Clarke, 1963, 'Acting-out and its significance for the residential treatment of delinquents', *Journal of Child Psychol. Psychiat.*, vol. 14, pp. 283–91

Norman Tutt, 1974, *Care or Custody?* Darton, Longman & Todd

Norman Tutt, 1975, *Care or Control?* MoPP Discussion Paper no. 5

Michael Zander, 1975, 'What happens to young offenders in care?' *New Society*, 24 June

8 Sordid Normality

A.E. Bottoms and F.H. McClintock, 1973, *Criminals Coming of Age* Heinemann, for Cambridge Institute of Criminology

J. Campbell, 1965, 'Success rates of T.S. *Formidable*', *Approved School Gazette* 59, p. 298

Ann M. Clarke and A.D.B. Clarke, 1959, 'Recovery from the effects of deprivation', *Acta Psychol.*, 16

Ann M. Clarke and A.D.B. Clarke, 1976, 'The Formative Years?' in Ann M. Clarke and A.D.B. Clarke, Eds, 1976, *Early Experience: Myth and Evidence*, Open Books

D.B. Cornish and R.V.G. Clarke, 1975, *Residential Treatment and its Effects on Delinquency*, HMSO

M. Davies, 1974, 'The Persistent Offender', *The Lawbreakers*, BBC

Wayne Dennis, 1973, *Children of the Crèche*, Appleton-Century-Crofts, New York

J.W. Eaton, 1955, *Culture and Mental Disorder*, Free Press, Glencoe

D. Farrington, 1974, 'Explanations of juvenile delinquency', *The Lawbreakers*, BBC

S. and E.T. Glueck, 1940, *Juvenile Delinquents Grown Up*, Commonwealth Fund, New York

S. and E.T. Glueck, 1968, *Delinquents and Non-Delinquents in Perspective*, Oxford University Press

A. Kadushin, 1970, *Adopting Older Children*, Columbia University Press, New York

J. Kagan and R.E. Klein, 1973, 'Cross-cultural perspectives in early development', *American Psychologist* 28, pp. 947–61

J. Kagan, 1976, 'Resilience and Continuity in Psychological Development', in Ann M. Clarke and A.D.B. Clarke, Eds, *Early Experience: Myth and Evidence*, Open Books

J. Kagan, 1976, in Ann M. Clarke and A.D.B. Clarke, Eds, 'The Formative Years?' *Early Experience: Myth and Evidence*

Patricia Morgan, 1975, 'Scientific Credentials of Psychoanalysis', in *Child Care: Sense and Fable*, Temple Smith

W.E. Roper, July 1950, and April 1951, 'Comparative Study of the Wakefield Prison Population', *Brit. J. Delinq.*, vol. 1, pp. 15–28, 243–70

Michael Rutter and Nicola Madge, 1976, *Cycles of Deprivation*, Heinemann

I.A.C. Sinclair, 1971, *Hostels for Probationers*, HMSO

N. Walker, 1965, *Crime and Punishment in Britain*, Edinburgh University Press (2nd edn. 1968)

9 *What Right Have We?*

R.L. Akers, 1967, 'Problems in the sociology of deviance: social definitions and behaviour', *Social Forces* 46, pp. 455–65

S.E. Finer, 1976, 'On Terrorism', *New Society*, 22 January

Melanie Guyler, 1976, 'School Label', letter to *New Society*, 9 Sept.

Joanna Mack, 1976, 'Disruptive Pupils', *New Society*, 5 July

Prof. F.M. Martin, 1976, 'Children's Hearings', *New Society*, 12 Feb.

P. Rock and M. Macintosh, Eds, 1974, *Deviance and Social Control*, Tavistock

Edwin Schur, 1974, *Radical Non-intervention: Rethinking the Delinquency Problem*

Laurie Taylor and Stan Cohen, 1972, *Psychological Survival*, Penguin

Laurie Taylor and Stan Cohen, 1976, *Escape Attempts: the theory and practice of resistance to everyday life*, Allen Lane

10 *Getting Their Own Back*

Dane Archer and Rosemary Gartner, 1977, *American Sociological Review*, vol. 4, no. 6, p. 937

J. Baldwin, 1974, 'Problem housing estates', *Social and Economic Administration*, vol. 8

W. Belson, 1975, *Juvenile Theft: the Causal Factors*, Harper and Row

A.E. Bottoms and J. Baldwin, 1976, *The Urban Criminal*, Tavistock

A.E. Bottoms, 1976, 'Crime in a City', *New Society*, 8 April

Tyrrell Burgess, 1975, 'Why can't children read?' *New Society*, 3 April

Sir Cyril Burt, 1925, *The Young Delinquent*, University of London Press

Stan Cohen, 1973, in *Vandalism*, Ed. Colin Ward, Architectural Press

David Downes, 1966, *The Delinquent Solution*, Routledge & Kegan Paul

Frederick Engels, 'The condition of the Working class in England', in *Karl Marx and Frederick Engels on Britain*, 1953, Foreign Languages Publishing House, Moscow

G. Fiegehen and S. Lansley, 1977, *Journal of the Royal Statistical Society*, vol. 139, part 4

Ken Fogelman, Ed., 1976, *Britain's Sixteen-Year-Olds*, preliminary findings from the third follow-up of the National Child Development Study, National Children's Bureau

Tom Forester, 1977, 'Do the British sincerely want to be rich?', *New Society*, 28 April

Paul Harrison, 1975, 'The Children Act Under Attack', *New Society*, 12 June

Household Food, Consumption and Expenditure, HMSO

B.J. Knight and D.J. West, 1977, *British Journal of Criminology*, vol. 15, no. 1, p. 43

Hermann Mannheim, 1940, *Social Aspects of Crime in England between the Wars*, Allen & Unwin

Tony Marshall, 1976, 'Vandalism: the seeds of destruction', *New Society*, 17 June

D. Matza, 1964, *Delinquency and Drift*, Wiley, New York

R.I. Mawby, 1977, *British Journal of Criminology*, vol. 17, no. 1, p. 30

Mirror Group Newspapers Household Readership, Income and Consumption Study, 1975

No Place to Grow Up, 1977, A Shelter Report on the effect of bad housing on children by Zoe Fairbairns and Jim Wintour

Geoffrey Pearson, 1976, 'In defence of hooliganism: social theory and violence', in *Violence*, Ed. by Norman Tutt, DHSS

Probationers in their Social Environment, HMSO

Social Trends, no. 6, 1975, HMSO

Nigel Walker, 1965, *Crime and Punishment in Britain*, Edinburgh University Press

Gavin Weightman, 1977, 'The Glasgow Murder Mystery', *New Society*, 17 March

Gavin Weightman, 1977, 'God lets me pickpocket', *New Society*, 7 July 1977

Paul Wiles, 1974, 'Explaining Violence and Social Work Practice', *The Lawbreakers*, BBC

Paul Willis, 1976, 'Lads, Lobes and Labour', *New Society*, 20 May

Peter Willmott, 1966, *The Adolescent Boys of East London*, Routledge & Kegan Paul

Peter Willmott, Ed., 1976, 'Sharing Inflation?', *Poverty Report*, Temple Smith

11 *New Jerusalem*

J. Baldwin and A.E. Bottoms, 1976, *The Urban Criminal*, Tavistock

A.E. Bottoms, 1976, 'Crime in a City', *New Society*, 8 April

Norman Cohn, 1957, *The Pursuit of the Millennium*, Secker & Warburg, 2nd Edn, Temple Smith, and Paladin

C. Cox, K. Jacka and J. Marks, 1975, *The Rape of Reason*, Churchill Press

J.W.B. Douglas, J.M. Ross, W.A. Hammond and D.J. Mulligan, 1966, 'Delinquency and social class', *British Journal of Criminology*, vol. 6, pp. 294–302

David Downes, 1966, *The Delinquent Solution*, Routledge & Kegan Paul

M.L. Kohn, 1959, 'Social class and parental values', *Amer. J. Sociol.*, 64, 4, pp. 337–51

M.L. Kohn, 1963, 'Social class and parent-child relationships: an interpretation', *Amer. J. Sociol.*, 68, pp. 471–80

Ian Taylor, Paul Walton and Jock Young, 1973, *The New Criminology*, Routledge & Kegan Paul

Ian Taylor, Paul Walton and Jock Young, 1975, *Critical Criminology*, Routledge & Kegan Paul

Robert G. Weeson, 1976, *Why Marxism?*, Basic Books and Temple Smith

12 *The Parents and the Leisure Child*

Albert Bandura, Dorothea Ross and Sheila A. Ross, 1963, 'A comparative study of the status envy, social power, and secondary reinforcement theories of identificatory learning', *Journal of Abnormal and Social Psychology*, LXVIII, p. 527

Urie Bronfenbrenner, 1964, 'Upbringing in collective settings in Switzerland and the USSR', *Proceedings of the International Congress of Psychology, Washington DC*, Aug. 1963, pp. 159–61, Amsterdam: North Holland Publishing Company

Urie Bronfenbrenner, 1967, 'Response to pressure from peers versus adults among Soviet and American schoolchildren', in Urie Bronfenbrenner *Social Factors in the Development of Personality*, Symposium 35, at the XVIII International Congress of Psychology, Moscow, Aug. 1966, pp. 7–18, reprinted in *International Journal of Psychology*, 1967, II, pp. 199–207

Urie Bronfenbrenner, L. Siman and J.C. Condry Jr, 1968, 'Characteristics of peer and adult-oriented children' (Department of Child Development, Cornell University) reported in Urie Bronfenbrenner, 1971, *Two Worlds of Childhood: USA and USSR*, Allen & Unwin; Penguin Education, 1974

Jerome Bruner, 1975, 'The beginnings of intellectual skills' (I and II), *New Behaviour*, 2 and 9 Oct.

Jerome Bruner, 1976, 'The styles of teaching', *New Society*, 29 April

Children and their Primary Schools, Plowden Report, 1967, HMSO

L.D. Eron, Leopold O. Walder and Monroe M. Lefkowitz, 1971, *The learning of Aggression in Children*, Little, Brown

Ken Fogelman, 1976, 'Bored Children', *New Society*, 15 July

David Herbert, 1977, *Transactions of the Institute of British Geographers: New Series*, vol. 1, no. 4, p. 472

Serita Kendall, 1975, 'Street kids of Bogotà', *New Society*, 16 Jan.

Melanie Klein, 1932, *The Psychoanalysis of Children*, 3rd edn reprinted, Hogarth Press

Margaret Mead, 1930, *Growing Up in New Guinea*, published 1963, Penguin Books

John and Elizabeth Newson, 1968, *Four Years Old in an Urban Community*, Penguin

John and Elizabeth Newson, 1976, *Seven Years Old in the Home Environment*, Allen & Unwin

M. Parry and H. Archer, 1974, *Pre-School Education*, a Schools Council Research Study, Macmillan

R.R. Rodgers, Urie Bronfenbrenner and E.C. Devereaux Jr, 1968, 'Standards of social behaviour among children in four cultures', *International Journal of Psychology* III, no. 1, pp.31–41

G. Sykes and D. Matza, 1961, 'Delinquency and subterranean values', *American Sociological Review* 26, pp. 712–19
Jack Tizard, Jane Perry and Peter Moss, 1976, *All Our Children*, Temple Smith

13 *School and the Leisure Child*
Neville Bennett, 1976, *Teaching Styles and Pupil Progress*, Open Books
B. Bernstein, 1971, *Class, Codes and Control*, Routledge
Urie Bronfenbrenner, 1971, *Two Worlds of Childhood: USA and USSR*, Allen & Unwin, also Penguin Education, 1974
Urie Bronfenbrenner, 1973, 'Children, Families and Social Policy: An American Perspective', in *The Family in Society: Dimensions of Parenthood*, A report to the seminar held at All Souls College, Oxford, April, HMSO
Thomas Cottle, 1976, 'School suspension in America', *New Society*, 30 Sept.
A.M. Kallarackal and Martin Herbert, 1976, 'The happiness of Indian immigrant children', *New Society*, 26 Feb.
W. Kessen, 1975 edn, *Childhood in China*, Yale University Press
Thomas W. Laqueur, 1977, *Religion and Respectability: Sunday Schools and English Working-Class Culture*, Yale University Press
Colin MacInnes, 1973, 'That Other Culture', *Times Educational Supplement*, 5 Oct.
Dennis Marsden, 1976, 'The Rough', *New Society*, 11 Nov.
Terence Morris, 1957, *The Criminal Area*, Routledge & Kegan Paul
Michael Power, 1967, 'Delinquent Schools?', *New Society*, 19 Oct.
David Reynolds, Dee Jones and Selwyn St Leger, 1976, 'Schools do make a difference', *New Society*, 29 July
Harold Silver, 1976, 'Teaching: the death of a meal ticket', *New Society*, 16 Sept.
M. Stacey, Rosemary Dearden, Roisin Pill and Daniel Robinson, 1970, *Hospitals, Children and their Families*, Routledge & Kegan Paul
Carole Striker, 1976, 'Helping children to read', *New Society*, 5 Feb.
David B. Tyack, 1977, 'A Choice of Education?', *New Society*, 7 April
Martha Vicinus, 1975, *The Industrial Muse: A Study of Nineteenth Century Working Class Literature*, Croom Herm
The West Indian Community, 1977, Commons Select Committee on Race Relations, HMSO

14 *Setting an Example*
John Archer and Barbara Lloyd, 1974, 'Sex roles: biological and social interactions', *New Scientist* 21 Nov.
Robert Ardrey, 1963, *African Genesis*, Collins
Albert Bandura, 1965, 'Influence of model's reinforcement contingencies on the acquisition of imitative responses', *J. of Per. and Soc. Psychol.* 1, pp. 589–95
Leonard Berkowitz and Russell G. Geen, 1966, 'Film violence and the cue properties of available targets', *J. of Per and Soc. Psychol.* 3, pp. 525–30
Leonard Berkowitz, 1962, *Aggression: A Social Psychological Analysis*, McGraw-Hill
Leonard Berkowitz, 1970, 'The contagion of violence: an S-R mediational

analysis of some effects of observed aggression', in William J. Arnold and Monte M. Page, Eds, *Nebraska Symposium of Motivation,* University of Nebraska Press

Leonard Berkowitz, 1973, 'The case for bottling up rage', *New Society,* 27 Sept.

Leonard Berkowitz, 1973, 'Words and symbols as stimuli to aggressive responses', in John Knutson, Ed., *The Control of Aggression,* Aldine

Urie Bronfenbrenner, 1971, *Two Worlds of Childhood: USA and USSR,* Allen & Unwin, Penguin Education, 1974

L.D. Eron, 1963, 'Relationship of TV viewing habits and aggressive behaviour in children', *Journal of Abnormal and Social Psychology,* LXVII, pp. 193–6

S. Feshbach, 1956, 'The catharsis hypothesis and some consequences of interaction with aggressive and neutral play objects', *Journal of Personality,* vol. 24

S. Feshbach, 1966, 'A study of catharsis of aggression', *Journal of Personality,* vol. 4, no. 6, pp. 591–6

S. Feshbach and R. Singer, 1971, *Television and Aggression,* San Francisco: Jossey-Bass

C. Gerbner, 1972, in *Television and Social Behaviour* vol. III, *Television Adolescent Aggresssiveness,* Eds G.A. Comstock and J.P. Murray, US Government Printing Office

M.A. Hanratty, R.M. Liebert, L.W. Morris and L.E. Fernandez, 1969, 'Imitation of film-mediated aggression against live and inanimate victims', *Proceedings of the 77th Annual Convention of the American Psychological Association,* pp. 457–8

O.J. Harvey and J. Rutherford, 1960, 'Status in informal groups: influence and influencability at different age levels', *Child Devel. 31, pp. 377–85*

D.J. Hicks, 1965, 'Imitation and retention of film-mediated aggressive peer and adult models', *Journal of Personality and Social Psychology,* vol. 2, no. 1, pp. 97–100

D.J. Hicks, 1968, 'Short and long term retention of effectively varied modelled behaviour', *Psychol. Sci.* 2, pp. 369–70

William Kessen, 1975, *Childhood in China,* Yale University Press

R.M. Liebert et al, 1973, *The Early Window: effects of Television on Children and Youth,* Pergamon

Clemens A. Loew, 1967, 'Acquisition of a hostile attitude and its relationship to aggressive behaviour', *Journal of Personality and Social Psychology,* vol. 5, no. 3

Konrad Lorenz, 1966, *On Aggression,* Methuen

I.O. Lovaas, 1961, 'Interaction between verbal and non-verbal behaviour', *Child Devel.* 32, pp. 329–36

J.J. McIntyre and J.J. Teevan Jr, 1972, 'Television violence and deviant behaviour', in G.A. Comstock and E.A. Rubinstein, Eds, *Television and Social Behaviour,* vol, III; *Television and Adolescent Aggressiveness,* pp. 383–435, US Government Printing Office

J.M. Mcleod, G.K. Atkin and S.H. Chaffee, 1972, 'Adolescents, parents and television use: adolescent self-report measures from Maryland and Wisconsin samples', in G.A. Comstock and E.A. Rubinstein, op. cit., pp. 239–313

Peter Marsh, 1975, 'Understanding Aggro', *New Society*, 3 April
Desmond Morris, 1967, *The Naked Ape*, Cape
Desmond Morris, 1969, *The Human Zoo*, Jonathan Cape
Anthony Storr, 1968, *Human Aggression*, Allen Lane the Penguin Press
G. Sykes and D. Matza, 1961, 'Delinquency and subterranean values', *American Sociological Review*, 26, pp. 712–19
R.H. Walters and E. Llewellyn Thomas, 1963, 'Enhancement of punitiveness by visual and audiovisual displays', *Canadian Journal of Psychology* XVIII, no. 2, pp. 244–55
W.D. Wells, 1972, 'Television and aggression: a replication of an experimental field study', University of Chicago (Mimeographical abstract)
Fredric Wertham, 1964, 'School for Violence', *New York Times*, 5 July
Fredric Wertham, 1968, *Violence and the Mass Media*, Harper & Row
D. Zillman, 1971, 'Excitation Transfer in Communication-Mediated Aggressive Behaviour', *J. Exper. Soc. Psychol.* 7, p. 419

15 *Opportunities and Repercussions*

Apprentices in Crime, 1974, Society of Conservative Lawyers
W.A. Belson, 1975, *Juvenile Theft: the Causal Factors*
A.E. Bottoms, 1976, 'Crime in a City', *New Society*, 8 April
A.E. Bottoms and J. Baldwin, 1976, *The Urban Criminal*, Tavistock
Crime as Opportunity, Home Office Research Study no. 34, HMSO
Clive Jones Davies and Ronald G. Cave, 1976, *The Disruptive Pupil in the Secondary School*, Ward Lock Educational
Hammersmith Teenage Project, London Borough of Hammersmith with NACRO
Charles Holahan, 1976, *Journal of Applied Social Psychology*, vol. 6, no. 1, p. 48
Bernard Ineichen, 1975, 'Teenage Brides', *New Society*, 7 Aug.
Intermediate Treatment, A community-based action-research study, 1977, National Children's Bureau (Aryeh Leissner, Terry Powley, Dave Evans)
Nicola Madge, 1976, 'Treatment for a few', *New Society*, 3 June
Tony Marshall, 1976, 'Vandalism: the seeds of destruction', *New Society*, 17 June
Oscar Newman, 1974, *Defensible Space*, Architectural Press
Mary Priestley, 1976, 'Camberwell Rhythms', *New Society*, 22 Jan.
Subcommittee of the House of Commons Expenditure Committee on the Operations of the Children and Young Persons Act 1969, Report vol I; Minutes of Evidence vol. II
Laurie Taylor, 1976, 'Vigilantes—Why not?', *New Society*, 4 Nov.
Norman Tutt, 1975, 'Care or Custody?' Pamphlet for MoPP
Peter Wilmott, 1966, *Adolescent Boys of East London*, Routledge & Kegan Paul

16 *Asking For It?*

Susan Brownmiller, 1975, *Against our Will: Men, Women and Rape*, Secker & Warburg
John Howells, 1974, *Remember Maria*, Butterworth
Erin Pizzey, 1974, *Scream Quietly–or the neighbours will hear*, Penguin
Julie Vennard, 1976, 'Justice and Recompense for Victims of Crime', *New Society*, 19 Feb.

Index